Yves Congar

**THEOLOGY IN THE SERVICE
OF GOD'S PEOPLE**

JEAN-PIERRE JOSSUA, O.P.

Yves Congar

THEOLOGY IN THE SERVICE
OF GOD'S PEOPLE

THE PRIORY PRESS, CHICAGO, ILL.

Revisores Ordinis: Thomas C. Donlan, O.P., S.T.D.; Bernard O'Riley, O.P. *Imprimi potest:* Gilbert J. Graham, O.P., Provincial. *Nihil obstat:* Thomas C. Donlan, O.P., S.T.D., Bernard O'Riley, O.P., Censores Deputati. *Imprimatur:* Rt. Rev. Msgr. Francis W. Byrne, Vicar General, Archdiocese of Chicago, October 30, 1968.

This book is a translation of *Le Père Congar: La Théologie au Service du Peuple de Dieu,* by Jean-Pierre Jossua, O.P., published by Les Éditions du Cerf, Paris. English translation by Sister Mary Jocelyn, O.P., Rosary College, River Forest, Illinois.

Library of Congress Catalogue Number 68-29599
© Copyright 1968 by *The Priory Press*
1165 East 54 Place, Chicago, Illinois 60615
Manufactured in the United States of America

Foreword

I do not intend to write a panegyric on Father Congar. To the servant of truth the only fitting tribute is the truth. Father Congar is not a universal genius; he is a Christian, a priest, a Friar Preacher. He is, moreover, a theologian who, in the service of the Gospel and through an affinity that developed gradually over the years, made himself *the* man of a particular phase of the Christian mystery: the renewal of Catholic ecclesiology with a view to the reunion of divided Christians. He enjoys great influence today because the field of his study and efforts in the Church (a field, as he loves to say, that is militant by its very nature) is that of Vatican II, the very field which characterizes our time in the History of the People of God. It is his humble but proud conviction that he was chosen for this work; it is also my conviction.

In great part these pages are the fruit of interviews with Father Congar, and of gleanings from his notebooks which he graciously allowed me to study. While perhaps I have been inclined to develop a certain aspect of his writings which seems important to me personally, I have sought also to be impersonal so that I could set down the true image of the man and of his work which emerged from these direct contacts.

The Author
The Saulchoir, October, 1966

5

Table of Contents

8

Yves Congar

THEOLOGY IN THE SERVICE
OF GOD'S PEOPLE

CHAPTER ONE

Life and Work Prior to 1965

1. PRELUDE: CHILDHOOD AND YOUTH
Family Background

Yves Congar was born April 13, 1904, at Sedan (in the Ardennes) to a middle-class family of four children. Of the three boys and one girl Yves was the youngest. He had a happy childhood: games in his own courtyard, playmates, the radiant presence of his mother whose influence on him was far-reaching. She sewed while the children worked in the quiet of the family study. Often, especially during the war years of 1914-1918, she read to them in the evening. On Saturday evenings she used to open a book of the Gospels and the children stood to hear the gospel of the following day. The expression "at that time" was unfamiliar to little Yves and he would ask what it meant. And so, although the family was not especially "pious," it is evident that it had sincerity and faith. While life was easy, the home training was somewhat austere; its emphasis on duty was to leave its mark on the young Congars. On one of the walls was the inscription "Know thyself." Its meaning was not too clear, yet it seemed to have universal significance as an appeal to conscience and the inner life. The adage had been taught Mme. Congar by her old Alsatian teacher who had taken refuge "into the interior" in 1870. It was to her home that Yves went on Sunday mornings, to her that he had to relate the Gospel read the previous evening—". . . the secret of happiness is to do one's duty and try to find one's happiness in it." This strong discipline was to fortify from within a character which was violent, stubborn, and irascible, one which

11

once led the child to sit on the streetcar tracks rather than do something that was asked of him.

A word must be said about the sentiment in Sedan during World War I, for its climate of opinion, quite foreign to us now, left its mark on Yves who was then ten years old. The people there, having endured many misfortunes, were very unhappy (a fact which was to have serious consequences); they had been humiliated by the occupation, and were intensely, ardently patriotic in a way hard to imagine today. Proof of this is found in a little journal which the child kept during the war. It is full of hatred for the "chleus" who had entered Sedan on Tuesday, March 25, 1914, and had exhibited true savagery by burning and shooting. The child's journal begins in a naïve and moving way: "Here begins a tragic story, a sad and somber story written by a child who at heart has always had both respect for his fatherland and a just and tremendous hatred for a cruel and unjust people." Such things leave their mark on a man; those who lived through World War II know it only too well.

To Call Men to Conversion
When he was ten, Yves wanted to be a doctor and asked for a microscope for his first communion gift; because of the war he did not receive it until 1918. In the spring of that year, however, he had changed his mind—he wanted to become a priest. This aspiration was born in a kind of lonely emptiness, an intense feeling of solitude which had lasted two or three months. Nor was the decision to be a source of comfort. For the first time the young boy experienced a feeling which was to engulf him at moments of decision throughout his life, a feeling of dread, of withdrawal, a fear of not measuring up, of being overwhelmed by things, of not being as good as others— in particular, a fear of studies, of Latin. He was to experience this fear in 1921 when he entered the Institut Catholique, again in 1925 on beginning the Dominican novitiate, when he was a prisoner of war, and even as a *peritus* at the Council.

At the very core of his vocation was the desire to preach so as to call men to conversion—a vocation already quite Dominican. But a seminarian soon to be ordained (he will be referred to here as Father X), in whom Yves confided, told him: "Your task will be to administer the sacraments, visit the sick, etc." The boy was not entirely convinced, but accepted the reply. Seeking an exterior sign he opened the *Imitation of Christ* to a passage which at the time seemed decisive and confirmed the priest's opinion. Today it would seem banal to Father Congar; a sign is a sign for someone, at such and such a moment. Father X, then professor at the Institut Catholique in Paris, had a great influence on Yves Congar over a long period of years. As early as 1935, however, the intellectual interests of each differed considerably.

Early Influences

Father X taught the young man, directed him, then introduced him to the university seminary of Paris. After two mediocre years at the minor seminary, Congar hesitated on the threshold of the major seminary from fear of a narrow and closed seminary life. Father X, entirely dedicated, profound, a man of prayer, succeeded in awakening in young Congar a sense of inwardness and an appreciation of the demands of the spiritual life. Strongly intellectual, he oriented him toward Thomism by first making him love the person of St. Thomas Aquinas. But the young disciple felt a certain resistance to the expression of some supernatural considerations that seemed to view life and the world too negatively. He hesitated too over the formulation of some Marian devotions he could not accept. Father Congar wanted a spiritual life, but he desired one that would not have any aversion to the life and world of men; one that would not have an excessive fear of "naturalism."

Even though Father X never actually accepted the principles of Maurras' philosophy (of which he made a lucid critique after its condemnation by Pius XI), he followed the publication *L'Action Française* with sympathy; but then so did a good number of the French clergy, especially the younger members. This movement aroused an attraction and a sympathy in Yves Congar, but no real passion. Its condemnation, if hard to accept, actually brought an unexpected liberation to the young man, as it did to many others. He was later to see in it one of God's greatest mercies. Henceforth he freed himself progressively from its influences. But he was to draw from it a twofold lesson: to know that it was necessary to put the absolute where it had to be and not elsewhere; and that in politics mental constructs were to be distrusted. Therefore he resisted any transposition to the left of the totalitarianism of *Action Française*. This evolution as well as certain circumstances connected with the Civil War in Spain sufficed later, in 1939, to widen the gulf between him and Father X, although Father Congar has never ceased to have an affectionate and profound gratitude toward him.

During his three years of philosophy in the seminary, where he followed the courses of Jacques Maritain, of Father Blanche, and of Father X, Congar familiarized himself with Thomism. Father X often took him to Maritain's home where met a group whose history should some day be written, so representative was it of a particular milieu and time (in which it had much influence), and so typical of that clannish spirit which springs up periodically. There was found an exclusive love of St. Thomas, interpreted according to the tradition of the School (especially John of St. Thomas), united with a regard for contemplation. We find a profound echo of this in the books of Jacques and Raïssa Maritain. For the Maritain of *Antimoderne* and *Theonas,* however, the entire adventure of modern thought, all of its "errors," came from not having understood "the adamantine distinctions" of Father Poinsot (John of St. Thomas). Father Garrigou-Lagrange was the usual retreat master for this circle. Yves Congar joined it with enthusiasm and drew many riches from it, for there were many to be had. Father X finally gave him something else. He brought him to

the Benedictines at Conques, near Herbemont, for Vespers of
the Transfiguration. There the young seminarian had a decisive
experience in the liturgy of the Church—an experience which
was to nourish him for many years and present a problem about
his vocation.

2. FORMATION OF THE THEOLOGIAN

During his military service at Saint-Cyr, and later at Bingen-
on-the-Rhine, alone in a romantic countryside, the monastery of
St. Hildegard opposite him, he questioned the path he should
take. He wanted to be a religious; would he be a Benedictine?
a Dominican? He came back to Paris in November, 1925, to
decide. After consulting Father X, Congar presented himself
to Father Louis, provincial of the Dominicans. He entered
the novitiate at Amiens. Here he had a fervent, happy novitiate,
free of problems, free even of any difficulties in adaptation, so
prepared was he by his clerical formation.

"He Is a Thomist Already"

Such was not to be the case when he arrived at the house
of studies, the Saulchoir, at Kain-la-tombe in Belgium. Here
the Dominicans of the French province, expelled at the beginning of the century, had established their house of formation.
Coming from the novitiate Congar was repelled by the in-
exorable factory-like spirit, by a schedule more narrow and
inflexible than a corporation's. It took him at least two months
to become adjusted. And yet, knowing the influences at work
on him while in Paris, the priests at the Saulchoir said, "He is
already a Thomist." Actually his was not entirely the same
Thomism he was going to find at the Saulchoir. The entire
effort of Father Ambrose Gardeil (1859-1931), a first-rate
theologian and regent of studies, had been to bring the level
of studies at the Saulchoir up to university standards. In this
he succeeded, at least for theology. An excellent dogmatist,
Father Héris, assured good classical teaching. The influence
of Father Lemonnyer, a former pupil in Jerusalem of Father

Lagrange and regent after World War I, of Father Mandonnet, of Father Roland-Gosselin, and above all of Father Chenu, a young and brilliant professor, was to secure the school a place in historical method, especially in the field of scholarly research (Institute of Medieval Studies, *Revue des Sciences philoso-phiques et théologiques*). The teaching of the house of studies was also to leave its mark on at least a certain number of pro-fessors and to affect the general climate. Thus, without ceas-ing to identify itself essentially with St. Thomas, the Saulchoir was to strengthen the study of biblical and patristic sources and of Greek philosophy. It took care to situate St. Thomas in his period, thanks to a study of medieval life. In the develop-ment of this study, the team was to collaborate with Etienne Gilson. This was to assure certain differences in regard to the Thomism of the commentators, of the School, and of the neo-scholastics. The apologetical concerns of Father Gardeil and other pre-war professors were already sensitive to the necessity of a sufficiently broad historical culture and of an understand-ing of the critical problems in the science of religions.

As the young Congar sensed on arriving, the milieu was per-vaded by an atmosphere of highly intellectual, even speculative, life. Among the most brilliant students were Brothers Thomas Philippe, Maydieu, Simonin, Dominic Dubarle, and H.M. Féret. Brothers Avril, Maydieu, and Couturier brought a balance by their broader, less theological, cultural interests. For the most part, life at Kain was removed from the world at large—few outside lecturers came, the professors had little or no contact with anyone beyond their walls. This kind of exile certainly provided the impulse to survive, to prepare for a return. The members seized upon the books and magazines that the *Revue des Sciences* received. But a certain insularity was only too evident. This was offset for the most part by the apostolic zeal with which they kept up a regular correspondence with the missions in their province, especially Norway which held great interest for Congar. There was also the "Russian Seminary" at

Lille, established by Fathers Omez and Dumont, which enjoyed great prestige at the Saulchoir.

Meeting with a Master

In describing the development of Brother Congar, emphasis must be given to the influence of Father Chenu. Not that the latter actually launched him on the way that was to be his or that he delineated his paths of research; rather he enabled him to share some major human and intellectual options. Perhaps Chenu's most decisive influence was in making him aware of history. The young man had always been interested in history, but his close association with Father X did not favor a development along these lines; this influence was undoubtedly beneficial in keeping him from an erudition pursued for itself and from a taste for an anecdotal history. But Father Chenu was extraordinary in awakening in others the vocation of the historian—historians who like himself would be attentive to the actuality of the past and to its repeated interrogation by the present. After having been his teacher of Greek—Father Chenu taught little and was satisfied to give courses at the secondary level—he was again his teacher in the history of doctrines. Father Congar likes to recall the ". . . marvelous impression of being awakened, of entering into the understanding of what has been thought, of the living steps of the development . . ." and above all that, the scholarship itself, especially in the personal contact with Father Chenu, "the brilliant brother, generous, open to everything, sympathetic and cooperative, whether one was just stammering or doing research—then one met a master, a friend, an incomparable brother, unceasingly trying to understand the other, to help him to understand himself, to encourage and often to enrich his work." With a documentation that often enough was infinitesimal, the genial intuition of Father Chenu enabled him to mine some of the richest veins in the past or in the present history of the Church.

In the austere setting of the Saulchoir, marked by many harsh observances (rising during the night, fasts, recitation of the Office, and many devotions—scarcely lightened by some modifications resulting from a certain rediscovery of the liturgy), Brother Congar had to take only one short year of philosophy because of his previous studies. He was to enter rapidly into the four-year theology cycle, during which time his ecclesiological and ecumenical preoccupations were soon to emerge. Without a doubt, the preaching of his pastor in Sedan and the formation given by Father X already partook very much "of the Church." The reading of *The Mystery of the Church* by Father Clérissac, a work remarkable for its time, also greatly influenced Congar in a way not entirely free perhaps of a touch of estheticism.

I shall return to the awakening of the ecumenical vocation, but here I must at least mention that Brother Congar prepared for ordination by meditating on the Gospel of St. John (with the commentaries of St. Thomas and of Father Lagrange), and on Father Masure's *The Christian Sacrifice*. It was while reading the seventeenth chapter of St. John that his "ecumenical" concern (which was to become primary in his life) took definitive shape.

3. THE GOOD YEARS: PRE-WAR

Yves Congar was ordained on July 25, 1930. I must stress that, from that day, Father Congar was first of all a priest of the Gospel. The number of sermons (or series of sermons), retreats, conferences (or series of conferences), over and above his regular teaching duties was to increase steadily over the years: 161 from 1930 to the war; 553 from his liberation in August, 1945, to his arrival in Strasbourg in 1957; 947 from December, 1957, to August, 1965! After a stay in Germany Father Congar came back to the Saulchoir to prepare his lectorate thesis on the unity of the Church; this was a somewhat academic task, but its preparation was an indispensable step in his development. Very early he had copied a page from Father Schwalm on what ecclesiology ought to be. It was taken from the article "The Two Theologies."[1] This text is important enough to warrant taking a moment to examine it. It will pinpoint themes that are familiar in Father Congar.

If St. Thomas Came Back

The article of Father Schwalm has evident limitations. In his third paragraph, "The treatise on the Church from the scholastic point of view," he clearly noticed a fact on which Father Congar will later insist—the treatise on the Church developed only in the fourteenth century under the pressures of disputes concerned with the juridical order of powers. But Father Schwalm does not ask what St. Thomas' own outlook was or if this author conceived the essence of the Church along juridical lines (which was the thought of the late Middle Ages and of the Counter-Reformation), or rather along the line of the New Testament and of the Fathers. However, the quotation he gives from Ambrose Gardeil could have put him on the path toward the sacramental and anthropological ecclesiology of St. Thomas, to which Father Congar will love to return. Father Gardeil had written: "If St. Thomas came back and saw the dogma of the Church as it has developed, I do not doubt that he would give it a large section in the third part of the *Summa Theologica* between the treatise on Christ and that on the sacraments."[2] Instead, Father Schwalm seeks in St. Thomas the elements of ecclesiology that are the preludes to subsequent controversies—questions of an institutional and social order. Hence the method and the ecclesiological plan which he proposes will again be entirely characteristic of an ecclesiology like Bellarmine's, that is, a reconstructed one. The Thomistic analysis of society applied to the Church as a society—this is to be the Thomistic treatise on the Church: "One would apply the ra-

---

[1]"Les deux théologies," *Revue des Sciences philosophiques et théologiques* (1908), 674 ff.
[2]*La crédibilite et l'apologétique* (Paris: Gabalda, 1912), pp. 147-48.

tional means of the scholastic method to social matters of a special and supernatural kind."

As I shall point out this approach was to leave its mark for a while on the young theologian, but it did not take him long to recognize the limitations of these perspectives. On the other hand, a very fine page from Father Schwalm was to give him lasting inspiration:

> Like every great work of doctrine, the future ecclesiology will synthesize the scattered acquisitions of centuries. Would that God might animate (if indeed he has not already done so) some young theologian to consecrate "the long hopes and the vast thoughts" with which youth is illuminated, to the patient and humble maturing of the hoped-for synthesis. This young theologian should preferably be a professor teaching these matters and hence steeped in the thought of the Fathers, of popes, of the theologians who were elaborators of the doctrine to be exposed—someone studious, recollected, knowing the real value of contemplation and of solitude, long-suffering, and generous. If it is true that every fine and fruitful life realizes in its maturity an enthusiasm of its twenties, what could be a worthier achievement of a professorial and university ministry than this treatise on the Church, this treatise on the Son of God in his social dimensions?[3]

Someone was to hear this call and devote his life to an attempt to respond to it.

First Teaching

Father Congar passed his lectorate in theology on June 7, 1931. When he went back to his cell he found everything topsy-turvy and on the table a farewell note from Father Chenu containing some pleasantries and the remark, "The end of the good old days!" Nevertheless, before beginning his teaching of apologetics, Father Congar received permission for a year of personal study. But since Father Chenu had to go to Canada to open the Institute of Medieval Studies at Ottawa (later transferred to Montreal during the war), a school to which he was

---

[3] *Art. cit.*

to give more and more of his time in the following years,
Father Congar was to give in his place the introductory course
in theology. It was at this time that he came into serious contact with the thought of the modernists, especially that of
Loisy, whose *Mémoires* had just appeared. In reading these
three volumes, the conviction (and at the same time a very
strong critical reaction) was born in him that the mission for
his generation was to bring together *in the Church* all that was
good in the demands and problems posed by the modernists.
He thought especially of the application of critical techniques
to the Christian deposit and, in religious philosophy, of "the
point of view of the subject."

For the six months of freedom left to him, Father Congar
hesitated between Berlin and Paris. He had already replaced
Father Delorme at Berlin during the vacation of 1931 and
so preferred to spend from January to June, 1932, in Paris. He
followed courses at the Institut catholique (Father X's courses
in sociology) and at the Hautes Etudes (Gilson's course on
Luther and a course with B.L. Bras) in the Protestant Faculty
of Theology. Because of this latter study and because of his
contacts with some Protestants, many Parisian Dominicans were
scandalized, thinking that in authorizing all this the father
provincial was precipitating Father Congar into apostasy. He
was forbidden to attend one of Loisy's courses. But Cardinal
Verdier, who had been his superior at the seminary, approved
everything. Father Congar assisted at French-Russian friendship reunions and became acquainted with Emmanuel Mounier
at Maritain's home. Then he returned to the Saulchoir and
prepared for his teaching of apologetics. His way of teaching
differed from that of his predecessors in the chair. Father
Congar never believed in a rational apologetical demonstration.
Even before reading and studying Pascal in prison, he was
profoundly Pascalian in this domain. He was also to insist on
the problems of inter-confessional apologetics and to contribute

in a more general way to developing this discipline to the status of true fundamental theology.

He was to teach *De Ecclesia,* which at that time was still included in the apologetics program; beginning the following year, however, it was to alternate with theology, fulfilling a vow made in 1905 by Father Lemonnyer. From this moment came Congar's concern to construct a treatise on the Church, a concern which was to become a lifelong desire—then almost a regret as each passing year delayed the realization of his plan. Strictly speaking, in spite of a considerable ecclesiological work, this plan has not yet been completed. Today Father Congar willingly admits that he congratulates himself for not having written it in the thirties or even after the war: "It would have been miserable. Now I would do better; but shall I ever do it?"

In 1932 he had to find a point of view and a plan for his course. What I have already said of Father Schwalm's article and of the fact that Father Congar followed Father X's sociology courses help one to understand how the young professor quickly decided to construct the mystery of the Church by applying to it the categories of the Thomistic philosophy of society. But, as he advanced, he realized that these categories, with their rigor and their type of philosophical approach to reality, were not sufficient to give a complete account of the reality of the Church. A good deal of his later effort was toward ridding himself of these categories. In 1947, however, he remarked that he was glad he had done this work.

Teamwork at the Saulchoir

The following years were to be satisfying ones. Father Congar worked in complete harmony and intimate friendship with Father Chenu and with Father H.M. Féret, who was two years older than he in the Order. A fearless Bordelais, Féret was a Church historian endowed with a fine theological sense. As early as 1932, after some decisive conversations, the three priests were aware of their total agreement on some essential options. The desire to liquidate "baroque theology," to return to the sources, seemed to them to establish a common purpose. They had conceived the ambitious notion of writing a history of theology; with this in mind they took notes and exchanged ideas and references. The work, however, was never seriously undertaken, in spite of several decisions to abandon everything else in order to give themselves to it entirely. Moreover, Father Chenu's increasingly frequent trips to Ottawa and the growing specialization of Father Féret and Father Congar soon made a truly common work difficult, for at the same time their work and different obligations became more overwhelming. Yet, as late as 1947, Father Congar remarked: "We still have the idea that some day we shall be able to cooperate in a common task, the fruit of these twelve or fifteen years of work which, while keeping us apart, nevertheless always brought us to similar preoccupations, options, and orientations." Undoubtedly they were at that time in a very strong psychological position. Conscious of their concern for openness they were at the same time backed up by an unchallenged fortress—the work of St. Thomas Aquinas. Each one went his own way relying on this support. Little by little certain limitations, certain distances, certain needs to move beyond it appeared, as did unexpected cracks, but it seemed that the work was done.

"To Give an Understanding of What One Is Doing"

It was in theological methodology that Father Congar was most influenced by Father Chenu, who in turn owed much to Father Ambrose Gardeil. This subject was held in great honor at the Saulchoir and Father Congar touched on it especially in teaching the introduction to theology and the "development of dogma." That is why (if I may anticipate a little) Bishop Amann, in 1938, was to ask him to write the article "Theology" for the *Dictionnaire de Théologie Catholique*. Its writing took him a year. Bishop Amann cut a part of the text which he considered too long. This article, which was to become famous, was in 1962 collected with various questions of fundamental theology, in the manual *La Foi et la Théologie* ("Le mystère Chrétien," fasc. 1). Now it appears outmoded to us because of the renewal of the theological problematic, and no one is more aware of this than Father Congar himself. Certainly he had always read and loved the Bible, but it was only during and after the war that an assiduous biblical study was to renew many of his perspectives and help him in an evolution of the very methodological questions themselves. His reading of Father Allo's commentary on the *Apocalypse* was decisive. If truth be told, at the pre-war Saulchoir the Bible played a larger part in the personal lives of the fathers than in their elaboration of theology. And this reflection brings us to the laborious and fruitful period during which Father Congar wrote numerous articles and for many years (as successor to Father Chenu) undertook the direction of the *Revue des Sciences* with all that this work implies—doing up packages, proofreading, filling vacancies, etc.

That is not all that was done at the Saulchoir; the fathers were very open to the life of the Church. For example, as early as 1929, the chaplains of J.O.C. and of Catholic Action came regularly to Kain where they were received, listened to, and assisted by Fathers Chenu and Congar. One day, either Abbé Cardijn or Abbé Guérin said to Father Chenu, "You give us an understanding of what we are doing." Father Chenu loves to recall those days, with their meetings, the apostolic activity, the awareness that theology is at the service of the Church and ought to be "engaged."

The first secretary of the French episcopate, Bishop Chappoulie, had written to the faculties of the Saulchoir to ask what professors would agree to give help in their specialties to the nascent secretariat. Most of the professors were hesitant. Would this "practical" work not turn them from their "speculative" studies? Three (Chenu, Congar, Féret), however, immediately volunteered; nevertheless the project came to nothing. In spite of distance, Father Congar also had a certain number of Parisian contacts, especially some ecumenical meetings of which I shall speak later. There were others which I cannot enumerate here.

The Church, Humanization of God

At the end of 1934 the Dominicans of *La Vie Intellectuelle* asked Father Congar to formulate a theological conclusion to a study (which the review had conducted for three years) on the causes of unbelief. His beautiful text was lucid and vigorous, but had tremendous repercussions, causing an important crisis of conscience in Father Congar's life. In this work the young theologian exposed the share of responsibility which the Church had in contributing at least to a state of affairs that could be described thus: the humanistic and atheistic world in its totality confronting the Christian totality. Has not the Church presented a disfigured countenance to men? Has it not been too juridical? insufficiently humanistic? too much on the defensive? not faithful enough? not incarnate enough? not sufficiently attentive to progress? Whereas in the design of God:

> To every growth of humanity, to every bit of progress, to every extension of the human in any one of the domains of creation—whether of knowledge or action—there should correspond a growth of the Church, an incorporation of the faith, an incarnation of grace, a humanization of God! That is the Church. That is Catholicity. The Church is not a small social group, isolated, a separate entity remaining untouched among the evolving realities of the world. The Church is the world insofar as it believes in Christ, or, what comes to the same thing, it is Christ dwelling in the world and saving it by our faith. The Church is religious humanity. What am I saying? It is the universe as transfigured by grace to the image of God.[4]

In 1963, the Preface to *Chrétiens en Dialogue*,[5] Father Congar, recalling these "Conclusions," wrote even more profoundly along these same lines: "The divorce that has to be denounced is that of God and man, of theology and anthropology. Because Christians adore a God without men, many men—without ex-

---

[4]*La Vie Intellectuelle* 29 (1934), 247.
[5]*Dialogue between Christians,* trans. Philip Loretz (London: Chapman, 1966).

cluding a possible revolt of pride or of cowardice—believe they cannot affirm man without denying God." I shall return to this important theme which, of the many that preoccupy Father Congar today, is the dearest to him.

The Collection Unam Sanctam

Two years later, after various activities (notably a stay in England), Father Congar took a still more important initiative in launching for Editions du Cerf the ecclesiological collection *Unam Sanctam.* It was joined to the "Conclusions" by the idea that the way to answer atheism is to change the face of the Church insofar as that depends on us. This collection was to have for its first number *Chrétiens désunis; Principes d'un oecuménisme catholique,*[6] which was to mark a turning point in the ecumenical attitude of the Roman Catholic Church. One need only recall the ecumenical vocation and work of Father Congar. From the same period comes the first edition (published in 1941) of *Esquisses du Mystère de l'Eglise.*[7] The book includes a first study, "The Church and Its Unity," a synthetic presentation of Catholic ecclesiology; a second, "The Idea of the Church in St. Thomas Aquinas," sets forth the elements which, in the work of the Dominican Doctor, express his fidelity to the patristic heritage and at the same time provide guidelines for present-day ecclesiological research—we are already far from Father Schwalm; a third is a short spiritual, rather than theological, study on the mystical body. There was, finally, another equally short, but important, essay entitled "Vie de l'Eglise et conscience de la catholicité" ("Life of the Church and Awareness of Its Catholicity"), on the relation between the life of the Church, its riches, and the consciousness which the Church has of them at a given moment of its history: there were more

---

[6]*Divided Christendom: A Catholic Study of the Problem of Reunion,* trans. M. A. Bousfield (London: Bles, 1939).

[7]*The Mystery of the Church,* trans. A. V. Littledale (Baltimore: Helicon Press, 1960).

riches lived in the primitive Church than were formulated in
the New Testament; she will not be fully conscious of all those
she bears in promise until she will have fully achieved her
Catholicity. Two studies, on Möhler and on heresy, complete
this collection. These were replaced in the 1952 edition by
another, equally valuable essay entitled "Le Saint-Esprit et le
corps apostolique, réalisateurs du l'oeuvre du Christ" ("The
Holy Spirit and the Apostolic Body, Continuators of the Work
of Christ"). This insistence on the actuality of God, on the
pneumatological aspect of ecclesiology, was to bear fruit twenty
years later.

4. THE WAR. THE GREAT YEARS: 1945-1953

The war was to put a stop to everything. Mobilized, then im-
prisoned for five years, Father Congar was to have the feeling
of losing years of work when he was at his peak, for, because
he was anti-racist, anti-Nazi at heart—but not anti-German—he
was considered as "hard" by the enemy and treated so as a
consequence. Did he truly lose these years? Much has been
made of the decisive importance that the intimate association
of priests and laymen, of believers and non-believers, was to
have in a mutually beneficial way for each of the groups and
for France herself. Congar carried on his work of chaplain, of
giving biblical conferences; but did he know how to derive
much from these contacts? At the beginning, undoubtedly, he
did derive much, but it seems that at Colditz he dried up and
became withdrawn. In his Preface to *Chrétiens en Dialogue*,
he stressed the opposition that existed between the spirit of
war and an ecumenical attitude. Later, at Lübeck, he even
had moments of trial. But the detachment of the pre-war days,
human maturity, and evangelical wealth were to fashion a
stronger and freer man for the trials to come. In 1948 Father
Congar was to draw up a memorial (for private circulation)
in honor of his escaped fellow officers who had died for France.
It was entitled *Leur Résistance*.

To Rejoin the World Evangelically

After the Liberation, in the extraordinary blossoming of ideas, of initiatives, of movements which characterized this period in France, especially in the life of the Church, Father Congar was to know new fruitful years. He himself described this climate in the Preface to *Chrétiens en Dialogue*:

> Anyone who did not live during the years of French Catholicism (1946-47) has missed one of the finest moments in the life of the Church. Through a slow emergence from misery, one tried, in the great freedom of a fidelity as profound as life, to rejoin in an evangelical way a world of which one had just become an integral part for the first time in centuries. We have since rediscovered that the future of the Church is linked to the future of the world, but then the evidence of this was given in the experience itself. Although cut off for five years from the very great deal of work done at home during the war, I had, nevertheless, been in earlier agreement with these orientations: the biblical movement; the liturgical movement conceived in a pastoral, not a ritualistic, sense; the renewal of the Christian community; missions (even priest-worker); research among the clergy for a theology illuminating the most authentic researches of the apostolate.

It was at the service of this reform "which certainly had its dangers but was sound in its roots and aims" that Father Congar was to write *Vraie et fausse réforme dans l'Eglise*. In my estimation this is his finest work—the one, according to Father Chenu, in which Father Congar gave of himself more than he did in any other work. In the years 1946-1947 he was to branch out in many other directions. These are the years of numerous contacts. In particular, Father Congar took charge of the theological part of the "days" for priests at the convent of St. Jacques in Paris. There he was to discover how mutually profitable theology and pastoral care were. From these conferences and from others that he gave to the chaplains of the J.O.C. or to the laymen of St. Séverin parish were to come *Sacerdoce et*

Laïcat,[8] *Le Mystère du Temple,*[9] and *Les Jalons pour une théologie du laïcat,*[10] which were to appear little by little during
the years to come. A series of courses on Christianity was
likewise to be the source of partial publications and serve as
a basis for others. Circumstances played an enormous part in
this work—they hindered certain realizations and helped others
along.

Before discussing these books, recall the return of Father
Congar to the Saulchoir—since 1937 re-established in France
at Etiolles en Seine-et-Oise, 25 kilometers from Paris. While
in prison he had learned with consternation of the condemnation of Father Chenu's little book *The Saulchoir, A School of
Theology,* and of its author's disgrace. Twenty-three years later,
reflecting on this episode, he was to write: "Even today, after
having questioned and sought, having learned many details, I
come up against so many contradictions and incomprehensible
details, that I can see in this affair only an error or an unfortunate step that cannot be justified."[11]

In any case, the priory was without a head, in full internal
conflict, the object of a distrust that was to prove tenacious.
Father Congar, suspect as early as 1939 because he encouraged
the "return to the sources" (which some—not without a certain
"flair" in a sense—deemed extremely dangerous), escaped Father Chenu's fate only because of his absence. The publication
of Möhler's *Unity in the Church* in *Unam Sanctam* (1939) had
almost caused trouble. In 1948 the new edition of *Chrétiens
désunis* was to be judged impossible, and was to appear only
in 1965 in facsimile. In 1945 Congar hesitated: would he teach
again? Then he accepted and again took up his teaching of

---

[8]*Laity, Church, and World,* trans. Donald Attwater (London: Chapman, 1963).
[9]*The Mystery of the Temple,* trans. Reginald F. Trevett (Westminster:
Newman Press, 1962).
[10]*Lay People in the Church,* trans. Donald Attwater (Westminster: Newman Press, 1957).
[11]*Chrétiens en dialogue* (Paris: Editions du Cerf, 1964), Preface. See
footnote 5, above.

fundamental theology and the treatise on the Church. However, he was to remain apart, without much responsibility in the educational field, his sphere of influence restricted.

Curtailment

Moreover, the years from 1948 on were to be years of intense intellectual labor, years during which he willingly curtailed many things and retrenched enormously in order to complete his work; this was contrary to what he had always done and was to do later—to be always at the beck and call of all. The wear and tear of his years in prison and the sadness of the trials he had endured accompanied him in his retreat. He planned to construct his treatise on the Church: *L'Eglise, Peuple de Dieu et Mystiquement Corps du Christ,* his eight essays on the communion of persons, which were to follow *Vraie et fausse réforme* and which were announced in the Preface of that book; different studies on religious knowledge and tradition; and finally works on Protestant and Eastern orthodoxy. How much of this was he to realize? Undoubtedly numerous partial studies published as articles (which were to constitute a good part of the collections of 1962 and of the years following) but especially four books saw light: *Vraie et fausse réforme dans l'Eglise; Jalons pour une théologie du laïcat; Le mystère du temple; Le Christ, Marie et l'Eglise.*[12] This latter work, which appeared in 1932 for the fifteenth centenary of the Council of Chalcedon, exposes the theological principles that underlie Christology, ecclesiology, and Mariology, binding them in a solidarity both for the traditional faith and for error. Let me add an important study, the German translation of which was to encounter difficulties: "Neuf cents ans après— Notes sur le 'schisme' oriental,"[13] which appeared in the publi-

---

[12]*Christ, Our Lady, and the Church,* trans. Henry St. John (London: Longmans, 1957).
[13]*After Nine Hundred Years* (New York: Fordham University Press, 1959).

cation *1054-1954, l'Eglise et les Eglises* (Collection Lambert Beauduin).

Preceded by a very fine Preface, an excerpt from which I shall give later, and with an Introduction that describes the major characteristics of the contemporary religious mentality, *Vraie et fausse réforme* (1950) consists of two rather different sections. The first two theological parts, which are not at all outdated and which comprise some of Father Congar's finest writing, expose, after a description of ecclesial structure, the meaning of reform in the Church and the regulation of the reforming prophetism within itself, then the conditions of a reform free of schism. The third part, somewhat different, studies in principle the meaning of reform in Protestantism, of which in fact it presents a condensed ecclesiology. Without criticizing anything in it, I might suggest that the understanding of Protestantism, and especially of Luther, which Father Congar was to acquire would have led him some years later to a greater positive appreciation. None of the studies on the communion of persons, foreseen as a result of this work, was to see the light of day in book form.

Jalons pour une Thélogie du Laïcat

Without doubt *Jalons pour une théologie du laïcat* is as important a book as the above-mentioned one, both for its immediacy and for the influence of its views on the theology of the laity, on the relations between the Church and the world, on the Christian priesthood (especially the baptismal priesthood and the spiritual sacrifice of the baptized), on the prophetic function of the laity, and on their holiness in the world. One might add, however, that this work is perhaps (in spite of appearances) less rigorously constructed than the other. It contains lengthy passages and even sections that seem outmoded to us today, like the theology of earthly realities or that of the apostolate of the laity and of Catholic Action. Father Congar himself had already returned to these two last questions in the studies published in *Sacerdoce et Laïcat*.[14] One cannot write on matters of such immediacy that contribute so much to awaken concern and awareness in the ecclesial consciousness (which in great part is the heart of the matter itself) without quickly outdistancing one's own thought or seeing it outdistanced (in part at least) by others. A beautiful biblical study, *Le Mystère du Temple*, completed in exile in Jerusalem while he was giving his course on the primacy, was published in 1959 and was to carry out a promise made in *Jalons*.

5. OBSCURITY, REINSTATEMENT, THE COUNCIL

The difficulties, only too real during the years just mentioned, were to multiply and again interfere with his work. No one is unaware that for ten years, from the end of 1947 on, the atmosphere was to grow progressively more and more stormy, especially in France, until breathing was almost impossible. Father Congar was to write later: "As far as I was concerned in this regard, from the beginning of 1947 to the end of 1956 I was to know nothing but an uninterrupted sequence of denunciations, warnings, restrictive or discriminatory measures, suspicious interventions."[15] Refusal for a new edition and translation of *Vraie et fausse réforme* (only the Spanish translation appeared), articles not published, conferences suppressed, an end to all ecumenical activity—these were but a few elements of the program. And Father Congar, whose integrity was beyond reproach and who refused to write under a pseudonym, asked for, and was often refused, authorization for the slightest undertaking. Then in 1953 there was the "case of the priest-workers," an experiment stopped by a decision from Rome. In the September twenty-fifth issue of *Témoignage Chrétien*, Father Congar published an article which he himself was later to consider insufficient and mediocre. "I redeemed this medi-

---

14*Priest and Layman* (London: Chapman, 1966).
15*Chrétiens en dialogue*, Preface. See footnote 5, above.

ocrity," he added, "by suffering with them." But the article did not lack courage; let it speak for itself: "Thanks to those men, the Church was again heard by the poor, and perhaps the most important thing yet, the poor were again heard in the Church. . . . You can condemn a solution if it is false; you don't condemn a problem—the problem remains."

Actually, Father Congar, unlike Father Chenu, had been only slightly involved in this missionary undertaking. Nevertheless he was attacked because of the animosity directed against the whole movement—the very one which was to result in the Council. Also aimed at were Fathers Chenu and Féret, as were the Dominican provincials of the three French provinces, and the Jesuit scholasticate of Fourvière at Lyons (an illustrious theological center).

Fidelity Responds to Distrust

These were to be somber years—Father Congar was exiled from the Saulchoir (itself threatened), even his most insignificant writings subjected to a central censorship which was neither understanding nor effectual, sent to the Holy Land where he resided at the *Ecole Biblique de Jérusalem,* hindered from accepting the Chair which was offered him at the *Hautes Etudes,* blocked for four inactive months in Rome where he was the victim of the pettiness of overzealous subordinates. Such was to be the case too at Cambridge, where he was assigned for almost a year without being able to exercise his priestly functions. As Father Laurentin (speaking of Fathers Congar, Chenu, de Lubac, Féret) wrote in the December 9, 1964, issue of *Le Figaro:*

> Their fidelity, their exemplary submission, their evangelical serenity, at the moment that everything conspired to push them out of the Church, triumphed over every hope of the system which was stifling them. But those who observed them knew that such a fidelity was impossible without a human and Christian quality and without an exceptional grace. Probably we shall never know what price has been paid for Vatican II.

Father Congar had already been spared some added nuisances by the very personal kindness of Father (now Cardinal) Browne, then Master General of the Dominicans. Another comfort came to him when Bishop Weber of Strasbourg invited him to seek asylum in his diocese. Assigned to the Dominican convent at Strasbourg, Father Congar led a very intense pastoral life—courses, retreats, conferences, preaching—without ever being introduced into the faculty of theology at the university. It was with greater freedom of spirit that he resumed his work.

The Dawn of John XXIII

And then came the pontificate of John XXIII; the very rapid evolution of the ecclesial situation; the announcement of and the preparation for the Council. I must insist here on two series of happenings: the reinstatement; the new series of publications. Very soon after the convocation of the Council, Father Congar was named consultant to the preparatory commission, and then he became official expert of the theological commission of the Council itself. Thereafter, in spite of certain muffled suspicions which remained, his situation improved rapidly—becoming even exceptionally outstanding. John XXIII, and especially Paul VI, gave him conspicuous evidences of trust; invitations, requests for collaboration multiplied to a point of exploitation, of oppression. Late in 1964 the Dominican Order named Father Congar a Master of Sacred Theology. This was the traditional crowning of the career of a professor in the Order, the recognition (with scarcely any privileges) of a brother's theological knowledge and teaching. On this occasion two very simple and very warm reunions were to bring his friends together. The first was a gathering at the Saulchoir of some of his brothers. Among them was Father Chenu, who gave an eloquent, affectionate address; Father Congar replied, saying that he owed him everything. The second, at Strasbourg, was a representative group from all ranks—bishops, priests, laymen, Catholics, Orthodox, Protestants. They described what Father Congar represented for them. Later I shall quote some excerpts from these addresses. In 1965 Father Congar was named a member of the Catholic commission for official dialogue with the world-wide Lutheran Federation which held its first meeting in Strasbourg in August of that year. That year too he was chosen by the Holy Father to be a member of the academic Council of the "Institute for the Study of Salvation History" in Jerusalem.

Continued Intensity of His Work

Although his time was more and more taken by the Council, Father Congar published a great number of works during these years, the greater part evidently being the fruition of research begun much earlier, or collections of articles or contributions to miscellanies dating from different periods of his activity. A quick survey of them, at least of those I have not yet noted, shows the following: first, a number of small books of pastoral interest, some of which are remarkable. *Vaste monde, ma paroisse*[16] (1959), a very fine book, from a collection of articles which had appeared in *Témoignage Chrétien; La Pentecôte*[17] (1956) and *Si Vous êtes Mes témoins*[18] (1958), two booklets which, though small, had repercussions; *Aspects de l'Oecuménisme*[19] (1962), a collection of some conferences on practical ecumenism; *Pour une Eglise servante et pauvre*[20] (1963), a combination of two important studies on the hierarchy as service and on titles and honors in the Church. The first had appeared in the collected volume *L'Episcopat et l'Eglise Uni-*

---

[16]*The Wide World, My Parish,* trans. Donald Attwater (Baltimore: Helicon Press, 1961).
[17]*The Church and Pentecost,* in *The Mystery of the Church.* See footnote 7, above.
[18]In *Laity, Church, and World.* See footnote 8, above.
[19]*Ecumenism and the Future of the Church,* trans. John C. Guinness and Geraldine F. McIntosh (Chicago: The Priory Press, 1967).
[20]*Power and Poverty in the Church,* trans. Jennifer Nicholson (Baltimore: Helicon Press, 1964).

verselle[21] which also contained the important study, "From the Communion of the Churches to an Ecclesiology of the Universal Church." Let me add to this list four volumes of chronicles from the Council, *Le Concile au jour le jour*,[22] grouping the notes which had appeared in *International Catholic Information* during the conciliar session. Finally there was *Jésus-Christ*[23] (1965), a collection of different studies varying in kind and interest. The first, "Christ, the Image of the Invisible God," and the last, "The Lordship of Christ over the Church and the World," are among the most beautiful and most characteristic pages of Father Congar.

Four large volumes brought together a whole series of studies (often unobtainable), two of theology in general and of spirituality, two of ecclesiology and ecumenism. *Les Voies du Dieu Vivant* (1962) contains short articles dating back, for the most part, to the pre-war era; while some are admirable, others are dated. More important, *Sacerdoce et laïcat* (1962), the indispensable complement to *Jalons,* contains studies on the priesthood, the laity and priests, and presence to the world and what it supposes. *Sainte Eglise*[24] (1963) is of interest especially to the theologian because it is a work which contains a certain number of important articles on collegiality—fragments of a treatise which has never been completed—on the nature of the Church or the functions and powers in the Church. The first study (after a short note on the Church as an article of faith), "Can the Church Be Defined? Destiny and Value of Four Concepts Which Claim to Do This," is typical of Father Congar's writings which played a large role in the preparation of the constitution *Lumen Gentium*. In this volume (which also contains articles of less importance) the ecclesiologist will find with satisfaction thirty years of ecclesiological articles written by

---

[21]In *Unam Sanctam* (Paris: Editions du Cerf, 1962), XXXIX.

[22]*Report from Rome,* trans. Lancelot Sheppard (2 vols.; London: Chapman, 1964).

[23]*Jesus Christ,* trans. Luke O'Neil (New York: Herder and Herder, 1966).

[24]In *Unam Sanctam* (Paris: Editions du Cerf, 1963), XLI.

Father Congar for the *Revue des Sciences Philosophiques et Théologiques*. There remains *Chrétiens en dialogue* (1964), an answer after almost thirty years to *Chrétiens désunis*. To these four large volumes two collections of studies on tradition must be added, *La Tradition et les Traditions*[25]—1. "Essai historique" (1960); 2. "Essai théologique" (1963)—and a short synthesis on the same subject, *Tradition et la vie de l'Eglise* (1963)[26] in which Father Congar intentionally and definitively moves the question of tradition from the field of apologetics to a field that is strictly theological.

For the future Father Congar plans (if editors and directors of conferences give him some respite) to complete two comprehensive ecclesiologial studies: to complete the series on the "four marks" of the Church, which together will constitute a treatise on the Church; draw up a history of the concept of the Church and of ecclesiology, a study which is ready, at least on his index cards and in his files. There are also other long-range projects, such as certain studies on the Church as communion, announced in the Preface of *Vraie et fausse réforme dans l'Eglise*. As of now, important contributions to collected works appear, especially in the collection *Unam Sanctam*.[27] This collection has taken Father Congar an infinite amount of time and caused him countless difficulties; perhaps it is his greatest success. It is actually this collection which issues the series *Vatican II, Textes et Commentaires des Décrets Conciliaires,* which Father Congar directs and to which he has made many contributions.

A life which continues, fruitful in spite of age and sickness, has no need of a conclusion.

---

[25]*Tradition and Traditions,* trans. Michael Naseby and Thomas Rainborough (New York: Macmillan, 1967).

[26]*The Meaning of Tradition,* trans. A. N. Woodrow (New York: Hawthorn Books, 1964).

[27]Of special interest: *Collegiality,* LII; *Church and Poverty,* LVII; *The Deacon in the Church and the World Today,* LIX.

CHAPTER TWO

The Man, The Theologian

1. ROOTS

It is important to know the man in order to understand a work as personal, as committed as Father Congar's. The man: his roots, his vocation, the direction he wished to give to his life, the work of the Lord in him. The man: his greatness and his limitations. Father Congar is not well known; one imagines him very different from what he is, much more original, much more revolutionary, much more cerebral, much less simply evangelical in his Catholic tradition. These imaginary views, these personalities constructed from a distance have done him much harm and explain a number of the difficulties he has encountered.

"I Am a Celt of the Ardennes"

Father Congar is from the Ardennes. This is significant. He himself writes in a notebook:

> I am profoundly a Celt and I recognize myself in the picture of the Celt that Renan gives in *Souvenirs d'enfance et de jeunesse.* I am wholly a native of the Ardennes and typify the characteristics of such a people as portrayed by Hardy in the *Revue de Psychologie des Peuples.* . . . I am a Celt of the Ardennes. By culture, formation, thought processes, I am decidedly Latin and strongly Roman.

This indicates a brusk disposition, tempered, concealing a keen sensitivity. In his case this trait goes so far as to make him hot-tempered and stubborn, quick to "fly off the handle." But I have already remarked on, and it is very important, how much Father Congar was fashioned by the education he received, a formation exacting much from conscience, a sense of duty, a very lofty notion of loyalty, of integrity, without however a trace of Jansenism.

This was to have many consequences in his life. First, it resulted in an absolute delicacy in the practice of obedience and in total submission. This was observed even in his most trying experiences, including the stupid pettiness of ecclesiastical censure. How many others, with reason perhaps, would have turned away, thinking it useless to show zeal in such cases. Then came a very rigorous sense of duty which forced him to work furiously, even to the point of producing extremely detailed outlines, minute schedules, etc. Of course, this guaranteed the production of a considerable amount of work, but perhaps was detrimental to a certain cultural development, to a certain appreciation of the worthwhile things in the life of men. In all his life Father Congar has never done anything impetuous or just for pleasure—even his relaxations were taken from a sense of duty.

More serious, and this is a real limitation, while Father Congar loves man in the abstract very much, he finds it a little harder to love a person. He finds it hard to have sympathy for the other who just happened to drop in. He is, in fact, more of a professor than a pastor, more of a prophet than a doctor—to find the two in one person is so rare! This does not hinder ideal friendships, but to have fashioned them more closely he would have to have had more time, more relaxation, less of a feeling of compulsion. At home in Sedan one did what one had to do. True charity certainly compensates for any shortcomings—but I refrain from hagiography. Let us leave to the Lord and to posterity the task of distributing various crowns. If Father Congar does not have the charism of personal contacts, like Father Chenu for example, nevertheless he believes in the passage of ideas by osmosis, in communication through shock; and undoubtedly something strong passes from him in the encounter. But this limitation in his character has had a rather serious consequence from which he has suffered: to find that even if he has felt certain things keenly, certain human aspirations, certain realizations of the Church in its growth, still he had let pass by, at the start at least, certain others that were no less important—the real greatness of Father Couturier's spiritual ecumenism, encountered at Amay in 1932, and the importance of Taizé, whose founders, Brothers Schutz and Thurian, had visited the Saulchoir in 1947.

One must look back to his origins, to the notion of the provincial, middle-class type, devoid of meanness, traditional but without any stupid conservatism. It helps to understand that Father Congar is essentially a man of tradition. Later I shall speak of the theological importance he accords to this concept and also how the decision to speak of it "from a less profound tradition to a more profound one," as Péguy expressed it, orders all his theology. But here I need insist only on the simply human meaning of the word tradition to which Father Congar is equally attached. Of the traditions that a man finds in his own milieu Father Congar writes:

> [They] fashion him, surround him, express him, and in some way clothe him, at the same time leaving him his profound spontaneity and all the force of an interior freedom. These traditions lead us to suspect that tradition is not only a force for conserving, but also a principle of continuity and of identity with a spirit through successive generations.[1]

A Man of Tradition

For Congar tradition goes far, comprising Western classical culture, the clerical formation received in the seminary—at least the great Latin traditions, for Father Congar has a horror of the ecclesiastical style and spirit of the French seventeenth century. But more and more Father Congar has become a man of tradition, one who is attached to what he has received, who

---

[1]*La Tradition et la vie de l'Eglise* (Paris: Fayard, 1963), pp. 9 ff. See Chap. 1, above, footnote 26.

gladly takes things as they are, who loves the past, the only possible source of a present rooted in it and receiving life from it in preparation for a future. This is the very opposite, in fact (the irony of it!), of a revolutionary. When one thinks of the ideas, the attitudes, that have been attributed to him! But a polemic is not always precise in its appraisal, it calumniates purposely. Even recently an Italian newspaper accused Father Congar (through his relations with Hochhuth and the *Editions du Seuil*) of being at the source of the *Deputy* scandal. Father Congar had never seen the author in question, never read nor seen his article, never been an editor of the *Editions du Seuil*, never met its director. It could be laughable—but a man of integrity is always hurt by hatred and lies. And when you think that he has even been accused of communism! What stupidity! In fact, having broken once for all his connections with *Action Française*, Father Congar has remained a moderate. He is a democrat, he is for liberty, for social justice. Republican? Since there is nothing else. Socialist? Secular? Not decidedly—I even sense a certain distrust of these themes which are so dear to others. Could it be said that he is a "dyed in the wool" patriot? I have shown the ardent patriotism of his childhood—strengthened by life on a frontier—the shock of war, attachment to the French past; decidedly, however, the word does not apply; Father Congar is too free to be so described.

Finally, one aspect of Father Congar's personality, to which I have already referred in speaking of his youth, should again be mentioned here, for it too is the result of having had roots in a human milieu that was simple, real, and healthy. I am speaking of his love of life, a taste for the things of the earth, a refusal of idealism, of evasion, of gnosis, of a disembodied spiritualism, of a supernaturalism which condemns (or at least suspects) the human. This is what left him uneasy about Father X's spirituality—profound surely, but very speculative and somewhat antihumanist. It was this that caused him to hesitate on the threshold of the seminary. It was this that

tempered, with a true love for man, a rather austere character
and a rather bookish professional work. It kept Father Congar
from being merely cerebral because he loved life too much and,
rightly, life in the concrete.

2. THE VOCATION OF AN ENVOY

It is hard to enter a realm as personal as that of a vocation;
but from a sense of gratitude God's work must be recognized.
Father Congar is a modest man who considers himself insignificant as a theologian. He has never taught "dogmatic" theology, that is, the ensemble of the Christian mystery, and says
that he doesn't know it well. There is no use exaggerating, but
there is some truth in this. Father Congar has never considered
himself a thinker. His great respect for speculative philosophy
leads him to conclude that he has renewed nothing essential
because he lacks the powers of reflection which enable one to
thrash out, to bore through, to plumb with systematic persistence.

I shall come back to the idea he has of his theological task.
Meanwhile, without in any way underestimating the importance
of research and of the philosophical underpinnings in theology,
I would be inclined to think that, in Father Congar's judgment
of himself, there remains a bit of the scholastic *a priori* as to
what theology ought to be, a little of those oppositions between
"speculative" and "positive" which date from his 1939 article.
I think he is a greater theologian than he claims to be. But
that should not hide the essential from us—granted that he has
limited means, the fact remains (as I shall point out), that
he has had a very great influence, especially in regard to the
Council. Perhaps there is a touch of exaggeration in Father
Laurentin's conclusion of the aforementioned article in *Figaro*:
"Father Congar's life can no more escape history than could
Newman's. As of now it does not appear less significant whether
it is a question of the man, his work, or his trials."

The Humble Sense of His Vocation

For him, for us, it is very simple: he has entered into salvation history. When a man, no matter how poor, is chosen and answers the call, something happens. What he thought he ought to study, to defend, to renew: ecumenism, ecclesiology, the role of the laity, missiology—that was to be the task assigned by the Lord at the Council. Modest as a man, Father Congar has a humble sense of his vocation. He must have the sense of his place in the whole, for one is not called alone. He is humble, even to the point of withdrawal, even to fear itself—I have already noted this moment of hesitation before each big step in his life, each new decision—but without shirking. It must be noted that this lack of self-confidence, the timidity which had again overcome him in prison at Colditz, disappeared in this milieu to give place to a more balanced outlook, one more magnanimous in the ancient sense of the word: the feeling of being no worse than another (or rather that others are neither more stupid nor less good than oneself), but also of being as strong and of being as sure as another. Life teaches this, if it doesn't bruise one too much and too quickly; when this is understood one does not hesitate before an undertaking.

I must return to this sentiment of a personal vocation. Father Congar is quick to quote in this regard the words of John the Baptist: "No one can receive anything unless it is given to him from heaven. . . . He who has the bride is the bridegroom; but the friend of the bridegroom, who stands and hears him, rejoices exceedingly at the voice of the bridegroom. This my joy therefore is made full" (Jn. 3:27-30). As a young religious he recited with fervor the quotation, "And thou, child, shalt be called the prophet of the Most High . . ." from the Canticle of Zachary without any notion of an exceptional vocation; rather, he recited it as any priest, any Christian, might say it to keep his place, however modest, in God's design. Rather than quote here from the Preface to *Dialogue between Christians* which develops this theme in two places, I shall quote

from an unpublished work the response Father Congar gave
to one of the tributes given him in Strasbourg in December,
1963:

> If you like, I'll tell you a little secret. I believe that, if I had
> to say on what word of Scripture, of the Lord, or on what adage
> I have built my life, I would have to enumerate several—I have
> already referred to one or two of them in these conferences—but
> there is one that I have rarely mentioned and which, in the final
> analysis, is perhaps the most influential; that is the attitude of
> John the Baptist: to know that each one has what was given him
> and must be content with that. The words of John the Baptist,
> "I am not the spouse . . .". No, I am simply in the vestibule,
> where it is a little cold, the door opens, etc., I lead into the mar-
> riage chamber—this is the role given to me. I apply it to myself,
> I apply it to others, many others. Each one has his vocation and
> that is the one which is most beautiful. I do not compare myself
> absolutely to anything—that's silly moreover—and I wouldn't want
> anyone to compare himself to anyone else. Yes, each one's is
> the finest for him. And finally it is evident, if one believes that
> everything is directed and there is a kind of unity, that the
> Holy Spirit leads toward a goal and brings everything together.

As early as September 17, 1930, Father Congar composed a
long prayer which seems significant to me as an example of
his preoccupations at that time. Although it does not in any
way contain the idea of such a distinct personal vocation, it
does suggest what God can do in one's life. It asks of God a
more embracing Church, one less quick to condemn (even
then!), less centralized, less exclusively Latin. It becomes a
vibrant tribute to the diversity of the human creation as a
manifestation of God's glory and then quickly turns into a
supplication for the catholicity of the Church, whose message
ought to be accessible to all men. All men, therefore, should
first have been understood and received by the Church. Then
the prayer continues: "My God, I am poor and insignificant
. . . but you can expand and enlarge my heart to meet the
immense needs of the world." Finally, to an expression of
suffering because of the division of the Churches and of the

often discouraging countenance of the Catholic Church, he gives this answer: "In reality we are the countenance of the Church. We render it visible. My God, make in us for your Church a truly living countenance." One could think you were reading the invocations of John XXIII assigning as the aim of the Council the revivifying of the Church.

"Instrument of Christ"

But, modest as one may be, is there not a little presumptuousness in attributing a truly personal place to oneself in the Church, in the economy of salvation? To answer this reproach one could recall (as Karl Rahner loves to do) that each Christian, absolutely every one without exception, has his irreplaceable spot in the design of God. But let me call on witnesses more qualified than myself—two of the participants at the friendly gathering at Strasbourg, already mentioned. And first, that old traveling companion, Father Féret, who in the long address he had prepared at the request of the French Provincial, said:

> Well! To the observer, to the witness that I have been along your path for more than thirty years, it is striking to see how in your personal journey you have been led from your youth in intimate association with the entire history which God directs. Progressively, in the place destined for you, you too have taken charge of this history and have accomplished it with God. From the start, though not realizing it, you were in the axis of the living tradition. From my vantage point I observed that the beauty of it was that at each stage of your life God prepared you for your witness by external circumstances as well as by the seeds he had placed within you.

In the afternoon meeting, when Professor Cullmann's turn came, he said to Father Congar:

> You know that the question of salvation history is close to my heart—especially the question of post-biblical salvation history, for there is where the problem lies. At the Council one morning some weeks ago I discussed that point with a member

of the Secretariat for Unity who was seated in our tribune and with my Catholic interpreter. I spoke precisely on the relation between the role of prophet and that of the Institution in this salvation history. And I remember that my interpreter, in order to make me understand that there is place in the Catholic Church for the prophetic role, said to me: "Look at the importance of Father Congar in our Catholic Church for more than thirty years." Well and good. First I want to go on record as agreeing with this testimony. . . . I shall add that you have likewise played a major role for those Christians who are not members of your Church, which proves that behind the history of the different Christian Churches there is only one history of salvation.

And Professor Cullmann concludes this passage of his discourse in a way that exemplifies precisely the point under discussion:

In talking about man's role within the context of salvation history there is no danger of exaggerating the human element in it—for it is understood that, in this history, there are only instruments of Christ, and we all know that what we owe to you we owe to an Other who has made use of you.

3. AT THE SERVICE OF THE PEOPLE OF GOD

Man is free, not only because he can refuse God's call but also because if he consents it is up to him to arrange his own life, to choose the means. Father Congar chose to live his as a service. His conception of the role of a theologian flows from this. I have already remarked that his awareness of his own professional limitations (he had never taught dogma) as well as personal ones, and his great respect for a theology rationally organized and conceived as a synthesis, made him say that he was not a real theologian, that he had not produced an intellectual work in the strict sense of the word, that he was an intellectual apostle rather than a scientific theologian. He was an admirer of St. Thomas, but he did not think that he was in the theological line of descent as far as intellectual temperament was concerned. He would gladly define himself as "a doctrinal servant of the People of God."

A Doctrinal Servant of the People of God

At the outset, let me say that this is a personal option which does not involve a judgment on what theology ought to be. In fact Father Congar realizes more and more that the distinction between pastoral and scientific theology has been exaggerated, that according to subject matter theology necessarily has degrees of intelligibility, and that his way of working is authentically theological. On the other hand, this idea of service, if it always implies an apostolic aim (and what truly living theology does not?) should not mean that the ideas must be forced to serve apologetical aims as was the deliberate intention of defenders of devotion in the past. In fact, some theologians, exclusively concerned with furnishing the militants of Catholic Action with a dynamic spiritual nourishment (the examples are Father Congar's) still put the apologetical first. In the last analysis Father Congar truly has confidence in the work of the intelligence, including his own. He thinks his particular talent is for history. If certain characteristics of his intellectual temperament which limit him on the philosophical side result in his not having realized a great architectural theological work, on the other hand his profound conviction that " . . . nothing is more apostolic than the service of truth," his rejection of a theological science closed in on itself, as well as of an insufficiently structured spirituality, make him perhaps a new type of theologian, closer to the Fathers than to the medieval scholastics.

What is a theology whose center is not the Christian experience and the life of the Church today? What is a theology that is not concerned with the great demands and the great aspirations of the world, with the signs of the times? One day at the Council, during a meeting of the Commission, Father Congar said to a great dignitary of the Church: "I've just been walking in the outskirts of Rome—what a contrast to our beautiful conciliar room where we met yesterday!" The other replied: "That is no concern of ours—we make the doctrine, others apply it."

One cannot help thinking of that other word: "Go and report to John what you have heard and seen . . . the poor have the Gospel preached to them" (Lk. 7:22). I shall come back soon to the meaning of the poor and to other aspects of the idea of service. But I must sketch a parallel that Father Congar once suggested, but did not develop, to describe (with a touch of modesty) what his theology is or is not: "I am not like Karl Rahner."

Yves Congar and Karl Rahner

One could insist on the points of interest common to the two theologians: the care of renewing ecclesiology and missiology, of re-introducing biblical categories into the theological elaboration, of including in theology sections formerly abandoned by the "dogmatists" to apologetics, and of giving a decisive place to anthropological considerations. Perhaps I should again state that Father came to anthropology through ecclesiology and not vice versa, a fact significant in itself. But even while stressing the identity of their views on the role of the theologian in the Church as doctrinal servant of the People of God, it is more interesting for my purpose to note the differences as well. Doctrinal service is rendered by Karl Rahner in the realization of a much more structured, much more synthesized work— yet as a "devoured" man, he, like Father Congar, is hindered from realizing the work along the vast proportions which he had envisaged—a work which would have presented in a complete and intricate way the ensemble of a thought whose homogeneity and force can be sensed. Is it a question of a more speculative temperament? a question of a philosophical formation deepened in the living milieu of the philosophy of the German university? a question of apologetical concern accentuated by its confrontation with contemporary unbelief? a question of opportunity through professional application of dogmatic theology to teaching? No doubt there is a little of all this and through it all a charism—a word each of them likes to use—which is different for each.

The Will of the Gift of Self

The desire to make one's life a service implies for Father Congar a total gift of self without taking back or reserving anything; a gift conceived with the inflexible rigor which helps one understand what I said of his formation in the line of duty. The gift of self to his work: an immense solitary labor for thirty-five years, from seven o'clock in the morning until ten at night with clock-like regularity, in a room where the library shelves, the table, the furniture (even the bed and chairs) collapse under the weight of books, notes, index cards, and the over-whelming pile of correspondence. His organization is unbeliev-ably like that of an artisan, without assistants, without modern files. ("A paper is there, between two books. . . . I tell you it is there. . . . What? It isn't there? Oh, I moved the pile five years ago; it's up there, above my head." The paper is pulled out, everything tumbles down with it.) He didn't even have a secretary until very recently. This is quite a contrast to the staff of assistants and of modern secretaries that other theologians have today—but Father Congar has no desire to change systems.

The gift of self to others, to the least interesting, to the most boring, with of course the first moment of irritation against having to waste his time, then the reaction: No one takes my time from me, I give it. A fixed decision to refuse nothing. Even to the detriment of the work to be done? "It's crazy. Others can do that. Cut down!" No, even at such a cost. Scorn no one, answer everyone, serve everyone, don't take oneself seriously. More profoundly, the decision not to become his own end, not to choose his life himself, to accept whatever happens. This is why people love him and love him very much in spite of his abruptness and bluntness. Let me quote another excerpt from Father Féret's address to Father Congar:

Even in the midst of your intense labor of study and of editing innumerable articles and books, you have accepted the humblest tasks. If today you are induced to make all these collections of your former production, those who do not know you cannot possibly understand their genesis. Only those who have followed you closely know the real explanation. From a spirit of service you have made it a rule never to refuse a contribution, never to refuse to collaborate, when someone requests an article for some collection or some *Festgabe*. You were often overburdened, but you always accepted saying: "After all, this is my stint for the Church, I ought to do it." And then an article for somebody's sixtieth birthday, a contribution for something's centenary, a question of finishing up or wrapping some of the volumes of your collection *Unam Sanctam,* to say nothing of articles for the daily newspaper or weekly magazines, nor of the innumerable conferences and congresses, unity weeks, social weeks, etc., nor of the ordinary preaching you do here and there by chance during your travels or to meet the demands of your conventual life. All your life there has been this permanent weight of the Church's requests, to which you believed yourself bound to reply, like a servant wanting to give to the fullest of his service. In a calm and quiet spot you could have produced a beautiful work, purely scientific, brilliant, polished, but you would have had to withdraw from the mainstream, withdraw from the daily service of the Church.

4. A CERTAIN "PROPHETISM"

The Icon of St. Dominic

All that has been said of him above plus his evangelical liberty and a concern to find the great reformist inspiration of the prophets of Israel converge to produce an impression of the whole that a certain reticence prevents me from specifying precisely; I prefer to suggest it by taking refuge behind the testimony that the lamented Professor Léon Zander, Orthodox layman, theologian of the Institut Saint-Serge of Paris, a very humble and very profound man, a delightful friend, brought back to me from Strasbourg in 1963 (small matter if it leads me to anticipate a bit Father Congar's ecumenical role). I wish to render this text with all its savor, and hence am willing to leave in it some clumsiness due to its spontaneity. Professor

Zander spoke of the importance of encounters with personalities of the Roman Church who reveal by their radiance what a Catholic priest can be. By destroying barriers they contribute something decisive toward a reconciliation. He continued:

> Indeed I think, Father Yves, that you are one of these people! Not only while listening to you, while having the joy of considering you as a friend, we come nearer Catholicism, we see the spiritual riches that it has and that it can reveal in its faithful, but we have many things to learn, to imitate, to discover, which completely change our attitude toward this Church which was closed for us because of historical misunderstandings. Allow me a personal example; you probably do not recall it. If you remember how we collaborated at the Saulchoir when there was the Catholic-Orthodox meeting on the "Filioque." During dinner or lunch someone brought this reproach against you, that you reply to every demand made on you, that you work too hard, that you are overburdened. And your reply was: "I cannot refuse them." Moreover you said, "St. Dominic would not have, either." Do you know what my reaction was? I said to myself: "There is the application of the general rule of iconology, the identification of the type with the prototype." I saw in you the icon of St. Dominic, and naturally, in St. Dominic, the icon of the Catholic. A word, probably almost unconscious—you uttered it without thinking of that—revealed a very important thing to me. And of this I can say that I try as much as I can to follow you and never reply with a "no" when a request is made of me; to make an effort, even if it is beyond my possibilities. It is a purely personal example to tell you what a role priests like you, without knowing it, play in our lives; and we, without knowing it either, come nearer to you. In rethinking about all that, after many years, we say: "Lord, give us some of these examples, give us some of these incarnations of the holiness of the Roman Church in these living and beloved personalities so that, through them, we might be able to work to the great reconciliation of traditions and to the unity of love which seems to us to be the source and the end of all ecumenism."

Pride in the Truth Which Frees

A complete love of the truth, an absolute faith—a little unbending, a little totalitarian (already seen in the child who didn't like Jules Verne: "Since it isn't true it doesn't interest me")—in

the *truth* on which one stakes his entire life, that is what makes
prophets in the Church. This is especially so in a Church which
had, which has, such a great need of resources, of purification,
of revivification, of openness. When something is true, whether
authorized circles say so or not does not change anything, all
that can be added is that a modest man ought to distrust his
own lights, ought not to draw conclusions too hastily. The fact
remains that it is not authority which makes truth, it is truth
which judges authority. True enough, it is not through our lips
that Truth pronounces this judgment, but to have understood
this does away with platitudes, fear, mental contortions. This
Christian liberty, this inalienable right founded on the blood
of Christ to adhere to the truth and be its servant, and to
pronounce it before and against all else, or to be silent (but
without contradicting oneself), this pride of the truth which
frees—so Dominican—is incontestably one of the great axes of
the life and thought of Father Congar. Nothing could show
this better than a reading of one of his most beautiful pages,
taken from the Preface to *Vraie et fausse réforme dans l'Eglise*:

> This book having been submitted to the examination of
> friendly censors, and then to a complete revision, is offered to
> the appreciation of all who really want to read it. But above
> all, and in the spirit of the second part, it is submitted to the
> judgment of the holy Church. She will understand, I am sure,
> that it is not a book of negative criticism but of love and of
> confidence. Above all, of total love and of absolute confidence
> in regard to truth. Not in vain has the Friar Preacher received
> the charge to defend this truth with all his strength. It alone
> can subjugate and at the same time fill and exalt the spirit. Here
> as elsewhere it has been believed possible to serve it only by
> an absolute and total sincerity. Absolute, that is to say without
> any mixture of cleverness, without camouflage, without timidity;
> total, that is to say honoring truth in all its dimensions, accord-
> ing to all its aspects, thus discovering, not an added artificial
> touch of "prudence," but from the very interplay of things the
> respect for everything which ought to be respected: a respect at
> once proud and humble, the respect of a man standing erect but
> realizing that he is dependent and willing to submit to an order

since order is but a particular name for truth. This is why there are no innuendoes in this book, nothing that is not loyal, nothing which cannot be heard and loyally upheld by every honest and informed man. Subtleties of thought and style deceive only those who are unworthy of the plain truth because they do not seek her unconditionally. Rather a completely confident freedom is the only attitude conceivable among children of God who have been established in the liberty of Christ and who celebrate unceasingly the unleavened bread of sincerity and truth.

Prophet of Tradition

In this remarkable text a prophetism *of a special kind* (for there are many) will have been sensed. For example, it is not a bitter, passionate, intransigent prophetism. I must try to make this distinction more precise. In the first place, as I have already said, Father Congar is essentially a man of tradition; I shall have occasion to return to the mutual interaction of a reforming prophetism and fidelity to tradition—two attitudes, two ecclesiological concepts which (according to Father Congar), far from excluding each other, mutually involve each other. But one can already understand that Father Congar's reformism will be well-tempered by this continuous reference to tradition. Under certain aspects one can be a man of reform, and under others a man of tradition, not according to a material division of the areas but according to the intimate bond between these values. In the Church the man of tradition is to the conservative what the man of reform is to the revolutionary. There is truth in the first members of the alternatives (hence no contradiction), incompatible caricatures between the second members.

Secondly, in the Preface to *Vraie et fausse réforme* I am aware that, if "truth" and "liberty" both come under the pen of Father Congar, the accent undeniably falls on the first; the second is but a consequence of it. The idea of "Christian liberty," which truly polarizes the thought of men like Father Chenu, Father Féret or Father Liégé (who in certain aspects is so like Father Congar he could be considered a disciple), has not the same intensity in Father Congar's thought.

Finally and above all else, it has been no surprise while reading this text to see the Church recurring time and again, not as a subject of discussion but as a frame of reference for the discussion, the backdrop of the entire Christian life and of all theological activity—the Church, its love, its service. Other faithful servants of the Gospel, especially during difficult years, have somewhat condoned certain failings, certain deficiencies of the Church. They figured that the survival in her of "high priests, scribes, and pharisees" constituted part of her mystery. Intellectual scepticism, pessimism concerning man, constant attendance on history, anti-organization temperaments, a greater awareness of "the world," all managed sufficiently well to live in the Church, even in submission to the Church, a little to the side of structures and in spite of them.

The attitude of a man like Father Congar is entirely different. He is truly a man of the Church, fighting from within her to help make her countenance more evangelical, suffering from her slightest defects, even from the most dreadful blows that could come to him through her—not so much from the hierarchy as from integralist pamphleteers, neurotic anti-communists, or anti-progressives. Naturally, in the face of such narrowness, such deformation, such doctrinal or devotional excess, he was to appeal from the Church of this given moment to the eternal Church, to the inalienable treasure—which, however, is not wholly complete during each consciously lived moment. In spite of everything he was never to give in to compromise, to the mutilation of Catholicity. Traditional reformism, intra-ecclesial protest, freedom in and through the truth, this prophetism is completed by an existential note which actualizes in daily life one of the points of the program proposed to the Catholic reformer at the end of *Vraie et fausse réforme*: patience. In delaying somewhat over this, I bring to a close this portrait of the theologian. It seems to me that it should be helpful to an understanding of his thought, to which, as I have gone along, I have given more attention than is apparent.

"The Patience Which Engenders Hope"

Renewal through a return to the sources, through the free projection into a new world, absolutely implies patience; that is a fundamental conviction of Father Congar who at the same time admits that men almost always lack this quality. To have a feeling for the delays necessary for the maturation of a living thing, this is not a question of mechanically substituting one thing for another, but of letting live, and that demands time. It requires work too, without wanting to gather immediately the fruit of one's labor. To know how to wait an entire lifetime: that is not the result of a relaxed psychology but of a sense of history. Sometimes one is disappointed; nothing ever comes of it. This was not so in Father Congar's case. In 1939, calculating the probable delays of the renewal, the priests at the Saulchoir said, "It will take thirty or forty years." The deeper the trough of the wave, the more quickly it passes. Father Congar loves to recall John XXIII: "Without him, we would not have had this." In conclusion let me quote here a passage from *Dialogue between Christians,* which shall soon be exemplified at each step as I trace the ecumenical career of Father Congar.

> Those who know me know that I am impatient in little things; I can't wait for a bus! I believe I am patient in big things, with a certain active patience about which I'd like to say a word here. It is entirely different from just marking time, from a certain faculty of chronological expectation. It is a certain quality of the spirit or rather of the soul, which has its roots in the profound and existential conviction first, that God is directing the game and is accomplishing a work of grace in us, and secondly, that for every important thing a delay is necessary for maturation. One cannot dispense himself from working with his time, provided he acts not in an empty time but in a time in which something happens, to know the maturation of that thing whose seed has been confided to the earth. I have often thought of the words of St. Paul: ". . . knowing that tribulation works out endurance, and endurance tried virtue, and tried virtue

hope" (Rom. 5:4). One would almost expect the reverse; it would seem that one could wait patiently if one had hope in his heart. In one sense that is true, but the sequence indicated by St. Paul reveals a more profound truth. Men who do not know how to suffer do not know how to hope. Neither do they know how to hope who are too eager, who wish to seize the object of their desire immediately. The patient sower, who entrusts his seed to the earth and to the sun, is the very man of hope. If patience is the patience of the sower, it is necessarily accompanied by the cross: "They that sow in tears shall reap in joy" (Ps. 125:5); but sometimes they do not reap at all, for ". . . one sows, another reaps" (Jn. 4:37). The Cross is the condition of every holy work, God himself is at work in what is a cross for us. Only through it do we reach a certain authenticity and profundity of existence. Nothing is wholly serious unless one agrees to pay this price. Only he who has suffered for his convictions attains in them a certain force, a certain quality of the irrevocable, and also the right to be heard and respected. *O Crux benedicta.* . . .[2]

---

[2]*Chrétiens en dialogue,* pp. lvi-lvii. See Chap. 1, above, footnote 5.

CHAPTER THREE

Ecumenical Vocation and Doctrine

1. THE CALL

Into the framework that this study of the life of Father Congar prior to 1965 prepared, I can easily put the highlights of his vocation and endeavors for the reunion of Christians. To carry out this task I shall rely heavily, even if I do not always quote it, on his Preface to *Dialogue between Christians,* to which I have already referred several times. I shall add to it some incidents not included in it: an analysis of the great ecumenical works of Father Congar; and a reflection on the fruits of the exchanges which for thirty-five years he has carried on (through books or personal contacts) with Christian brothers separated from the Roman communion.

"Who Sowed This Seed in Me?"

Preparations for the ecumenical vocation go far back into the life of Father Congar, a man in whom, as has been observed already, things have deep roots. One must not forget that Sedan was one of the great centers of French Protestantism in the sixteenth and seventeenth centuries, illustrated by the teaching of Jurieu, de Bayle, and others. Yves Congar was born into a country of mixed religion, where his parents knew some Protestants, where as a child he played with little Protestants (even having "theological" discussions on the Mass with the minister's son), where he shared with the Calvinists the chapel which the minister offered to the Catholic pastor whose own church had been burned by the Uhlans.

It was at the Saulchoir, when he was already aware of the problems of the Church and of a theology of the Church, that

57

Father Congar truly acknowledged a call to work for unity. Indeed, the existence of the "Russian Seminary" at Lille, mentioned previously, directed by the French Dominicans, and certain courses of Father Chenu's in 1929 on the "Faith and Order" movement and on the Lausanne Conference, helped to deepen this awareness. But as I said earlier, it was during the young deacon's preparation for his ordination, while meditating on the seventeenth chapter of St. John's Gospel, that he recognized his vocation to work for Christian unity. From the time of his ordination the young priest frequently offered Mass "for Christian unity." In one of his chronicles from the Council at the time of its second session, Father Congar describes the tense expectancy felt by those dedicated to unity at the moment that the schema on ecumenism was introduced. Then he reviewed his own past:

> It is an historic moment. On this morning of November 18 we gather in prayer, we listen, we wait in hope. The Church is about to engage in dialogue in a definitive way. Perhaps she will be surprised to find herself so firmly convinced of things she scarcely realized only a few years ago. Who sowed this seed? And who sowed it in me some thirty-five years ago? One might as well ask who makes the dawn succeed night, or spring follow winter.

Father Congar made known to his superiors his desire to work for the cause of unity. The first to whom he confided this was Father Chenu, who expressed his complete bewilderment. He could not see why this brilliant student would leave his medieval studies where he constituted the greatest hope of a team weakened by illness and the absence of some of its members; he regretted somewhat that Father Congar chose to "specialize in ecumenism." He was not slow to understand that it was not a question of specialization but (an idea dear to Father Congar) a veritable congeries of everything in the Church. There indeed is a major ecclesiological principle: in the Church its "in-itself" cannot be separated from its "with-the-other" or "for-the-other." Neither ecumenism, nor mission, nor presence to the world are adjuncts or appendices, rather they are of the very essence of the Church. She is defined only when they are evoked. He also made his interests known in a letter to his former regent of studies, Father Lemonnyer, who had meanwhile become closely associated with the Master General of the Dominicans. Father Lemonnyer replied in 1929 or 1930, encouraging him and assuring him of his complete confidence. Coming from a man as sceptical and as cold as Father Lemonnyer, this assurance carried considerable weight.

How to Listen to the "Others"

A patient man, docile, respectful, Father Congar's first move was to listen. And to listen first of all to those who had already blazed the trail which he hoped to follow. He inquired about the Malines Conversations, about Father Portal, Cardinal Mercier, in order to live in communion with these pioneers. Later on, he was delighted to meet others more or less suspect or exiled. He was listening, too, to the "Others," discovering their books, their centers. Immediately after his ordination he left for Düsseldorf where, in the library of the Dominican convent, he found Friedrich Heiler's review *Die Hochkirche,* and was struck by its enthusiasm and openness. The following year he visited places made famous by Luther—Wartburg, Erfurt, Wittenberg. Personal contacts were to follow soon.

I must insist, however, even if I return to it in a more theoretical consideration, that there is more than just listening at the heart of Father Congar's ecumenism. From the outset there was a fundamental attitude without which no dialogue is possible (and in which a whole ecclesiology and even an entire conception of truth were involved), a readiness to encounter others with the thought of finding in them an element of truth and the willingness to embrace it. It was absolutely necessary to repudiate confessional apologetics, a "ghetto" spirit whose

own bent is to absolutize everything current in a certain milieu
and thus destroy the very possibility of discovering others and
surpassing oneself. This involves an absolute confidence in
truth and implies risking everything on the principle of St.
Thomas that no truth can be contrary to another truth. Consequently, whatever truth one finds, wherever one finds it, it
must be gathered up. One can be sure that in the end all will
harmonize. According to Father Congar this can undoubtedly
be done only little by little, knowing how to go one step in
advance of one's present position. And thus one is led to see
that this finally involves an ecclesiology in which the idea of
catholicity holds a decisive place: catholicity in depth, to be
sure, a true universality and not a simple geographical cos-
mopolitanism. It is an idea of an all-embracing unity, global—
gathering ideas, things (especially in Father Congar's pre-war
perspective), and people (he would insist more on this today)
into an all-encompassing fullness. The entire ecumenical orienta-
tion of Father Congar rests on this concept of catholicity. A
modest beginning in the 1930's attests to it—the foundation at
the Saulchoir of "nuclei of catholicity," where the differences
and varieties (Nordic Christianity, Mediterranean Christianity,
East-West, etc.) were studied in view of a reconstitution of
unity.

2. TO APPROACH DIVIDED CHRISTIANS

Before retracing briefly Father Congar's intense pre-war ecumenical activity let me examine for a moment the relationship
between ecumenism, ecclesiology, and theology as seen in his
work of this period. Let me note in passing that the word "ecumenism" was then quite new in Catholic circles; it appeared
only within quotation marks in the subtitle of *Chrétiens désunis*:
principes d'un "oecuménisme" catholique. But in the conciliar
document, *Ecumenism,* Catholic principles of ecumenism are
spoken of; the adjective is displaced and the quotation marks
have disappeared. When one has learned from Father Chenu

to attach decisive importance to words and to their history one cannot but be struck by this rapid evolution.

Ecumenism Is Not a Specialty

Ecclesiology and ecumenism are inseparably connected. It is useless to try to establish formal priorities. It is at the heart of an ecclesiological awareness that Father Congar discovers ecumenism, which is itself only one dimension of a much broader reality. But since, and rightly so, it is a dimension in the strict sense, signifying a certain state and spirit of all ecclesial mentalities and realities, then if one wishes to advance ecumenism one must grapple with the state and conception of the Church at every level. At the same time, listening to others is provocation for the Church, as much for a purifying return to the living evangelical sources as for a more truly Catholic opening. In the Preface to *Dialogue between Christians* Father Congar writes:

> I felt keenly the strong link between the total stripping demanded by ecumenism and the whole ecclesiastical, pastoral, biblical, and liturgical movement. I quickly realized that ecumenism is not a specialty and that it presupposes a movement of conversion and reform coextensive with the life of all communions. It seemed to me, also, that for each individual the ecumenical task was to move the Catholic Church a few degrees on its own axis in the direction of a possible convergence and unanimity with the "others," in accordance with a more profound and honored fidelity to our unique Source or our common sources.

Why is ". . . the most profitable ecumenical work accomplished at home and pursued in one's own Church?" A passage from the introduction to the conciliar document *Ecumenism* tells us. Father Congar writes:

> Every time an effort in the evangelical order is made for a greater authenticity of things, or in such a way that, had one acted thus before the fatal catastrophe of the final break it would have been avoided, then one does his part to heal the wounds of the Christian body; one gives life and power to the movement which works for encounter, reconciliation, a regrouping in unity.

But let me return to *Dialogue between Christians* where, having enunciated these principles, Father Congar shows the concrete ways of carrying them out:

> Hence the program outlined in *Divided Christendom*, successive applications of which resulted in other works such as *Vraie et fausse réforme, Lay People in the Church, Tradition and Traditions*. Over and above these works, however, hundreds of conferences, meetings, courses, were formally consecrated either to different aspects of the cause of unity, or planned to assist it in some way. In the final analysis, indeliberate, unintentional ecumenism, an ecumenism which was so only because of an internal dimension or quality, was the most efficaciously ecumenical.

Note the nuance: great ecclesiological works have been conceived in terms of and in favor of ecumenical action. This causes me to suggest that, in this period of Father Congar's work, ecumenical interests held first place. They indeed represent his fundamental vocation. With time, circumstances will displace the center of greatest interest.

In any case, one thing certain is that Father Congar was to accept during this period numerous theological undertakings and conferences in various fields. He accepted them very deliberately, less from immediate personal attraction than from a desire to advance the cause of ecumenism by drawing attention to it. "By means of studies of unquestionable scientific and theological value I wanted to gain enough credit to cover and support my position on ecumenism, and thus any credit or honor that might come to my humble person from theologians, clergy, or hierarchy could be turned to the advantage of the cause I served."[1]

To Encounter Others

I shall be rather brief on the ecumenical activities of Father Congar from 1932 to 1940. Greater detail can be had by refer-

---

[1]*Chrétiens en dialogue,* Preface. See Chap. 1, above, footnote 5.

ring to the Preface already cited which describes at length numerous encounters. I shall consider only those that had lasting influence. Father Congar, without the shadow of a doubt, purposely sought out these contacts. Many pioneers in ecumenism, many Protestant and Orthodox theologians, saw this young Dominican descend upon them. Such was the case for Oscar Cullmann who tells of the fear his old servant had of this "monk." A native of one of those exclusively Protestant villages of Alsace, she was sure he would bring harm to her master.

I have already alluded to the first meetings of 1932: the courses at the Protestant Faculty of Theology, whose teachers were W. Monod, A. Jundt, A. Lecerf. Having broken with an anemic liberalism they were the moving spirits of a return to the sources of the Reformation. Their pupils were Roland de Pury, Louis Bouyer, Jean de Saussure. I have also mentioned the Franco-Russian circle animated by Berdyaev, with its retreats at which Christians of all persuasions could be found. Father Congar still tells of his visits to Abbé Gratieux, a specialist on Khomiakov and on the Slavophile movement, and to Dom Lambert Beauduin, the moving force behind the liturgical renewal, founder of Chevetogne and friend of the future John XXIII. Like Abbé Gratieux, Dom Beauduin was under suspicion, indeed exiled, which fact undoubtedly explains the reserve with which he greeted his enthusiastic visitor. At Amay (where Dom Beauduin had founded a monastery dedicated to the cause of unity and characterized by the simultaneous celebration of the Office in the Latin and Oriental rites) Congar conversed with Dom Clément Lialine who gave him much in the way of knowledge of Slavic orthodoxy. Here too he met Father Couturier. This priest, by promoting the celebration of the octave of prayer for unity, was soon to bring something decisive to the true evangelical implanting and flowering of the cause for reunion. His activity, centering especially at Lyons under the sponsorship of Cardinal Gerlier, was to be somewhat paralleled during these years by the more doctrinal work of Father Congar. At the same time, however, Father Congar had served dutifully at the Church Unity Octaves and found much encouragement in discovering more and more fervent listeners. For his part he gave them solid ecclesiological foundations, and a keen realization of the obstacles that charity alone could not overcome.

By 1934 Father Congar was well enough known to take the initiative and to plan some ecumenical activities, usually rather modest but contributive to a reconciliation between Roman Catholics and Protestants. In May, 1934, at Juvisy, when Karl Barth was visiting in Paris, Father Congar assembled two groups: his confrères from the *Vie Intellectuelle* (the future team of the *Editions du Cerf* at Paris, whose importance in the development of French Catholicism has often been remarked) and his Protestant friends. There were Etienne Gilson, Jacques Maritain, Gabriel Marcel, Pierre Maury, Denis de Rougement, and Alexandre Marc. Somewhat similar, though more pretentious, was the ecumenical gathering held in 1937 at Bièvres, in view of a common preparation of themes to be discussed at the "Life and Work" Conference at Oxford and at the meeting of Catholic ecumenists at the Saulchoir in 1938. I should note here that as early as 1933 Father Congar had felt that in Protestantism, even French Protestantism, the future belonged to Karl Barth and his followers. He had given a course on him at the Saulchoir which Pastor Maury, a disciple of Barth, now endorsed, expressing the agreement on Congar's interpretation of the Swiss theologian's thought. The dominant note in Barth's thinking was the purely "vertical" and personal character of the relationship with a transcendent God to whom all causality in salvation seems jealously reserved. Barth was afterwards to evolve, in the sense of the "humanity of God."

To Know and to Recognize One Another

To make the reformed Churches known to Catholics and vice versa, to cope with prejudice and ignorance, Father Congar undertook to publish regularly in *La Vie Intellectuelle* sections devoted to Protestantism and ecumenism. While recognizing the value of these efforts, Father Congar is today more than aware of their limitations: they failed to convey an understanding of the complexity of the spiritual worlds that were invaded. Greater opportunity should have been given the Protestants themselves to explain their own positions, rather than have them explained for them. Other collaborations with *La Vie Spirituelle, Sept, Irenikon,* and *Russie et Chrétienté* were added to this program for the diffusion of ecumenical ideas. At the same time Father Congar was the moving spirit behind two intellectual groups interested in working for unity: one under the patronage of Père Portal; the other, called "L'Amitié," was restricted to members of the teaching profession.

Last but not least, in 1935 he decided upon and announced the formation of the series *Unam Sanctam,* a project to which I shall return when speaking of the principal ideas of his ecclesiology. It would be difficult to exaggerate the role this series has played, and one may conclude that Paul VI was thinking of it and of its influence when he said that Father Congar was one of those who had the most to contribute to the preparation of the Council. In any case, the importance of *Unam Sanctam* in the ecumenical field (my present concern) has been considerable. The first volume of the series was *Divided Christendom,* which I shall analyze shortly. But while noting that, in this volume, the part devoted to Anglicanism undoubtedly marks the greatest affinity with the spiritual milieu studied, and is the one that has aged the least, still I am led to recall, though briefly, the trip that Father Congar made to England in 1936. If the ecumenist was disappointed by the theological climate of the Church of England, which did not seem to him worthy of the exegetical and historic culture which for the most part is prevalent there, nevertheless he was profoundly affected by her spiritual heritage which truly still lives within her. "I love the Anglican Church for its admirable patrimony, its cult, and its ethos, at once both religious and humanist, reverent and free. . . . How could one prevent the riches of its moral and religious heritage from perishing if it should eventually unite with Rome? That is a possibility which belongs neither to tomorrow nor the day after" (Preface to *Dialogue between Christians*).

1937: *"Divided Christendom"*

Divided Christendom is a book whose historical importance (a Protestant author wanted to use it as the dividing line separating Catholic participation into a "before" and "after") must be stressed as frankly as its senescence is admitted. From afar Father Congar judges it thus:

> I am well aware of the limitations and even of the defects of *Divided Christendom*. I was then too close to a scholastic Thomism, too close to the study I had made of Schleiermacher and Protestant liberalism. I was too quick to classify, categorize, and judge. . . . Even so, *Divided Christendom* had a great influence as I have often since realized. How many priests and laymen, how many bishops at the Council, have told me that they owe to it either their awakening to ecumenism or more often their conversion to a new meaning of the Church, a meaning that is broader and more traditional. . . . I think that the greatest advantage of *Divided Christendom* is that, for the first time, an effort was made to define ecumenism theologically or at least to situate it in this context (Preface to *Dialogue between Christians*).

As the diversity of testimonies just presented might lead one to expect, this book includes widely different elements: those which at the time of their composition were to comprise a small ecumenical *Summa*. First there were those elements that could be described as reasoned information. In this category there was first of all a historical study whose purpose was to explain (more or less) in their genesis and duration the stages in the ecumenical movement (Chapter 1). Then there was a somewhat detailed presentation of the ecumenical movement (Chapter 4) of which Father Congar was to say later in a kind of *retractio*: "I underestimated the importance of 'Life and Work'. . . . I did not see the profound truth concealed in the idea of working in unison; the missionary dynamism of the ecumenical movement also escaped me" (Preface to *Dialogue between Christians*). Finally there was a study of ecclesiology and of Anglican ecumenical theology (Chapter 5), and (with a more general introduction to Orthodox mentality) an exposition on Russian Slavophile ecclesiology and a criticism of it (Chapter 6).

Chapters Two and Three of *Divided Christendom* are of a very different nature from the rest of the book; they propose to establish the ecclesiological foundations of ecumenism by the study of the complementary concepts of *unity* and *catholicity*. Why should the Church be *one*? Because a unique divine life is given to her in the unique Christ (a divine logic of unity); but also because men need to express in social unified structures (those of a unique organized people), a profound unity of faith and of communication of life (a human logic of unity). One must understand thoroughly the line of reasoning in this second point: theological reflection is not a deduction, it begins with the economy of the incarnation effectively willed by God, but it applies to God (for purposes of convenience) an anthropology of corporal and social man. God, saving his creature, saves him as he is. When I begin to speak of Father Congar's ecclesiology I shall return to the ecclesiological "model" that this reasoning introduces.

But this unity is a unity of fullness and of riches bringing into a synthesis the infinite diversity of men, of cultures, of civilizations. This synthesis the Church should incorporate into herself, thus incorporating it into Christ (catholicity). Thus she adapts herself to all the differences but she also purifies the human diversities, and assimilating them to herself in order to incorporate them, she makes them die to their too specific peculiarities. In conclusion, Father Congar sketches the portrait of the truly catholic Christian and thus brings to a close these two beautiful chapters, whose somewhat idyllic nature contrasts painfully with reality; yet one can see how they lay the foundations for any ecumenical theology faithful to the nature of the Church of Christ.

> The catholicity of the Church is the universal capacity of its unity. It is the pleroma of Christ, his expansion and his accomplishment in humanity; the coming of his salvation and as it were his mystical incarnation in all the living flesh of humanity. The Church is, for every man personally, and for all humanity, the gathering, the accomplishment, the fullness in unity. She is our peace in Christ.[2]

An especially fine book, *Catholicism*, by Father Henri de Lubac, S.J., was to be number three in the series *Unam Sanctam*. This book was to support these views with an exceptional knowledge of patristic tradition and an appealing style which was both poetic and precise. The reverberations of this work in the French Church were to be considerable.

Finally, Chapters Seven and Eight of *Divided Christendom* wished to propose a properly ecumenical theology elaborated from a Catholic point of view, an organized discussion on the theological problems posed by the divisions and the search for unity. This was followed by a concrete program for action. It seems to me that these chapters are the most outdated of the work. They deal successively with the following: the status in the Church of separated Christians taken individually; a judgment on the value of the dissident communities as such; a theology of reunion (conceived with many nuances, such as the return of the separated brethren without any positive renunciation on their part, to the body of the only Church which, in the meantime, will have manifested its catholicity in its fullness); a reflection on the intellectual and psychological attitudes necessary to progress along the path to unity. This was all

---

[2]*Chrétiens désunis*, in *Unam Sanctam* (Paris: Editions du Cerf, 1937), I. See Chap. 1, above, footnote 6.

treated in a fresh, audacious way that was to be criticized because of its openness. But compared with the later writings of Father Congar, or even with the conciliar text on ecumenism, it is apparent that these chapters were soon to be outdated. In general their greatest limitation is that they are deduced too immediately from principles posited from above, from the unity-catholicity dialectic at the interior of the Roman Catholic Church. These principles suppose an ideal situation—something the fact of division belies. They can in no way be revoked because of this contingent fact, but only subsequent analyses, resting on the existence of the ecumenical movement interpreted as a "sign of the times" will permit an advance. To adopt a dynamic view of the search for a unity still situated in the distance, we must maintain that the Roman Catholic Church is the unique Church of Christ which substantially contains catholicity in its fullness, but we must transcend the negative judgment brought against the separated churches, the idea of a Catholic ecumenism centered in Rome, and the problematic of the return to the fold.

3. FOUNDATIONS FOR ECUMENISM

I Was Suspect

In 1937 Cardinal Pacelli, then Secretary of State to Pius XI, had refused Father Congar authorization to participate as an observer in the Oxford Conference which he had helped prepare with some Protestant participants. This was the first of a long series of rebuffs and suspicions. I have already mentioned the difficulties encountered in Rome in regard to *Divided Christendom* and to the French translation of Möhler's *L'Unité dans l'Eglise*, difficulties that were renewed from 1948 to 1950 when a question arose concerning a new edition of *Divided Christendom*. The publication of a new edition was then deemed impossible. Between these two events is situated the disappointment experienced in prison by Father Congar in regard to the ecumenical contacts he had with the simple average Catholic as compared with theology students interested in ecumenism. A certain number of incidents could even be cited here, to say nothing of the climate of opinion (very unfavorable to the irenic spirit) produced by the extreme combativeness and bitter struggle of these years.

After the war, contacts as well as work were resumed either directly in the area of ecumenism or indirectly through the renewal of the ecclesial conscience and of the theology of the Church within the Catholic communion. Father Congar had many encounters with Protestants and Orthodox, much work with Chevetogne and with *Istina,* founded and directed by Father C. Dumont, O.P., of whose remarkable ecumenical gifts Father Congar was later to say: "He had the faculty of truly seeing things in their context and development, combined with a shrewd appraisal of men and of things." Dumont also had the capacity of acquiring extremely accurate information, and above all of giving friendly support: "No dossier can tell what a friend, support, and counselor Father Dumont was" (Preface to *Dialogue between Christians*).

To avoid differences that might have proved harmful to the very cause of unity, the publication of numerous articles and books was renounced, as were numerous meetings between divided Christians or even with Catholic ecumenists. Two refusals were to disappoint Father Congar keenly in 1948: the refusal of the permission to publish an article on the Catholic position in regard to the ecumenical movement; and the refusal of authorization for him and nine other theologians (the list of whom had been requested of him by the office at Geneva) to participate at the Amsterdam Assembly as observers. This center was asked to deal instead with theologians who enjoyed the confidence of official representatives. This event proved, as Father Congar notes in the Preface to *Dialogue between Christians,* that "I was simply not made for any kind of negotiation whatsoever." He also realized that supervision had become so rigorous that he would soon have to give up all ecumenical activity: "I was irremediably suspect and under surveillance, my actions real or supposed were interpreted in advance in a reprehensible sense." At that time, the Instruction of the Holy Office defining the regulations for the participation by Catholics in the activities of the ecumenical movement, and the official conference of Catholic ecumenists organized at Rome under the direction of Father Charles Boyer, S.J., which was awaited with much apprehension, was not entirely negative. Yet shortly there was to come the publication of *Humani Generis,* and the promulgation of the doctrine of the bodily Assumption of the Virgin. It is known only too well the regrettable effect this was to have on ecumenical relations, especially for its champions.

The Time of Silence

For Father Congar the time of silence had come:

> For my part, I was as discreet as possible on strictly ecumenical matters, especially in regard to publications. I thought that the condemnation or formal disavowal of a book like *Divided Christendom* would set the cause of Catholic ecumenism back thirty years. It seemed to me that I could help most by keeping silent or in any case by publishing nothing. I limited myself to preaching during the Christian unity octave or to small groups (Preface to *Dialogue between Christians*).

He extended his activities too to the negotiations that were to result in inaugurating the "Catholic Council for Ecumenical Questions," a group of Catholic ecumenists who were later to supply most of the members of the Secretariat for Christian Unity. Its president, Monsignor Willebrands, was to become the secretary of the Secretariat. Soon, after a trip to the East where Father Congar was received by His Holiness the Patriarch Athenagoras, came the obligation to submit to Roman censorship even his most insignificant writing. This meant exile.

But the entire ecumenical climate during all these years was disheartening. An article in *La Vie Intellectuelle* by Father

A. J. Maydieu entitled "Christians in Search of Unity: The Road Blocked," sadly remarked on this sorry state of affairs and tried to discover its causes, to propose a view which would enable one to work toward its solution. After the constant meetings of the war years, fruitful without compromise or concessions, in intense human communion with conscious reference to the Lord Jesus, source of friendship and mutual understanding, one sensed a hardening from the end of 1946 on. "Progressively," Father Maydieu wrote, "the gains are lost, positions hardened, the road which led from one to the other seems blocked." Hardening on the part of the Catholic position was seen in the condemnation of a "false irenicism" in *Humani Generis*. In general, the way that this encyclical settled in advance the principle of authority and the dogmatic way in which it was promulgated contributed to the unease. A hardening was also observed on the part of the Protestants, insistence on divisive elements, a revival of old griefs, the lecture platform offered to turncoats. The generous considerations that Father Maydieu advanced, and which called for a study, within the faith, of these events, and to integrate proposals to overcome them did not succeed in hiding the painful impression of disillusionment and discouragement which then gripped men dedicated to the cause of unity.

But we know that, for Father Congar, ecumenism implies a renewal in depth in the life of the Church as well as in the doctrinal awareness she has of herself in the light of the Word of God. Therefore it is toward this that he was to work during all those years. As far as possible this work was to be simultaneous with his ecumenical activity, but it became exclusively ecclesiological when the latter ceased. Thus he thought to give solid foundations to the search for unity, at the same time realizing an ecclesiological work, the importance of which was to transcend its immediate ecumenical consequences.

In the following chapter I shall return to the great ecclesiological themes that constitute the wealth of the works of this period.

For the moment let me pick out two outstanding notions, whose repercussions in the field of theology were as immediate as those of the concepts of unity and catholicity.

God's Salvation and Man's Action

In his article, "Dogme Christologique et ecclésiologie,"[3] Father Congar says there is a connection, a profound interrelation between Christology and ecclesiology. He strives hard to define the limits of this parallelism: some have been tempted to insist too much on it in the field of the ontology of the Church, but he is very correct and very illuminating for the general meaning of the two dogmas and the internal equilibrium of their elements. Therefore it is not surprising that any aberration in one field will be an almost infallible sign of an equivalent deviation in the other. Father Congar exemplifies this equilibrium in a second article of the same collection on the Christology and ecclesiology of Luther, "Regards et Réflexions sur la christologie de Luther."[4] For Luther, the humanity of Jesus is less the cause of salvation than the place where God accomplishes his victory over sin; the Church is the assembly of those whom God has justified by reason of their identification with the Crucified through faith, without any institution which would be a human work.

In another work, *Christ, Our Lady, and the Church*, Congar takes up this theme showing wherein lies the profound reason for this vertical conception (in which the Church, in an economy of the new alliance, plays a purely prophetic role of a perfectly spiritual kind). He shows this to be the same reason for refusing to Mary any role in the gift of grace. She is found in a conception of salvation according to which it can be accomplished by God alone, beyond any human collaboration. The reasoning is that any human cooperation would detract from the transcendence

---

[3]Written in 1954 and reprinted in *Sainte Eglise*, in *Unam Sanctam* (Paris: Editions du Cerf, 1963), XLI, pp. 69-104.
[4]Written in 1954 and reprinted in *Chrétiens en dialogue*, pp. 453-489. See Chap. 1, above, footnote 5.

and sovereign causality of the Creator. This sequence has an anthropological aspect as well. Undoubtedly one can show today, better perhaps than when Father Congar wrote these works, that the theology of justification of Luther and Barth (whom Congar particularly had in mind in writing these pages), is very close to that of the Council of Trent because, very simply, it is that of the New Testament. But the fact remains that the idea of a "reward" for the cooperation of man in a salvation given however gratuitously and the conviction that the glory of God is not lessened by man's greatness but contrariwise, constitute anthropological corollaries of these ecclesiological, Mariological, and Christological positions which remain the chief stumbling blocks on the path to unity. This is not the place to expatiate on the historical reasons for these positions taken by the Reformation: reaction against a scholasticism which had lost all sense of the absolute of God; imprisonment in a philosophy which did not permit the conception of the relationship of two causalities at different levels; a too exclusive insistence on the great themes of the Epistle to the Romans to the detriment of other aspects of the New Testament; a dialectical temperament or system solving problems by a *sic et non*—all these and more were factors contributing to the position of the Reformers.

A very important section of *Vraie et fausse réforme*[5] develops these analyses to show clearly that the fundamental principle of Lutheran ecclesiology (which is also the main point of divergence), namely, the rejection of institution, of authority, of tradition, takes root in a still more fundamental principle which is situated at the level of the religious relationship itself. This is the notion that salvation is the work of God *alone*, excluding any assistance or cooperation. Consequently, the visible Church is nothing but a human thing, which gathers the faithful saved interiorly and directly from on high by the Lord. For its part,

---

[5]*Vraie et fausse réforme dans l'Eglise,* in *Unam Sanctam* (Paris: Editions du Cerf, 1950) XX, pp. 440 ff.

Christology itself is threatened by a kind of occasionalism, a trace of which Father Congar found at the level of the theology of the Eucharist; perhaps his position on this last point would be somewhat modified today. Here is the essential passage:

> Finally the critical point seems to me to be a certain inability of the Protestant mind to grasp the true significance of transcendence and immanence. It always seems to the Protestants that they can affirm immanence only at the cost of transcendence. They do not see that something can be *in us,* and so ours, even while being God's; for them it can be God's only by not being ours. As if divine sovereignty did not consist precisely in causing things to be and to act; as if it were diminished when, through generosity, it communicates to the creature the possibility of cooperating with it.[6]

This is evidently aimed at the chief of the moderns, Karl Barth and his followers, but at others too, like Nygren and Aulen who however had tried to escape the consequences of this position. On the other hand the years have allowed us to see the emergence of other tendencies in Protestantism, at the heart of which this problematic is perhaps about to be overcome.

Ready to Justify His Love for Luther!

I shall return to the admiration which Father Congar had for Karl Barth and which he so eloquently expressed in the Preface to *Dialogue between Christians*:

> In our opinion one man, in less than twenty years, has modified on a world-wide scale the theological map of Protestantism. To do that Barth had at his disposal not only a kind of prophetic power, but the resources of human genius: culture, tremendous industry, human sympathy, courage, freedom, sensitivity, and a poetic gift.

But it is especially about Luther that I must say a word in order not to conceive Father Congar's position regarding him

---

[6]*Ibid.,* p. 453.

as an essentially negative one. On the contrary he was much attracted to him from the start of his ecumenical years—I mentioned his pilgrimage to the major Lutheran places. Father Congar considers Luther one of the greatest religious geniuses of all time (which does not necessarily mean one of the most balanced). He puts him with Augustine and Thomas as the great figures in the history of the Western Church, seeing him possessed of extraordinary instinct, a purely biblical genius. Moreover he loves him very much and studied him much. That is something: to love the type of man that the Lutheran or Calvinist of the first and great generations was, to feel oneself fraternally close to his Christian effort, even if one refuses more than one doctrinal option! In his preliminary report to the Council, Father Congar said that he was ready to give his life to justify this love, this respect for a witness who reminds us that man is not a receptacle for grace, that it is necessary to remain unceasingly attentive to a God who, as subject, is always personally engaged in the religious relationship, always active and immediately present in everything.

Father Congar is aware that as a theologian he has benefited enormously from Protestants. There is no doubt that the Catholic biblical renewal owes much to Protestant exegesis and still more perhaps, at least in Father Congar's case, to the biblical theology of the Protestants who helped us rediscover the great themes of God's pedagogy and salvation history. An essay like the *Mystery of the Temple* and more than one passage on the plan of God in *Vraie et fausse réforme*[7] bear witness to this fact.

A Meeting with the Orthodox Church

If Father Congar, from the beginning until now, because of readily understandable geographical reasons, has been in his unionist activity much more oriented toward the reformed Churches, he has not been less prompt to seize the opportunities presented him

---

[7]*Ibid.,* pp. 133-50.

to know the Orthodox Church and to become enriched by his
contacts with it. I have already spoken of his relations with Abbé
Gratieux who taught him Russian and introduced him to the
thought of the Slavophile movement. Even before that, at Berlin
in 1931, some Protestants had brought forth as an objection
to Catholicism the legend of the Grand Inquisitor in *The Brothers
Karamazov*. This was the start of an assiduous reading of Dos-
toevski. I have also spoken of his numerous contacts with Russian
exiles—with the limitations that their very idealized view of
Orthodoxy entailed—visits to Chevetogne, the trip to Greece
after the war.

Father Congar loves Orthodoxy very much and understands
its attraction. The negation of the world, which Father Congar
criticizes sharply in what he calls Western "monastic ideology"
(and which, of course, must not be confused with the monastic
vocation itself), does not have the same meaning for the Orthodox. The negation is made from love of the world and is balanced
by the insistence on the cosmic aspect of the Paschal message.
And Father Congar thus owes the Orthodox a sensitivity to
"cosmism," while aware of the fact that with them it is relative
idealism, not according sufficient reality to things here below.
He also owes them a sense of community, of communion in love
in which each one is active—the most profound aspect of the idea
of *sobornost*. Finally, Orthodoxy brought him perhaps concern
for a certain transcendence of Latin conceptualism, in the sense
of the integral knowledge of Khomiakov: to know the totality,
one must live in the totality. One does not *first* believe and *then*
find the charity of Christ, but it is truer to say that we love one
another in order to confess together, "I believe."

How Brothers Become Strangers

An important text of Father Congar gives maturity to certain
intuitions or certain developments already present in *Divided
Christendom* but even more noticeable in the work to which I
refer: *After Nine Hundred Years, the Background of the Schism*

between the Eastern and Western Churches. This long study tries to make understandable the origin of the divisions between East and West by going beyond a very formal definition of "schism" which illuminates nothing and does not correspond to a historical reality which is infinitely more complex, since in some respects it goes back to the first centuries of the Church, while in other respects it has never been totally consummated. This last point is especially true from the moment the criteria of evaluation are sacramental and caritative rather than juridical.

Father Congar sets out to put in relief the historical causes of the divisions: the regime of a state Church dating from Constantine which was to make the East much more dependent than Rome on imperial control; greater fragmentation of Eastern Christianity into Churches relatively independent of each other; the Byzantine demand of the transfer of religious authority from the old to the new Rome on the principle that there is only one single center of the Christian world unified in the empire; barbarian influences in the West, especially the politics of Charlemagne; Islam's role in isolating the two groups; the unqualified aggression of the "crusades." Over and above these socio-politico facts there were some elements of a cultural and religious order: language, mentality, rites (in the sense in which these express a profound sensibility), and theological methods.

But more complex and graver were the ecclesiological questions: as early as 342 (The Council of Sardica), two worlds opposed each other, East and West, whose differences, reciprocal misunderstanding, and what Father Congar likes to describe by the word "estrangement," became accentuated. Without doubt Charlemagne's blunders (introduction of the *filioque* into the *Credo,* rejection of the *per filium*) played their part, as did the ambitions of the patriarchs, but even more profoundly there is opposition between the two ecclesiologies, constructed differently to live and to think the same mystery of the Church. If the East recognized the Roman primacy more than it wishes to admit today, it was in the sense of a primate *in* the communion of the Churches, at the service of the faith and discipline of all. Undoubtedly it was not in the sense of a primacy of a divine right over the universal Church, conceived as a continuation of the primacy of St. Peter, such as Rome was to claim very early. This is of a piece with a whole view of the Church: some think of it first as a local Church entering into communion with neighboring Churches through their bishops, while others think of it first as a universal Church. Father Congar was to develop this at length in his study, "De la communion des Eglises à une ecclésiologie de l'Eglise universelle." Everyone is in agreement on the universal and indivisible character of the profound unity; but at the level of concrete ecclesiastical structures this can be translated in two very different ways. It remains to be seen if the episcopal collegiality defined at Vatican II will be permitted to show, by its dialectic with the primacy, the possible reconciliation of the two ways; like an appeal addressed to Orthodoxy to recognize on its part that there is not any power *in* the communion which does not imply a power *over* the Church in the service of this communion and unity themselves.

But my intent here was to show the historical complexity of the divisions; any inventory of respective responsibilities is truly impossible. In *After Nine Hundred Years* Father Congar gives evidence of this in regard to the great ruptures under the patriarchs Photius (Ninth Century) and Michael Cérulaire (Eleventh Century), when an attempt was made to impose on the East the concept of primacy held by the West. Congar concludes by analyzing the distrust born of remoteness, and by showing that the Church is universal even in its very visibility, and, by the will of Christ, if wrongs are shared, they are not however equal: "In a quarrel between a father and a son, the charges are never equal. Authority can be wrong, it is never fundamentally wrong; there can be many good reasons against it. It possesses the fundamental, structural justification of legitimacy and law." Beautiful words, to which a life gives weight. His final appreciation of the difficulties between Rome and Constantinople is more subtle and more optimistic than that of *Divided Christendom;* everything comes back to the ecclesiological problem and ultimately to the problem of primacy. But if the "schism," above and beyond these real difficulties, is the fruit of an estrangement, everything that aggravates this increases the schism, everything that permits separated brethren to know each other diminishes it.

4. TOWARD THE CONCILIAR DECREES ON ECUMENISM AND RELIGIOUS LIBERTY

I have shown how Father Congar was forced to retreat from the ecumenical field and how he concentrated his efforts on his ecclesiological work. Strangely, unexpectedly, this evolution was irreversible. When John XXIII ascended the throne of Peter, when Father Congar could speak and publish freely again, when he was engaged to collaborate in the preparation and work of the Council, it was almost exclusively along ecclesiological lines. He was a *peritus* on the theological commission and not in the Secretariat for Christian Unity. It was only after considerable delay that the latter group appealed to him for the revision of the schemas on ecumenism and religious liberty. His recent appointment as a member of the Catholic delegation to engage in dialogue with the Lutheran Churches is the first important mission confided to him in the ecumenical field.

Why? I shall not expand on this phenomenon, to the growth of which many factors have contributed. For one thing, his mastery of ecclesiology and his great theological reputation argued strongly in favor of his presence on the commission which was to draw up *Lumen Gentium*. But, on his part too, he was greatly attached to the ecclesiological work that had occupied him for so many years, and somewhat detached, not from the cause itself, but from the practical aspect of ecumenism. When certain reverses overwhelm one, in the end it so happens that something is broken or at least wounded. Moreover, during all these years a new generation of ecumenists, new experts who had won their stripes, had proven themselves, especially in the framework of the conference of which I spoke, and came very naturally to take leadership. Of course, Father Congar, free to do as he pleased, was to resume considerable ecumenical activity, but at the level, so to speak, of conferences and unity octaves.

He was also to attempt, at Strasbourg (by a teamwork similar to the one that had produced Lalande's *Vocabulaire technique et critique de la philosophie*), a *Vocabulaire oecuménique,* one that would interest the two theological faculties of Strasbourg and of which he had been thinking since 1945. It was a question of defining precisely the theological terms of the different confessions, since one of the more delicate problems of dialogue is that, behind the same words very different realities are sometimes intended, while on the other hand, the same realities are expressed in very different ways. This working instrument, which would be of inestimable value, is still in the process of being prepared by Roman Catholic theologians, Calvinists, and members of the Confession of Augsburg.

Two of Father Congar's works, including older elements, date from this period: *Dialogue between Christians* and *Aspects de l'oecuménisme.* The first is a large volume that gathers together studies on history and practical ecumenism, a new series of historical analyses and critiques on Anglicanism and Protestantism, and some more specific articles on the theology of the schism and on the destiny of Israel. This is a volume full of riches but relatively weighed down by a number of repetitions—in a word, one that is not very serviceable.

On the other hand, the very small *Aspects de l'oecuménisme* is a collection of six lectures, several of which are excellent. It is easy reading and can open perspectives to anyone wanting to learn more about this subject. From these two works and from some of his conferences there emerge a historical view, a psychology, a pastoral ecumenism about which I must say a few words to complete the more theoretical views that have preceded. For ecumenism, like the divisions themselves, already has a history. Above all, the fact that Christians have stood up and started to move toward unity is of world-wide importance which means as much to the observer as the fact of the rupture.

Christians Stand Up for Unity

Father Congar presents the history of the ecumenical movement in the following way. After a pre-history, accomplished especially by a regrouping of missionaries (under pressure from the churches of the Far East who were scandalized by all the "isms") which resulted in 1910 in the world-wide Missionary Conference at Edinburgh, the Ecumenical Movement (the term dates from 1920) passed through its first stage from 1910 to 1936. This period could be styled "horizontal" in the sense that one worked on a plane laboriously trying to enlarge the area of harmony through "a gentleman's agreement," as one tries to put a puzzle together. There were two lines of thought, one more practical (*Life and Work*); the other, more doctrinal (*Faith and Order*), before long was to work with the Orthodox, although its dominant note was certainly doctrinal. For reasons I shall not go into here, the Vatican categorically refused to join.

But the political crisis of 1936-1938, a real period of transition, was to permit a progressive development to a new stage which could be called the stage of common references. In fact Hitlerian neo-paganism brought forth, in reaction, the confession of the Lordship of Christ and at the same time awakened the sense of responsibility for the world. I have already mentioned the role that Karl Barth played in this evolution at the same time that he contributed to an equally important doctrinal renewal. This two-way vertical reference, this position of the Church as a "go-between" of service between Christ and the world is, according to Father Congar, absolutely decisive. It is under its sign that the second ecumenical stage really began in 1949 with the union of all the associations and the Orthodox into the "World Council of Churches." In 1961 the World Council of Churches was united with the other great ecumenical body, the International Council of Missions. The new perspective consists in studying some great themes of faith between the two poles, Christ and the world: the Church is their living junction, and its unity like a grace, will come from on high. If one thinks of the major themes of Vatican II and of Paul VI's plan for discourses and encyclicals, he can see how influential these concerns were to be in fostering good will between the World Council and the Catholic Church when the latter, in 1958, decided to show interest. One can also see that when she did so, when she opened up to a spirit of dialogue, it was the beginning of a new era for the ecumenical movement— that of cooperation with the Roman Church. A first kind of real exchange was the presence of non-Catholic observers at the Council. The important role they played there is well known.

To Be Converted, All Together, to Christ

As far as psychology and the practical aspects of ecumenism are concerned, it seems to me that the teaching of Father Congar can be summed up in the enumeration of a few principles that are indispensable to any effort toward unity. They are requisites for all, near or far, who find themselves engaged in ecumenical work. This, ultimately, means all Christians. In the first place, it is imperative to pass from polemics to dialogue; the former strives for immediate results, it does not work with history, it gives credit exclusively to reasoning and to authority without considering psychological or sociological factors, it pulverizes debate by drawing up catalogues of errors without looking for the intuition which gives coherence to a thought. Dialogue considers the positive Christian elements, it consents to be questioned by others, it is in search of plenitude, it "works in the historical dimension." In dialogue, the game of *total* truth must be played. Its rules are: recognize one's faults, one's limitations, not only personal ones, but those of institutions as well; do the necessary historical work, exacting and faithful, and advance nothing that is not absolutely certain; possess a true humility, not only personal and religious, but intellectual, at the opposite pole from the collective pride of Orders, schools, churches; listen humbly, knowing that truth is transcendent. Granted the mistakes made by one side or the other in the past, and the prejudices to which they give rise, an absolute sincerity without any reservations must be manifested. To this end one must avoid all proselytizing and every appearance of calculation. Above all one should distrust interconfessional conversions, which ought to proceed from an exacting and pure conviction but will never represent an adequate solution to the problem of separation.

For we must be converted, all of us, and to Christ: it is he who desires and accomplishes this union; what he expects of us is that every day each of us deepens his own fidelity in order to be capable of one day surpassing his actual state in order to receive the gift of unity—even if each one does not have an equal distance to traverse. This presupposes a continued return to the source, to the Word of Christ: this return to the biblical Source can alone bring plenitude and purity. However, the most exacting intellectual work is still indispensable, for one can enter into dialogue only if one is strong; the most natural reaction of the weak is the defense mechanism. In its turn the contact of faith with the Word engenders *prayer*, an essential dimension of the search for unity, not only because it has impetrative efficacy but also because it alone can form for us "a heart of love," can change us within the very interior of ourselves. This prayer can be integrally common, asking of God, according to the formula of Father Couturier, ". . . that unity that God wills, through the means that he wills." A last decisive dimension is *common action;* if union comes through conversion to Christ, because the Church is for the Lord, it also comes through service to the world, because the Church is for the world. Thus with great hope we rejoin the great axes which are at one and the same time those of the World Council of Churches and of the Second Vatican Council.

A short text from Father Congar summarizes all this:

Whereas formerly one quarreled, cursed, banished, killed, sometimes very cruelly, today one desires first of all to understand ancient griefs. Many of these griefs were serious and had a meaning. And now, developing in a knowledge of truth, and pursuing a dialogue with all those who for their part pursue a similar aim, one desires to take a road which would finally converge at a point of light where we should be able to communicate in an integral fidelity with the One whom we all confess as our Lord and with the gift he made us of his covenant![8]

"What We Reformed Theologians Owe to Him"

Having described what the ecumenical dialogue brought to Father Congar, I would like to conclude this chapter by quoting a Protestant testimony to him which teaches us what he himself could give in dialogue to the "Others." It is from Pastor J.J. Von Allmen of Neuchâtel. It completes nicely the testimonies I have already quoted from Professors Cullmann and Zander, and seems to me especially significant.

What we Protestant theologians owe to him is that, like no one else, he has destroyed the equivalence which (since the national synod at Gap in 1603) we have been accustomed to establish between the bishop of Rome and the anti-Christ, between Roman Catholicism and the adversary of the Gospel. By his manner of calling upon us, by his manner too of listening to us, he has blessedly removed the illusion of being the most legitimate possessors, the particularly attentive and privileged hearers of the Word of God. We owe it to him to have shaken us in our confessional pride, and consequently to have freed us to confront with courage and hope the obligations toward unity and the outpouring of the Spirit which makes an appeal to the Church today. You have called upon us as brothers, that is to say with candor and hope. With candor, because you have never conjured away the problems, you have not cheated us, you have not tried to minimize what divides us. Moreover, and this is why your calling on us was commanded by hope, neither have you wanted to uphold your side in matters which divide and separate us, to banish us to a realm where we could be nothing but an object of scorn. Your hope is too strong for you to support the idea that we might be forever a contradiction, and you have re-engaged us in a living dialogue. In frequent readings of your work, in too

---

[8]"Pédagogie de l'oecuménisme," in *Aspects de l'oecuménisme* (Paris-Brussels: Pensée catholique, 1962). See Chap. 1, above, footnote 19.

infrequent encounters, I have learned that your love for your separated brother is stronger in proportion as he is more exacting, as he is more courageous, as he is more impatient to give priority to those theses where the division seems the most deeply rooted. It was to reach a solution of truth in charity, and not to condemn us, that you invited us to pick up, in a climate of opinion made serene by the Holy Spirit, the major themes of that painful dialogue of the sixteenth century.

But it is not only through the brotherliness of your call that for the last twenty-six years you have been slowing down the reflexes of a facile anti-Catholicism of the current Protestant tradition. You have done it as well by the quality of your listening; you have shown that you take seriously the questions we ask of your Church. In fact, instead of letting us ask them, as from memory, of a distant and deaf Roman Catholic Church, you and those who resemble you have forced us to ask them of an attentive and living partner. . . . You have listened so attentively to these questions that we often had the impression that you were making yourself a relay of them so that they might reverberate with courage, authority, and hope within the very heart of the Roman Catholic Church. Only, and perhaps this is why I personally am most grateful to you, since you have been listening as a brother to these fundamental questions we put to you, you have never ceased to make us clarify them, to rephrase them, to purify them. That is why, at least indirectly, you are at the source of so much of our research, of so many of our studies, and also perhaps of the salutary conflict which opposes in the Churches of the Reformation the supporters of the "catholicity" of the Reformation and the adepts of the "protestantism," that is to say, the laziness, alibis, and agitations which have disfigured the reformed Church since the eighteenth century.

CHAPTER FOUR

The Ecclesiological Work

1. THE ECCLESIOLOGICAL PLAN OF FATHER CONGAR

In this chapter I do not intend to develop the entire ecclesiological work of Father Congar, nor even to give a summary of each of his theses. And in what follows I shall not give his thought on other contemporary theological problems. I merely intend to stress some of his main lines of thought. My criterion will be the following: I shall keep what Father Congar himself considered the most important. To begin with, let me show, not what Father Congar tried to bring to the conscience of the Church, nor the essentials of his precise objectives, but rather the manner in which he wanted to proceed, the action he intended to take to fulfill his mission in the renewal of the Church.

I need not repeat in detail what has already been said about the connection between his ecclesiological vocation and ecumenical calling. However, at least the way it was carried out must be stressed, for its genesis is of major importance to understand precisely how Father Congar will carry on his research. His procedure will be guided more by spiritual and ethical interests than by intellectual demands, although intellectual positions are of course implied. Because he lived in the Church, loved it, and appreciated it, he wanted to meditate on its mystery and at the same time rejuvenate its countenance. As I have said, he has always been wholeheartedly "of the Church." In this he resembled his pastor, a man of the old French clergy, a great reader of Bossuet, very attached to the old traditions of the Church of France, as shown by his wearing the rabat, and his opposition to

Gregorian Chant and defense of the one then popular in the Rheims-Cambrai district. The war strengthened the fervor of the little Catholic community that closed in on itself. The "doctrinal" preaching of the pastor, commenting on the catechism, the creed, the history of the Church, made a profound impression on young Yves who retained throughout his life this love for the Church so keenly experienced in parish life. And it was to be always thus. It was in the contacts he had after the war years of 1939-1945, through the intense movement within the life of the Church possible at that time, that Father Congar was again able to move forward, to work out the theology of the laity, of the Church in the world, etc. His was not a research primarily speculative in its intelligibility and unity, but a concern to think in an organically unified way about a *reality* which is effectively one: The Church in its mystery. His was not a reforming concern of a cerebral kind, but an exacting love. Therefore it was in the beloved Church herself that he was to look for the principle of renewal, especially when the concern for unity was to lead him to see its urgent and many-faceted necessity.

When Father Congar was to come up against the juridical and authoritarian ecclesiology of the baroque period and even of late scholasticism, and wanted to reverse the movement, to overcome the evolution which many (either to rejoice in it or to overwhelm the Catholic Church with it) deemed irreversible, he proposed to do it by a return to tradition. When he was confronted by a closed system, jealous, stifling, which had lost all memory of any other state of affairs, which answered all questions put to it with the idea (assuredly correct, but partial) of the "living magisterium," he asked himself how to go beyond the position actually held without rupturing the Catholic communion. He saw that this could be done only by conceiving this Catholic communion as a communion not only with the teaching Magisterium as it is today (*with* it, of course), but with the entire past and even the entire future.

"To Draw from the Sources the Knowledge of the Church"

His plan concretely involved two steps—and one virtue. First, to study history, which corrodes simplistic certitudes, abstract reasonings, relative facts changed into absolutes, and the fiction in which one can live. When historical facts are brought to light, they compel a cleansing; they also clarify the sources of many misunderstandings. This certainly is only a minor role of history, but it is a very important one. Secondly, and more profoundly, by means of history he wished to bring back to ecclesial consciousness the buried layers of its treasure, to appeal to it from what is presently held to what is not "of the past" but sources of life now deep in the catholicity of the Church and seeking only to break forth freely again. It is a question of "rediscovering the present and the future with the help of the past and of vivifying this past in the light of the present to prepare the future." There is no denying these traditional riches, no matter how deeply they are buried. The Council shows this: one can be sitting "on top" of them for centuries, eventually even work with persistence to annul them, in vain; the Author watches over his work.

And finally, the beautiful virtue which these hopes and these works call forth, and to which I have previously referred, is patience. I have spoken of the place Father Congar makes for it both in his own life and among the major conditions of an authentic Catholic reform.

The idea of a great ecclesiological collection is a response to this project of returning to the Sources ("Revertimini ad fontes," said Pius X about the liturgy). It was not by chance that the prospectus announcing the launching of *Unam Sanctam,* drawn up by Father Congar himself, presented it in this light. A passage from this significant text follows:

> The idea of this collection comes from a twofold consideration. On the one hand, when one reflects on the big problems of Catholic life and expansion, of modern unbelief or indifference, finally of the reunion of separated Christians, one is led to think that an

amelioration of the present state of things (insofar as it depends on us), supposes that a notion of the Church as great, living, rich, full of biblical and traditional vigor penetrates Christianity: first the clergy, then the Christian élite, then the entire body. On the other hand, an incontestable renewal of the idea of the Church is manifested on all sides, where, moreover, as is normal, the thrust of the interior and apostolic life of souls precedes theology. Naturally the desire is aroused to respond to the need which was perceived and then to serve a movement manifestly inspired by the Holy Spirit. These two things call forth the same response from within: an effort of thought to produce a truly great, living, serious theology for the Church. It is this work that, for its part, and without detracting any merit from similar efforts, *Unam Sanctam* wishes to pursue. The intention determines the point of application and the extent of effort. . . . *Unam Sanctam* aims at making the nature, or if you will the mystery, of the Church better known; historical works can figure in it, and some liturgical and missiological considerations, and even some studies pertaining to divided Christendom and the problem of reunion, insofar as such research is to the interest of a more profound and richer knowledge of the Church in its intimate nature and the mystery of its life. In particular, since theology, according to its own law, lives only by an intimate and organic contact with its datum, a considerable part will be devoted to the study of the sources: Holy Scripture, the Fathers, the liturgy, the life of ecclesiastical institutions, etc., from which one should draw an authentic knowledge of the one, holy, catholic, and apostolic Church.

2. THE FOUNDATIONS OF ECCLESIOLOGY

The question is: What does one understand by the *Church* and what picture of the whole does one get of this reality? Several complementary approaches can be tried. One can ask what are the essential elements of the reality which is the Church, or better, what are the essential levels of analysis among which its living substance can be distributed? There can be constructed one or several theological "models" of the Church, to function in the particular problem that a theologian would wish to confront and resolve. One can also study historically and compare the thought contents contained in the word *Church* throughout the centuries, determining the great stages of the evolution of this consciousness which the Church has of herself. This is to propose to oneself an ecclesiology. Finally, one can study the *names* of the Church, reflect on the predominance of this or that designation at a certain epoch, and also test their capacity of conveying something of the mystery, thus bringing into play their complementarity. Father Congar has successfully tried all these approaches. Here I shall try to show the image of the Church which finally emerges from all of them.

The Ecclesiological Schemas

The great ecclesiological works of Father Congar thus present several of these fundamental "models" which allow one to think of the Church and to place within it a kind of partial reality, in order to confront a certain theological difficulty. Since these "models" are taken from different points of view, they do not harmonize perfectly, but it is not hard to show their compatibility and to establish their point of juncture. For example, we have seen the presentation of the Church proposed by Father Congar in *Divided Christendom*. It aimed at showing the profound causes of its unity by revealing the essential principles of its life: *Ecclesia de Trinitate,* the extension of the divine life, the communication of God's riches (divine logic of unity); *Ecclesia in Christo,* the mediation through Christ of this communication, the sacramentality (at the juncture of these two logics and comprising them); *Ecclesia ex hominibus,* the communication of God's riches accomplished not in an immediate, personal, and interior way, but in conformity with our terrestrial condition. It is incarnated and social, taking the societal form and countenance of the Church (societal logic of unity, because human). With a somewhat different purpose in mind, the meditation of the first of the studies in *The Mystery of the Church* is constructed in the same way. Thus, from the point of view of its formal causes, the Church appears at one time as constituting its members (the gift of life), at another as being constituted by its members (who need an organization of these gifts).

This duality "Church making"—"Church made" is found in another kind of analysis (in *Vraie et fausse réforme* and in *Lay People in the Church*) of the reality which is the Church, whether it is used for determining what is and what is not reformable in the Church, or the place of the laity. But this time the new distinction is made from a realistic, a concrete point of view. In it one opposes, on the one hand, the *institution,* the structure of the Church (the totality of the means destined to realize the communion, hierarchical pole of communication of God's riches) which is given by Christ and remains unchanged, holy, without admixture of sin; and on the other hand, the *community* of the members of the Church, its life (the *congregatio fidelium,* the pole of communal consent), holy but mixed with impurities and hence reformable. Midway between the two there is the "state of affairs in the Church," the concrete figure of powers, of sacraments, of dogmas, in their perishable garb at a given moment in history, or in the men who exercise them: at one and the same time *institution,* in the most banal sense, and *life;* all this is equally eminently reformable.

Rather than show precisely how these two complementary views are joined at the level of the *Ecclesia in Christo,* let me disengage the major ecclesiological lesson from the whole. The Church appears as being essentially one community which receives and lives the gift of God. (Through this it is eschatological, and in eternity it will not be anything but this.) At the service of this unique gift so that it might communicate itself, and at the service of this community so that it might receive this life in a way connatural to it (that is, Word and sacrament first, then a visible society), the ecclesial Institution exists as an intermediary or a vast sacrament which extends the mediatory mission of Christ. Completely relative to the two other terms, it is at one and the same time holy, founded and animated by the Lord, and yet assuming at each period of history a human countenance which is imperfect, modifiable, and reformable.

Historical Evolution

Although this view of ecclesiology is profoundly traditional, it was not always so clearly apparent in theology or in the thought of ecclesiastical authority, even though what it contemplates has never totally ceased to be lived. A brief historical sketch, made with the help of Father Congar's work, will help exemplify this. I take my inspiration especially from unpublished conferences, although a quick summary of these views could be found in Father Congar's Preface to *Ecclesia Mater*[1] by Karl Delahaye.

In the first three centuries—"Never was the Church more purely herself than at this epoch, filled with the vigor of its origins"—the ecclesiology is the ecclesiology of Christian man, it encompasses an anthropology. The word *ecclesia,* according to the meaning given it then, ought to be translated "a Christian community"; what was in mind is "the *we* of the Christians," the Christian *I* in the first person plural. Or rather, since the Institution is not in any way ignored, it is "the structured community." This is what is the subject of everything that is said about the Church, this that begets the faithful, this that has pastoral care. No special treatise is written on this subject, but it is mentioned with reference to great biblical themes: "She is humble, she is converted, she prays." Later, such themes will not make any sense: a system is not converted. We shall come back to another aspect, the presence, in full act, of the Holy Spirit. This too will be completely forgotten when the hierarchy is conceived as a mechanism cleverly set up by Christ who thus provided for the needs of the Church until the end of time. In the Middle Ages the patristic conception is still the generally accepted ecclesiology. In the twelfth and thirteenth centuries, with Thomas Aquinas, for example, even if it is true that more emphasis is put on the category of the Mystical Body, offshoot of the meditation on Christ the head and of the avatars of the

---

[1]In *Unam Sanctam* (Paris: Editions du Cerf, 1963), XLVI.

Eucharistic theology, the Church still has the meaning of a multitude of the saved from Abel to the last of the elect, fathered under the authority of one Lord: visibility is not yet inscribed in it as an essential element.

But soon, in reaction against the spiritualistic negations which terminated in a purely invisible Church, and especially since the *systematic* reflection on the Church was to be introduced into theology at a time when there was concern to defend the pontifical power against the encroachments of the secular power, there was more and more exclusive insistence on the societal, juridical, and organized aspect of the Church, with all the clericalism implied therein. This, viewed in the extreme, will be the ecclesiology of Robert Bellarmine who sees the Church as a visible society, subject to the Roman Pontiff, much like the kingdom of France or the republic of Venice. Instead of an anthropology linked with a pneumatology, to a doctrine of the Holy Spirit, which constituted the conception of the Fathers and of the great medieval doctors, there prevailed only an abstract theology of mediation, which is self-containing, without the terms involved (God and the Chosen People!) having any decisive importance. Therefore it is necessary to go beyond the seven centuries of unilateral emphasis on visibility and powers— without losing the benefit of clarifications advanced during this period—to an ecclesiology of man, baptized and living in the spirit. This is what Father Congar proposes; this is why he deems the volume of studies of New Testament anthropology, containing articles by Fathers I. de la Potterie and S. Lyonnet, S.J., an essential one of the collection.[2] But is this not the ecclesiology which, from all sides, has been imposing itself on us for twenty years? Is it not the ecclesiology of the Second Vatican Council? One last approach will enable us to realize this, the study of the *names* of the Church, the inquiry into the key-terms that

---

[2]*La vie selon l'esprit, condition du chrétien,* in *Unam Sanctam (Paris:* Editions du Cerf, 1965), LIV.

characterize one or the other period of the history of ecclesiology, to ask if any one of them is particularly apt to define the Church. To show this I shall rely chiefly on the first study in the volume *Sainte Eglise,* namely, "Can the Church be defined? The destiny and value of four theories which claim to do it."

People of God and Body of Christ

A definition of the Church being impossible, one might ask what are the great biblical images, the determinations: scriptural (people, body, temple, communion), theological (sacrament, society), which best express the mystery of the Church. Each one brings in its wake a host of associations, in such a way that, in analyzing them, one truly constructs an ecclesiology, but with the result, too, that the meaning given them is susceptible of variation, even in what concerns the New Testament. For example, *Church* expresses an assembly convoked by God and brings up the question of the links between the universal Church and the local Church, the latter being less a part of a whole than the already full manifestation of a more vast totality. The richer concept of the *People of God* suggests a multitude of men over whom God rules and who, in the world, are the sign of this reign of God to be realized everywhere; it connotes also, with all the riches implied, the link with the People of God of the Old Testament, and stresses the historic dimension of God's plan. It does not sufficiently express the difference of regime between the two Covenants (unless one makes it precise by saying the eschatological *People of God*), nor the decisive fact that "henceforth one cannot become the People of God except by becoming the Body of Christ, members of the Body of the beloved Son."

But if the biblical and patristic concept of the People of God was able to regain its place in the foreground of ecclesiology and even be given a privileged place by the Second Vatican Council which introduced it into the Constitution *Lumen Gentium* as a fundamental datum, the concept *Body of Christ* has a quite complex and confused history behind it. I have said that, with the Fathers and in the Middle Ages, the word did not at first signify an ecclesiological notion in its modern meaning; rather:

> [It is] a Christological and soteriological notion. It designates the multitude of spiritual beings, including angels, who under Christ their head enjoy communion with God. It includes, therefore, the just of all ages. . . . For the medievalists, *Corpus,* applied to a group of men, did not necessarily express visibility but simply a plurality ordained to one single principle . . . here God or Christ, to whom men are ordained by faith.

But in the context of a societal ecclesiology and wishing to combat a completely spiritualistic idea of the Church, a completely different meaning has been given to the word *body.* To pinpoint this reaction let me quote from Calvin's *Epistle to the King of France*: "Some always require a visible and apparent form of the Church. On the contrary, we affirm that the Church can exist without visible appearance."

The new meaning of the word *body* is "a sociological or corporative meaning including visibility and juridical organization." To establish this interpretation, the secondary meanings of the term in St. Paul were used. Modern exegetes have protested against the predominance of this meaning and put forward the soteriological meaning: "The Church is something of Christ, a presence, a manifestation. What is primary in the thought of St. Paul is the personal body of the risen Christ. But this body, which is his, has a role and a value for the entire world. Through it Christ is principle of a new creation."

The encyclical *Mystici Corporis Christi* of Pius XII, which marks an important epoch in the history of this concept, sought to combine these two perspectives. The conciliar text opted definitely for the second, which excellently expresses at one and the same time the unity and distinction of Christ and the Church, as well as the intimate bond of the members among themselves, their complementarity, and the cosmic dimension of the whole.

Temple of the Holy Spirit and Communion

Two other New Testament concepts on which Father Congar puts equal emphasis complete the ecclesiological picture. *Temple of the Holy Spirit*[3] is particularly valuable to express the interiorization, the spiritualization of the presence of God which is produced when, to the temple of Jerusalem succeeds the new Temple which is Christ, which in its turn will be each Christian, and which finally is the entire Church. Source of the holiness of the people of the new era, the Spirit coming from the risen Christ is also the source of the life of the Church and its builder; he is the soul of the Body of Christ.

The term *communion* (*Koinonia*), which Pilgram formerly restored to an honorable place, is both closer to precedents and more susceptible of assuring acceptance of a visible society in the Church. It starts out from the relationship which exists between people in the life of the community, but which must necessarily be expressed and organized into a society. To tell the truth, in the New Testament itself, the word, like *Body of Christ*, expresses a category of participation founded entirely on Christ and the Spirit, on *what* one shares; the idea of a social group is not present there. This was shown in *The Church Is a Communion* by Father Jerome Hamer, an ecumenical associate of Father Congar (presently assistant secretary of the Secretariat for Christian Unity). But the fact remains, according to Father Congar, that such a concept could be established as valuable and complementary to the others if, in elaborating it one took for granted "the valuable support not only of sociology, but of the interpersonal ontology of the personalist philosophy."

Society and Sacrament

The two theological terms *society* and *sacrament* are considerably different in their epistemological type. The first is completely characteristic of the "baroque" conception of the Church. Of

---

[3]Treated by Father Congar in *Le Mystère du Temple* (Paris: Editions du Cerf, 1958). See Chap. 1, above, footnote 9.

course, medieval ecclesiologists of the Mystical Body or of the *Congregatio Fidelium* had included the idea of society, showing that there exists in the *congregatio* both unity of the spirit and the multiplicity of organic, complementary functions. But this is entirely different from a theology of the Church *constructed* on the concept of society. The best proof that juridical conceptions did not yet dominate in the medieval period is that, "in these functions were mingled indistinctly offices that were purely spiritual, charismatic, or purely pragmatic, with properly hierarchical responsibilities arising from what we call public law." On the other hand, the anti-spiritualist or anti-Protestant ecclesiologies introduce into the very definition of the Church the social modality of its terrestrial existence. The ecclesiology was constructed on the philosophical concept of society within which was situated the Church, a supernatural society having its own differences. The result of this can be seen: an underestimation of the communal aspect, an overestimation of the aspect of authority, a failure to recognize the value of the evangelical dimensions of the doctrine—for example, the polar notions of Christ and his Church.

It is in an entirely different context that the term *sacrament* or *primordial sacrament* was put forward as expressing in a synthesis the mystery of the Church. As has been shown, Father Congar made a judicious use of it in *Lay People in the Church* in order to situate the role of the Institution in regard to the believing community, which, living from grace, then appears as the *res*, the holy reality. In a slightly different sense the term can be used to express the meaning of the presence in the world of the Church in its totality. Without seeing in it any one category sufficient in itself to express all that the Church is, Father Congar, in his reference to the writings which propose it, pronounced in its favor, whereas other ecclesiologists show themselves more reluctant to do so. But he himself has not made much use of it, whether in his theology of mission or salvation of infidels (which could be treated along this line) or in his presentation of the Church itself.

Because of these various approaches a certain image of the Church in its totality has been developed: a community receiving divine life thanks to an institution which structures it, and which is entirely relative to it; a People constituted of the baptized, on the march in history for the salvation of the world; the Body of Christ within which moves the Spirit which interiorizes the work of the Lord. Father Congar has helped to restore to a place of honor this biblical and traditional view of the Church, carrying out his plan of appealing, against anti-reformist theology, to more profound sources. Anyone who has read the constitution *Lumen Gentium* realizes what it owes, not to Father Congar who is only an instrument, but to these sources.

3. STRUCTURES OF THE CHURCH

The realm of interiorization, of the spiritualization which characterizes the New Covenant by contrast with the Old, is not complete here below. From this point of view the Church still has to await in the heavenly kingdom a consummation which, while not entirely like the one to which Jerusalem submitted in becoming the Church, is not entirely unlike it either. Why? First, because man is man, corporal and social, and God takes all these things seriously. I mentioned this fact in speaking of Lutheran ecclesiology, saying that God even went so far as to associate to the ministry of salvation the redeemed themselves. A second reason is the imperfection of men: entirely relative to the interior freedom of the elect, there cannot but remain in the Church some aspects of law and temple. Since it is impossible to do away with them, they must always be regulated and transcended. All this, therefore, justifies the existence in the Church of a structure, of an institution visibly extending the mediating role of Christ and of his authority over the people, while the Holy Spirit who animates this permeates the community to constitute it entirely in a state of vocation. Chosen in the People of God and for its service, men will be depositaries of the message addressed to faith, of the sacramental and hierarchic powers. The inevitable consequence of this design is known: the instrument thus established will at each moment of history combine its own limits and ungainliness with the irreproachable holiness of what is confided to it; and this not only in the personal realm but even in the exercise of the ministry.

For Father Congar, whose positions I have just briefly and partially summarized, the essential point in what concerns this structure is not only that it appears entirely relative to the mystery that it serves and to the men that it engenders to salvation, but also that it must reflect, in everything that it is, *this mystery* and *this community* in their most specific aspects. It is not a question of defining a priori law, society, authority, priesthood, and then of adjusting this definition in the case of the Church. It is a question of studying what apostolic authority, evangelical law, Christian priesthood, etc., are in themselves in a realm wherein it is proposed to awaken liberties, to give God, to arouse a communion of love among men. The facts are there moreover to show the need of such a study. According to Father Congar the proper genius of canon law, in spite of slight resemblances based on civil legislation, is completely different from profane law. It is different in spite of the rediscovery of Roman law which has marked the mentality of churchmen and the relations between Church and State more than the spirit of ecclesiastical law itself.

I shall now try to develop the consequences of everything that has just been said: for the theology of apostolic authority in general, for that of the priesthood, for that of the relations between collegiality and primacy, and for that of the pastorate. These are, to be sure, only examples.

Authority in the Church

Thus apostolic authority, according to the New Testament, is a humble, serving, fraternal authority which has only by abuse or an understandable, excusable, and reversible historical process, assumed imperial effects, or adopted the feudal style and courtly etiquette.[4] It is an institutionalized charism (neither of the two terms should be abandoned), in favor of an entirely charismatic community:

> Authority in the ancient Church was that of men who are like princes in an entirely holy community, *plebs sancta*, and visited by the Spirit of God: princes more conscious of their authority because they saw it as bearing the mystery of the salvation that God wishes to carry out in his Church. They desired to be and knew that they were moved by the Holy Spirit, but they also knew that the Spirit dwells in the community of Christians, and they remained closely linked to it in the exercise of authority.[5]

However real the authority in the Church is, it is not *primarily* juridical power but a service of charity to men, not only in its usage, in its practical mode, but also in its very essence because it is in and for *agape*, because it always makes a third intervene— God himself.

This charismatic and perpetually theological nature of authority, in contrast to a purely juridical concept, intervenes decisively in the theology of the Magisterium. In the doctrinal domain its first act will not be to define with authority but to witness with assurance; it believes what it itself transmits, and the Church adheres to its teaching because that is what it transmits. Certainly, in order that what it says might have authority, it does not need to consult juridically the whole Church, but it expresses in fact what the Church believes; if not it would have nothing to say. Thus it is even infallible—should one say indefectible?—in the sense that, even when fumbling, when deceived at times in the details of its endeavors, the *Ecclesia* in its hierarchical authority which expresses it has the words of eternal

---

[4]"Titres et honneurs dans l'Eglise," in *Pour une Eglise servante et pauvre* (Paris: Editions du Cerf, 1963). English trans., *Power and Poverty in the Church* (Baltimore: Helicon, 1964).
[5]"La hiérarchie comme service," *ibid.*

life and at the end will not fail; it will posit a final, infallible act. This change of perspectives in regard to a juridical and factual conception is found even in the doctrine of the vicarial role of the pope. Let me quote here an important passage on the expression *vicarius Christi* as a papal title. Taken from "The Hierarchy as Service," the quotation is only one of many examples of the juridicizing of terms, quotations, and concepts which at the start had an entirely different significance. In fact:

> [There was a] real change of content in the expression *vicarius* while the word remained unchanged. The former meaning of the word in Catholic theology was that of the visible representation of a transcendent or celestial power which actually worked through its terrestrial representative. The framework and the climate of the idea were those of the immediacy of God's action, of Christ and the saints operating through their representative: a very sacramental, iconological conception linked to the idea of the constant intervention of God and the saints in our terrestial sphere. It is also this actualist value of vertical descent and intervention which is originally found in the famous text, "He who hears you, hears me; and he who rejects you rejects me. . ." (Lk. 10:16).
>
> Although this value did not disappear with time, it was covered over by another value which, for its part, is not entirely new (what is new is its evident prevalence), that is, the idea of a "power" transmitted from the beginning by Christ to his "vicar," that is, to a representative who will replace him and who will transmit after him, according to a historical chain of transmission and of succession, the power thus received. Here there is a prevalence not of verticality, of immediacy, of iconological representation, but of horizontal transmission of a power inherent in a terrestrial representative and which, received from above, is however possessed by this representative who uses it in the way all authority can use the power attached to it.

From the nuances of the text, the judicious balance of Father Congar's ecclesiological thought can be recognized. The insistence on the Christo-anthropological themes, on pneumatism and charisms, does no harm to the classical view of the place of the Institution, of authority, of law, of which the traditional foundations are shown. At the same time Father Congar feels free to criticize subsequent excesses. This is far from reformation or Jansenism, even further from a cerebral reformism which rediscovers the "primitive Church" of a dream.

Nothing better expresses this balance than the beautiful study, "Le Saint Esprit et le corps Apostolique, réalisateurs de l'oeuvre du Christ," which dates from the period immediately after the war and is of great importance in the field of missiology. Here is its significant conclusion:

> The present task of ecclesiology (made easier by a great number of really valuable studies, the teaching of the Magisterium, and the present union of the spiritual and the apostolic) is to sacrifice neither of the two poles whose coordinates we have tried to recognize, even if a certain tension must remain between the two.

The author summarizes his ideas thus:

> 1. There is a duality of agents (or missions), doers of the work of Christ, the Spirit accomplishing internally with divine efficacy what the apostolic minister is doing externally. To do this he is aided by a bond of Covenant, in virtue of God's fidelity to his promises.
>
> 2. The Church is structured by the establishment of the means of grace, which are attached to the *acta Christi in carne*. It is fundamentally Christological.
>
> 3. But under the government of the celestial Christ the Church lives through the action of the Holy Spirit. Its life is thus a realm where the transcendence of its Head and the equally transcendent personality of the Spirit are characterized by the sovereign liberty of their names and of their interventions.[6]

The Christian Priesthood

Thus far I have spoken of authority in general in the Church, emphasizing the magisterial or doctrinal aspect and not touching the theology of the pontifical primacy except by way of example; there has been no attempt to treat the problem as such. Now I

---

[6]In *Esquisses du mystère de l'Eglise*, in *Unam Sanctam* (Paris: Editions du Cerf, 1953), VIII (2nd ed.; Paris: Editions du Cerf, 1966), pp. 139-40.

would like to say a few words about another aspect of the ecclesial Institution, of the power transmitted by Christ which is the evangelical priesthood, or *power of order*. This is distinguished from the *power of directing with authority* (doctrinal or disciplinary) to which in the West we have become accustomed to giving the debatable name of power of "jurisdiction." This distinction of two powers agrees more with my very succinct exposition than does the framework of the three "functions" (sacerdotal, royal, and prophetic) which Father Congar often applies to the evangelical Institution. This distinction agrees even more as this schema finds its best field of application in the domain of the universal vocation of the People of God. But a word of warning: if I have distinguished priesthood and Magisterium, it does not mean that priesthood is the equivalent of cult! On the contrary, Father Congar's entire theology aims at enlarging the doctrine of the ministerial priesthood according to the Gospel, of conceiving it as a pastoral and prophetic priesthood which includes the cultural and sacramental dimension without being summed up in it. To get this result, one must take as first analogue of the priesthood not the function of the priest in its secondary meaning but that of the bishop of which the priest partakes. More radically still, it is necessary to situate the priesthood-ministry in relation to the priesthood of Christ and to the universal priesthood of the baptized.

In Chapter Four of *Lay People in the Church* and in an excellent summary in "Notes sur notre sacerdoce,"[7] Father Congar presents things as I have just described them. One only is priest, Christ, offering to God for the salvation of the world his sacrifice of obedience and love; *all* are priests, all the baptized belonging to the priestly People and offering their persons to God in spiritual sacrifice (Rom. 12:1; 1 Pt. 2:9-10); *some* are priests of a ministerial priesthood, destined to serve that of the faithful,

---

[7]*Sacerdoce et laïcat*, in coll. *Cogitatio fidei* (Paris: Editions du Cerf, 1962), IV, pp. 109-22. See Chap. 1, above, footnote 14.

to put them in a state of spiritual sacrifice, to incorporate sacramentally their offering of themselves and of their entire life to the unique sacrifice of the Head. Thus is the ministerial priesthood itself a complex reality, comprising at one and the same time the announcement of the Word and the celebration of the sacraments. It is in fact relative to a sacrifice which is not first a cult, but personal, in faith: the "spiritual sacrifice" of the New Testament which signifies a personal gift, accomplished under the movement of the Spirit. And this is fully verified in the traditional theology of the episcopacy, in the Fathers of the Church; it is further verified when the priesthood of the bishop is shared by the *presbyterium,* the college of priests of the second order who help the pastor realize his ministry.

From a technological, theological point of view, it will be noticed that Father Congar defines the priesthood from an idea of sacrifice rather than from a too imprecise notion of mediation, or the too "spiritual" concept of consecration. He gives to this notion of sacrifice, and therefore to "priesthood" which is correlative, all of its personal evangelical dimension. This is an entirely different thing from a definition of the priesthood as the power of celebrating Mass, ready to complete it by a "power over the Mystical Body." The theologian writes:

> For our part we judge that we are faithful to Holy Scripture and to a sound theology when we define the priesthood as the quality which permits us to present ourselves before God to obtain his grace and therefore his communion, by offering a sacrifice agreeable to him. . . . When it concerns our true relationship with God, our Creator, from whom comes everything we are or have, it is we ourselves, the totality of our being, of our doing, of our having which ought to constitute this sacrifice.[8]

The sacramental, ministerial, or hierarchic priesthood which comes from above, from Christ, has no other end than to bring

---

[8]*Les jalons pour une théologie du laïcat* (Paris: Editions du Cerf, 1953), pp. 200-202. See Chap. 1, above, footnote 10.

sacramentally, visibly, to us the sanctifying action of Jesus Christ until everything is consummated in the kingdom, and to inscribe our sacrifice in his, singularly in and through the celebration of the Eucharist in which the priest is at one and the same time the minister of Christ and the representative of the assembly.

A Question of Leading Men to Meet God

This theology of the priesthood has some very important practical consequences in the realm of the missionary exercise of this function. To announce the Gospel in order to arouse a people to conversion is already an essentially priestly act, and can even be the only exercise of a priesthood for a long time (for example, that of the priest-workers before the birth of any Christian community), but it will have its full dimension only in the Eucharistic consummation, virtually present from the start. But here I prefer to emphasize its larger pastoral consequences by quoting a passage from Father Congar's preface to Delahaye's *Ecclesia Mater,* wherein is sketched a new vision of the pastoral. On more than one point this resembles Karl Rahner's thought as expressed in *Mission and Grace.*

> [In the Church today] we are still too inclined to proceed as if we believed it was a question of filling slots, or making a success of something (the Church). Actually it is primarily a question of succeeding in positing, or leading others to posit, *spiritual* acts, of leading to an encounter with God, of encouraging one to be converted to the Gospel. It is a question, then, not of making sure of the items on the program, but of eliciting a prayer which would be a prayer, a repentance, or a movement of "penance" (that is to say, of conversion), which would be a repentance and a movement of conversion, a communion which would be a communion, a faith which would truly be a faith! Often we use a pastoral of *things* in which men at all costs fill the pigeon-holes of a project which has already been laid out, as if their only role were to maintain a system, and if possible to assure its success. We make sure of the items on the program "religion," but there is practically no spiritual act, and *no Christians* are produced. Biblically and really there is a spiritual act, first when it is truly the act of *someone* who commits his living person to it, and when the Holy Spirit is at work in it. Such is the meaning of "spiritual temple," "spiritual

sacrifice," and of so many other analogous expressions in Christianity. To arouse, to provoke, to nourish such spiritual acts supposes that the one who is called to be a minister of it commits himself as a spiritual man.

And this not only at the level of good usage or of a virtuous exercise of priestly duties, but, "it is necessary to see these spiritual aspects in a more interior way, one more essential to the operations of the instituted ministry. St. Paul preferred to speak as a spiritual man rather than in the name of an authority that he was very conscious of possessing."

Collegiality, Form of Apostolicity

One last aspect of this ecclesial structure, inasmuch as it reflects the very mystery that it serves at the institutional and hierarchical level of powers, is that of episcopal collegiality which, Father Congar tells us, "expresses the profound nature of the Church."

The exposition of this notion would have been more appropriate a little earlier, but a historical scruple led me to defer its presentation until now, for even if the idea was widespread in pre-war or early post-war works, it is especially in the last few years that this theme, profoundly traditional as it is, has been restored to honor. Here it is no longer about an encroachment of seven centuries on a somewhat unilateral theology that I must speak, but of a jump of fifteen centuries. It is useful to underline the fact, rarely noticed, that it was Father Congar who first used the word "collegiality" to translate the Russian term *sobornost*. This term has a much broader sense than the one which now concerns us. What is important in the idea of episcopal collegiality is that it involves a collegiality of communion. I have already said how much this is the necessary complement of our classical ecclesiology, with its emphasis on the universal Church and on its principle of unity. I shall not return to this point. Let me insist rather on the articulation of this doctrine with that of the primacy and on its significance at the structural level of the Church, where it expresses organically the communion of love of all the ecclesial community, somewhat as concelebration expresses, at the level of hierarchical priesthood, the unanimity and unity of the entire Eucharistic assembly. I shall make use of Father Congar's explanation of collegiality which he gives in his notes from the Council.[9] It is a question of a conciliar teaching, of course, but the presentation which sets forth the main thoughts is his; it is a theological reflection.

What then is episcopal collegiality?

1. Peter was not the only one to receive the charge of feeding the universal Church, although he received it personally with a particular title which made him head of the entire Church, including pastors. But all the Apostles, constituted by the Lord as a college with Peter at their head, received this charge with him.

2. The bishops inherit this. In fact, if it cannot be said of each bishop taken individually that he succeeded in the ministry to a particular Apostle, yet the body of bishops as such succeeds, for the activities of the ministry, to the body or to the college of Apostles as such. Collegiality is, in its foundation, the very form of apostolicity.

3. One is incorporated into the body or college of bishops by episcopal consecration in which the sacrament of order is given in the highest degree, establishing in the People of God the obligations and dignity of the Head. It is a service of governing which comprises corresponding powers and graces.

4. Incorporated into the college, a bishop radically possesses a teaching authority and a pastoral conduct in regard to the universal Church. It is this authority which is actualized at the council when the pope convokes one and approves its decisions: for there is neither a true college nor a collegial act outside of participation in this quality with the pope, head of the college and head of the Church militant.

---

[9]*Le Concile au jour le jour,* Session III (Paris: Editions du Cerf, 1965), pp. 44-45.

5. Most often a bishop is not consecrated for the service of the universal Church only (which would be too indefinite), but for that of a particular church.

6. The pope himself keeps authority over the universal Church, but exercises it at a different level from the ordinary or daily administration of it—at the level of the great resources and great interests of the People of God, especially everything concerned with its conservation and with its growth in unity.

Collegiality, to be truly lived in the Church, will suppose a profound evolution of the mode of exercise of pontifical authority. Father Congar says that, even though this authority radically possesses the power of governing the universal Church in a centralized way, it is not obliged to do so, and without relinquishing any of its rights nor any of its essential powers, it can transform itself in an unforeseeable way. This is of tremendous importance for the ecumenical dialogue, where the style often carries greater weight than the principles. It will presuppose too a type of missionary bishop as different from the pastors who comprised Vatican II as the bishops of true pastoral style, desired by the Council of Trent, were from the feudal or seignioral type who were gathered there and expressed this hope.

I have talked enough of the foundations of the Church and of its structure; one must see what becomes of all of it when these realities are viewed, not in a horizontal cross-section, at a given moment in time, but in history—when one scrutinizes the life of the Church in time.

4. THE LIFE OF THE CHURCH, TRADITION, AND REFORM

In speaking of the Christian personality of Father Congar I observed that he had refused to choose between tradition (identified more or less with conservatism) and reform (synonymous for some with revolution); these attitudes are reconciled at a profound level. In studying the ecclesiological "model" of *Vraie et fausse réforme*, I have become familiar with one way of reconciling the following apparently antagonistic notions, namely, preserving faithfully a normative deposit and at the same time reforming oneself unceasingly. The solution consisted in discerning in the Church a traditional pole, the very thing which God has given and preserves faithfully. This does not change. It is transmitted in an irreformable fashion, and has no need of reform for it is objectively holy. I am speaking of the most profound elements of the ecclesial Institution, bearer of the divine life which at each instant creates the messianic community: Word, sacraments, and apostolic authority. To it there is opposed a reformable pole: the life of the community which is holy, but whose holiness is mixed with impurity and is unceasingly in need of conversion. Also as part of *life*, and so reformable, there are the institutions (plural) which have no other guarantee than the ecclesial Institution itself. Here it is a question of the state of things in the Church, of life concretized in institutions: temporal institution; administration; ecclesiastical customs and traditions; rites; and even the hierarchy, not in its irreformable powers, but in its way of living and of organizing these holy powers.

This first approach has the advantage of letting one discern what can or ought to be reformed or adapted at a given moment in the life of the Church. But it is inadequate, for it is not sufficiently aware of what tradition and reform are in themselves nor of what the life of the Church is in time. Only by looking at tradition and reform as two complementary dimensions of the life of the Church does one perceive a second and much more profound means of reconciliation between them.

The Work of God Is Not Static

According to *Vraie et fausse réforme dans l'Eglise*, one seizes a major axis of this life of the Church, and therefore of God's design for men, in understanding that the work of God is not static; it is a history and a development inserted into time and disclosing little by little its meaning and its value. There, as in nature (but allowing room for freedom), everything begins with a seed which already contains the fullness that it will attain, develops by stages, and arrives at completion. From the promises made to Abraham until the end of history when all humanity will be reconciled in God's embrace, the People of God are on the march, and if the "seed" does not directly attain its final plenitude it is because God does not act alone—we cooperate. What God gives must also be "done" by us; everything is given by him, but everything is still to be done by us to whom even the ability to be able to do it is given; thus, because of our part in it, this can be accomplished only in history. I shall have the opportunity in the following chapter to cite some of the most beautiful passages of *Vraie et fausse réforme* wherein these themes are developed.

Now let me place in this history Tradition (according to *Tradition and Traditions*) and Reform (according to *Vraie et fausse réforme*). In this movement it is not enough to say that tradition and reform do not exclude each other, not enough to say that each must be given its share. In this life which develops through time, tradition is the seed, the parting gift which is transmitted from age to age, and with it, at the same time, its very growth and development. Far from being the conservation of an inert deposit, it is the harmonious growth and fulfillment of what is transmitted. But this development, because of obscurity and sin as much as the sovereign freedom of God, has not an automatic continuity. It needs new departures and remains submissive to divine initiatives. Thus, says Father Congar,[10] when a man is converted under the influence of grace it is an event which interests the communion of saints. But when this man has a mission to launch a new departure toward the goal, then a prophet, a reformer, is born. And when, because of this

---

[10]Conference "L'avenir de l'Eglise," in *L'Avenir*, Actes de la semaine des Intellectuels catholiques (Paris: Fayard, 1963). See Chap. 1, above, footnote 19.

vocation, the entire Church—or a certain part of the Church—is converted, this is the reform which interests history. For the Church in its very life is aroused to be assimilated more closely to Christ and, in its relation to the world, to revise the style of Christ's presence. Thus, in the living tradition (itself in tension to be renewed), reform is this new departure of purification, of deepening awareness, and of adaptation. Since the Church is the Church of tradition and of the divine deposit, reform always first shows itself as a return to the source, as to a treasure at the heart of tradition.

The Church, Subject of Tradition

After these general introductory remarks I shall examine in detail some important questions in the theology of tradition and reform as proposed by Father Congar.

First, let me develop, thanks to the simple and illuminating presentation of *The Meaning of Tradition,* a reflection I have already made on tradition as a development of history. This general theme seems better adapted to our purpose than the fine distinctions between Scripture and Tradition. Yet I should at least indicate that the term *tradition* can be taken in three principal meanings: as the *act* of transmitting or passing on something, as in a relay race; then (and at the same time), as the *content* communicated—*what* one passes on—the reality of Christianity; and finally, a more specific meaning according to which there is distinguished in this total content the ensemble of the Scriptures, the Bible as a book, and tradition in the sense of transmission by some means other than writing, whether by what is found in the Book, but in a living and personal way (this is the essential), or by something else (which is possible but very secondary). In the brief development that follows, I shall use the word "tradition" in the usual meaning—which rules out the first two interpretations.

The subject of the living tradition is the community, the entire Church. In this process:

Tradition is not a purely mechanical transmission of an inert deposit; it implies in its very notion the handing on of an object by one possessor to another, and so from one living being to another. It is *received* in a subject and this subject is living. A living subject necessarily puts something of himself into what he receives. With him, a teaching, whether by word or by example, or even from a written book, always takes on a certain character of dialogue. . . . [But] it is not enough to say that there is a living subject—it must be added that this subject lives *in history* and that historicity is one of its proper characteristics. This in no way implies a relativity of truth, which would be nothing more than the successive and changing thought of men. This communication . . . of a definite object, which remains identical in its underlying nature . . . is accomplished during a history to which it is not a stranger. That is to say, this history is not just a stage-setting placed in the background and not touching the characters, as we find in the moving picture studios.[11]

Thus history shapes the deposit without changing it; the continuity of tradition is historical: "It is the permanence of the past in the present, at the heart of which it prepares the future."

How does tradition live in history? First of all by replying to the questions of time, "for this history is first that of men and of the world. It is not a tranquil revery. It is full of discoveries, questions, attempts."[12]

The Church is established to announce what she, as God's representative, is to contribute to the historical development. Man, to whom the Gospel is to be announced, does not wait unmoving, but he advances in time by many paths, with an abundance of questions. In the second place, profiting from the intellectual wealth of the times, and even from a certain elaboration of the virtual content of an idea (always previously held though not always explicit, i.e., a development of dogma), there resulted new expressions, new interpretations to give to the unique message. Thus tradition is at the heart of the Church as its very life,

---

[11]*Ibid.*, pp. 84-86.
[12]*Ibid.*, p. 87.

inherited but actual, fresh and living, replying from the fullness of the treasure to the new questions of the day, advancing in history toward fulfillment by developing with humanity itself.

Reform Replies to Temptations

To come back to the question of reform. I have shown how this development toward a goal does not operate in a continuous way. It experiences stages from which new divine initiatives, through individual men or small groups, promote the adventure of the kingdom, a recentering in relation to the major axes of the movement, a readaptation to the world. For this movement, this development, includes in the new economy (as under the Old Testament) a double risk which *Vraie et fausse réforme* analyzes at length.

In the first place, because this development of the work of God always goes from the exterior to the interior, from cult and the juridical to the personal and the human (transposition of sacrifice, of priesthood, of the temple, of law), there is a "temptation of pharisaism," which consists in forgetting that Christianity has truth only in men, in stopping at what is material, at means. The reform, then, is to desire, like the prophets of the Old Testament, to give back to things their spiritual truth, not to allow the ecclesiastical apparatus to obscure God's grace in men's minds by replacing ardor and the spirit with structures, however necessary the latter might be to contain the spirit. It is a question of avoiding the degradation of the "mystical" into the "political," of confronting pharisaism with acts which are things in themselves instead of being for something else, of refusing to strive for power and assurances of success, of rejecting a group spirit, of not letting proselytism substitute for evangelization. The prophet, in Christianity, is this man called by God who is opposed to turning means into ends, opposed to serving external form for itself, for he reminds us unceasingly that this form has its truth beyond itself. He ardently frees the spirit from the letter.

In the second place there are stages in this development which can refuse to let themselves be transcended; one becomes attached to the forms in which the idea was incarnated, whereas its very dynamism demands that it go further. The "temptation of the synagogue" is typically the refusal to make this transition because of fidelity to the form, which becomes infidelity to the principle; one clings to what is attained at a given moment. On the contrary, reform here will be the willingness to adapt the structure of ecclesial life to a new situation—to the missionary life of the Church, for example, or to its intellectual life. As opposed to the nearsighted ones who are faithful to the letter, true fidelity includes the development of the fundamental principle toward the perfect form. According to an expression of Father Montcheuil, which Father Congar loves to quote, "It is not those who are obsessed with the past who maintain tradition, but those who experience it in the depth of their being." And so here the prophet appears again like one who gives to the movement of time its true relationship to God's plan, revealing the meaning of events, seizing upon the provocation which they represent on the part of God, for the Church. He further serves the progress of God's plan toward its goal by refusing to let any stage be harmfully considered as definitive.

This appeal to a continual reform in the Church (which since it is reform within tradition is a very different thing from the Protestant *ecclesia semper reformanda*) has not ceased to cause scandal since the appearance of Father Congar's book in 1950. However, as Father Chenu observed in his address to Father Congar at the Saulchoir in 1963, the word "reform" has been heard incessantly at the Council, even on the lips of the two popes who presided there. "The triumph of one word," Father Chenu remarked, "is always something very significant." And he added:

> It is extraordinary that these intuitions which you have had, and which have been in ferment in a few others around you, reached full maturity so quickly and so definitively. Of course— there is a return in the continuity—it is the same Church, but pre-

cisely this *reformatio*, this coming to grips with its conscience on the part of the Church after the Counter Reformation [caused] the era of the Counter Reformation to be closed and many eras to be closed with it.

But in this life of the Church, in its "in-itself," its internal reform is inseparable from what is still very fundamentally itself: its aspect "for-the-world," which I must now broach. I shall point out at the same time (for it is correlative) the theology of the laity that Father Congar proposes to us.

5. CHRISTIAN LAITY, RESPONSIBLE IN THE CHURCH AND IN THE WORLD

The Specific Vocation of the Layman

Leaving aside the completely negative definitions of the layman, familiar to the last centuries of the theology of the liturgy of the Church, of spirituality and of law, Father Congar first tried to define the layman in an intra-ecclesial fashion, stemming from his baptismal membership in the People of God. This initiation prepares him in a very positive way to take his responsibility in the Church as a full-fledged member. A distinction of complementary vocations within the same community differentiates layman and cleric in a way to be determined in each particular area of the life of the Church.

But a second, though no less important hint, gives another criterion of discernment. In fact, in *Lay People in the Church*, Father Congar introduced a second element in the definition of the layman: interest for the world, in the very positive sense of an ensemble of responsibilities, tasks, commitments, which are the lot of man in creation and in the city. This interest, as the fundamental datum which becomes a divine vocation, specifies the layman as opposed to the cleric who is withdrawn from these temporal responsibilities by his particular service of the Word:

Laymen are in the world as Christians to do in it the work of God insofar as it is to be done in and through the work of the world. . . . The layman then will be the one for whom (in the very work God has confided to him) the very substance of things exists and is interesting . . . because, speaking in the Christian context, what is to be referred to the Absolute is, for the layman, the very reality of the elements of this world whose appearances pass.[13]

From this comes the idea, developed in the conference "The Future of the Church," that laity and world are correlative terms, and that the civilization of medieval Christianity was not only clerical but unconcerned about the positive reality of the world. Inversely, to an awakening of the world there corresponds an awakening of the laity in the Church.

It is on this second point of the vocation of the layman that Father Congar purposely dwells in his later writings, accepting the definition of Karl Rahner (though not adhering to all his views on the apostolate of the laity). According to this definition the layman is "the one who, inasmuch as he is a Christian, conserves in his being the determinations of his natural insertion into the world."[14] Certainly, the opposition "layman-cleric" would, in this realm, have to be pinpointed in a very precise and specific way. But Karl Rahner as well as Father Congar maintain, in opposition to some authors, that the distinction cleric-layman is not purely intra-ecclesial, but has repercussions at this level of rapport with the world. In view of this very service there is a certain "setting apart" of the servant of the Word. It differs from that of the monk and is at the very heart of a presence. Of itself, this setting apart is not opposed to the ordination of married men, although it is the strongest argument from suitability for the elements of religious life associated with the priesthood in the West. Even less does it exclude manual work and other subordinate tasks. In the domain of political responsibilities, however, it maintains certain important reservations. Why is this? To the best of my knowledge Father Congar has not expressed himself formally on this subject, but I can infer that it is because the basic differ-

---

[13]Les Jalons pour une théologie du laïcat, op. cit., pp. 38, 45.
[14]"Théologie de l'Action catholique" (1957), reprinted in Sacerdoce et laïcat, op. cit., pp. 329 ff.

ence between the Church, a means of salvation established from on high, and the world must be manifested visibly at the very level of the ministry.

Thus, for example, suppose that a priest-worker's refusal to take an office in a trade union beyond the basic one (an indispensable sign of solidarity) caused a scandal among his comrades. This scandal would be the occasion of manifesting the paradox of the Gospel and of the Church themselves. It is understood, of course, that it is not a question of evading a subordinate task which the Church in the past has approved without the slightest hesitation.

The Apostolate Is Natural to the Layman

Thus the first positive aspect of the condition of the Christian layman is his life and his responsibility in the Church. The great functions of the Church, as I stated earlier, concern not only the hierarchy, but the community as such: the community within which the hierarchy and the laity have their complementary roles. Father Congar also tries in *Lay People in the Church* to pinpoint these roles in the diverse realms of the life of the Church, then in that of its presence and its action in the world. I have already shown how these roles were articulated in the case of the priesthood; in the same way one can analyze the participation of laymen in prophetism, in authority, in the communitarian life of the Church. However, if one envisions the vocation of the Church in the world, if, for a start, one considers the first dimension of this vocation, which is the announcement to the world of the Gospel of salvation, the "mission" of the Church, again one is going to find interacting the two elements of the vocation of the layman, the two positive aspects of his condition: his full membership in the Church and his insertion into the world. On the other hand, the theology of the missionary activity of laymen should in turn indicate their proper role as members of a completely missionary Church, and the role of the hierarchy with its special responsibility for the mission of the Church.

Thus, in their place in the world, laymen will be missionaries by the witness that "every action which God's salvific plan in the world" constitutes, but without excluding the explicit witness of the world. On the contrary, "faith and baptism consecrate it and impose on it the duty, at the same time as the grace, of the *confessio fidei.*" For this, the duty of the apostolate is completely natural to laymen. They do not need to receive it from on high, it comes to them "from their ordinary quality as Christians. In its most common meaning it does not suppose any other dependence in regard to the hierarchy than the general dependence characteristic of all Christian life vis-à-vis the heads of the Church in matters of faith, sacramental life, and Christian conduct."[15] This notion is in opposition to certain abusive uses of the idea "mandate." But the fact remains that laymen can be called to a close collaboration with the hierarchical authority in the exercise of its apostolic mission in a more precise sense. A major means of this collaboration is Catholic Action, which Father Congar studies at length in *Lay People in the Church* and in the article "Théologie de l'Action catholique," from which the preceding quotations were taken.

The Entire Church Is Missionary

One might have gathered that the word "mission" in the last paragraph was taken in a broad sense, one common to all the Church, as well as in a second sense, more specific and proper to the ecclesiastical hierarchy. These meanings do not seem to correspond to what a secular education has accustomed us to understand by the word: the establishment by missionary institutes, under the direction of the Roman Congregation of the Propagation of the Faith, of new ecclesial structures in countries where Christianity has not yet penetrated.

This leads me to say a word about Father Congar's missiological conceptions. He has given much thought to these questions

[15]*Ibid.*, p. 345.

(which explains the role he played at the Council in the elaboration of *De Missionibus*), but he has published very few of the results of his research. One book, *Mission, sacerdoce, laïcat,* the outcome of a workshop and dialogue with the Mission de France. at Limoges in 1953, was withdrawn from publication by Father Congar himself in 1954 at the time of the priest-worker affair. Since then Father Congar has published *La Mission et la théologie de l'Eglise.*[16]

The essential is to show that it is the entire Church which is missionary. This involves at least two consequences. In his notes from the fourth session, Father Congar sums up his views as follows: In the first place, "missions (in the classical meaning) must be included in mission. Or, to say the same thing in a different way, must be included in ecclesiology pure and simple. For too long the Church has been identified in a practical way with the dioceses of the old Christendom; distant undertakings, the missions were, so to speak, projected beyond the Church." There will certainly be different modes, but the interior mission which confronts the de-Christianization (or better, the non-evangelization) of certain sections of so-called Christian countries has just as much right to the term mission as distant missions have. Let me note in passing that the old canonical definition of mission, *to establish the Church,* "retains its truth; however it cannot be interpreted in a strictly juridical sense, for missions are always geared to men, not to institutions. And it must be readily admitted that the Church is to be made effectively present, not in territories, but in regard to human groups for whom it does not really exist" and for whose conversion to the Gospel it strives. This is why Father Congar much prefers the old medieval expression *to expand* the Church to the term *to establish* the Church. The former has an entirely different connotation in which, it will be noticed, Church does not have an institutional

---

[16]In *Repenser la Mission*, 33e semaine de missiologie de Louvain, 1965.

and hierarchical meaning but a richer and more comprehensive one.

In the second place, the respective roles of the hierarchy and of all the People of God as such must be so delineated that mission will not appear to be reserved to the former. But neither is it a question of slighting the special responsibility of apostolic authority. Actually, one might ask why it would not be possible to apply mission in an undifferentiated sense, not to the hierarchy but to the People of God as such. The place of the hierarchy could then be situated at its very heart and at its service in the perspective adopted above to present the whole of ecclesiology. According to Father Congar, when it is a question of mission, one is led through the will of Christ to effect a necessary distinction, discerning two different meanings of the word mission, as I began to do above. Mission can be considered, he says, "as the *responsibility* of witness and of service which flows from the Christian quality as such: thus there is mission in the broad sense and this mission is equally incumbent on every Christian. All the disciples received the Holy Spirit and the gifts which render them responsible for God's cause. If, however, mission is taken in the sense of a definite command given by Christ to the Apostles . . . then it must be said that the apostolic body of bishops is the first heir. The entire Church cooperates with it."[17] Here again is found an ecclesiological principle previously discussed when presenting the theology of the *Mystery of the Church.*

The Lordship of Christ over the Church

Now comes the second great dimension of the vocation of the Church in the world—which is the work, the presence, the service, the sanctifying action in the creation of and in the earthly city themselves. Let me try to summarize the thought of Father Congar, which seems very important and remarkably balanced. Christ is the Lord of everything: of the Church and of the World.

---

[17]*Le Concile au jour le jour,* Session IV (1966), p. 61.

When he comes into the world the Creator transfers to Christ his universal mastery, by making him as man the Lord of everything. Thus everything is, in him, recapitulated—taken up under one single Head. He accomplishes God's plan, not only for Israel, but for all humanity and even for the whole of creation. God restores to the world, through Christ, the dynamism which allows everything to attain its end.

> The order of Redemption or of grace on the one hand, the order of nature or of creation on the other, have one identical foundation and are responsible to one identical sovereignty, to one identical government—those of Jesus Christ. . . . This unity of principle does not involve a unity of structure. . . . It involves, assuredly, a unity of plan and of purpose.[18]

In the Church as in the world this Lordship is substantially the same: restoration, reconciliation of all, love, truth, justice, that each thing might be what it should be—and not arbitrary domination, tyranny. At the end of the world that Lordship will burst forth, and there will no longer be any distinction between Church and world. But as of now this distinction exists, involving a different way of exercising the Lordship of Christ over each one. Why?

Father Congar tells why in an article entitled "Church and World."[19] In virtue of what was just said about the Lordship of Christ, the Church, which openly acknowledges it in faith, ought also to be at the service of its spread throughout the world.

> The Church should certainly be the animating power of the movement by means of which the world will attain its last end, which is in fact supernatural. But in itself it is something other than the movement of the world in its supreme aspiration. It is not only the crest of the wave, borne by the great mass of waters. . . . It comes from above from a series of divine initiatives which

---

[18]*Jésus-Christ* (Paris: Editions du Cerf, 1964), pp. 188-89. See Chap. 1, above, footnote 23.
[19]*Le Concile au jour le jour, op. cit.*, Session III, pp. 143-76.

are inscribed in history, and the most decisive of which has been the coming of God himself in Jesus Christ, who sent after him his Holy Spirit.

The Lordship of Christ over the World

Since then, there is Church *and* world. Over the Church Jesus Christ rules effectively, that is to say he is recognized as Lord. We know that he exercises this Lordship both through the apostolic Institution and through his Spirit which directs from within the entire community. Over the world the Lordship of Christ is exercised otherwise—it is not explicitly recognized, it does not impose itself with power and authority, it is neither visible nor immediate. How is it exercised? First, invisibly; it rules over the hearts of men who, without knowing Christ, have chosen freely to be open to his call which their consciences transmit to them: toward truth, toward good, toward all the values. Then, in regard to the structures and the very realities of this world, his Lordship is exercised in and by the creational structures of the world. What does this mean?

> To heal the sick, to know and to make known the natural truth of things, to make human justice reign, to suppress the various forms of slavery, and to free man to place at the disposition of others more of the goods of creation—any and every activity which, insofar as it is authentic, really accomplishes the work of God. . . . In its profound movement human history is, in short, a search for these two benefits, of cure or integrity, of unification or universal reconciliation. The kingdom will provide these for the creature, but by producing them from above; whereas history seeks to obtain them from below, starting from the resources of the creature himself . . . [working thus] for Christ who, eternal Wisdom, includes the intentions of creation in the work of his Redemption.[20]

From this it follows that the hierarchical Church has no temporal power but only spiritual powers of a religious nature. It

---

[20]*Jésus-Christ, op. cit.* pp. 213-14.

also follows that the official recognition of the Church by a "Christian" state, far from being a fundamental proposition implied in the Gospel (in view of which any other solution would be only a compromise or an "hypothesis"), is in reality only *one* of the possibilities of the unique evangelical proposition of the responsibility for everything which Christians have in the world, where they must make Christ reign. As I have said, if they must make Christ reign, it is not in a theocratic way but by the reconciliation of everything in love. In the actual pluralistic situation, this official recognition is an unrealizable hypothesis; another possibility remains for Christians: that of becoming involved in the human city not *as* Christians but because they are Christians, to make it as conformable as possible to evangelical objectives. It is seen that this theological reflection also brings real support to the doctrine of religious liberty, another decisive principle being the absolute liberty of the act of faith and the evangelical respect for the "other" which Father Congar analyzes in two studies in *Sacerdoce et Laïcat*: "Conversion" and "Proselytizing and Evangelization."

"A Church That Might Be in the World"

Father Congar has a positive attitude toward the modern world, with its human effort toward mastery and progress in which men of all types collaborate. He is without the enthusiasm which characterizes some of his brother priests and friends, but neither does he have any pessimism. His severe criticism of the "Christendom" of old, his willingness to free what is valuable in the actual rapport between Church and world (while they do not conceal from him the ambiguity of several contemporary aspirations or realizations), sometimes go so far as to express themselves with impressive force, which does not exclude a certain lyricism, especially when it is a question of the grandeur of the vocation of the lay Christian. To celebrate this, Father Congar rediscovers within himself a love of life, a confidence, a respect for man, a profound

emotion before the splendid types of humanity: "One understands that God became incarnated."

"What do laymen do?" he asks. I personally have heard him
reply: "They make man, humanity. It's tremendous: to advance
this project, each man brings something to the fulfillment of
human nature which others inherit. And everyone brings something; man is created every day." One could think he was hearing
Father Chenu's, "The more I work, the more God creates." In
the conference already referred to, "L'avenir de l'Eglise," there
is found in the rhythm of the dialectical "In the world but not
of the world" a beautiful exposé of these views, completely centered on the vocation of the Christian laity and on the correlation
between a world that is fully world and a Christian adult laity.
To conclude this section I will quote a significant passage from
this important text:

> What one must realize today is a Church that might at least
> be of the world, that might be nothing but Church, but that would
> *be* it. A Church that might be in the world and that to accomplish
> this might recognize, opposite it, the world for what it is. A Church
> whose entire existence (even that of pure praise which I have taken
> care not to forget) might have as a dimension accompanying it in
> everything that it is, the awareness, the obsession even, of being
> sent to the world. The future of the Church is full mission. The
> future of the Church is a true dialogue. The two things appear
> alien to each other only if they are considered superficially. . . .
> In the reign of Christendom the Church did not truly have any
> world opposite it; it had it as absorbed and fashioned in its image
> in such a way that there was scarcely any tension or dialogue ex-
> cept in the interior of the counterpart. Dialogue, like mission,
> always refers to another recognized as Other yet capable of com-
> munion. Today how could the Church not be aware of a world
> so full of vitality, of inquiry, and of question? . . . The Church is
> aware that, having been sent, it ought truly to meet that world.
> No longer being in the position of a monopoly, as formerly . . . the
> Church cannot thrust its message at the world without asking it
> what it is, what it bears within itself, and even what it offers. For
> twenty years, reflection on the interior Mission has brought one
> to see it not as an entirely unilateral contribution, but as involving

an aspect of welcome, of openness to the other, of receptivity, of exchange and reciprocity, and finally, of sharing.[21]

From the heart of the Church to the center of the world, such has been the itinerary into the ecclesiological work of Father Yves Congar. Now, in a briefer chapter, I must go back still further in his essential theological options in order to put in their right place certain positions already encountered, but not perfectly elucidated. To do this I shall, as far as possible, try to make use of little known or unpublished works of Father Congar. Thus I shall give the reader the opportunity of entering into an understanding of some decisive aspects of the thought of the theologian. In fact, because in the larger ecclesiological works these aspects are disengaged only progressively and upon reflection, they are not always evident, although they underlie them. On the other hand, these decisive aspects recur frequently in his recent writings, allowing me to cite him more frequently and at greater length than when it was a question of presenting the main lines of his ecclesiology. In so doing I was obliged to summarize or to simplify theories that were often lengthy and very complex.

---

[21]*Sainte Eglise*, in *Unam Sanctam* (Paris: Editions du Cerf, 1963), XLI, pp. 393-410.

CHAPTER FIVE

The Great Theological Options

1. THEOLOGY FOR MAN AND ANTHROPOLOGY FOR GOD

For ten years Father Congar has been meditating unceasingly on a theme which I broach here, somewhat bluntly, for the first time. I shall try to shed light on it gradually. He thinks that one can never separate in any domain the "in-itself" and the "for-men." For someone who has been so little concerned to notice contemporary philosophy or to accept its support, he has shown himself remarkably attuned to the thought of his time. After all, is not philosophy itself the elaboration and criticism of great intuitions? Moreover, when Father Congar as early as 1932 wished to integrate into Christian reflection the modern (and modernistic) preoccupation with *subject,* was he not already on the path which led him to his present interests? According to him, then, the "in-itself" and the "for-men" cannot be separated, not even in what concerns God. Of course creation is free as is Redemption, but there is something in God which brings him to creation in such a way that we discover in it something of what he is. Through man whom he creates, through the Man whom he becomes, something of God is revealed. Everything is there in this union of anthropology and theology. For us there is only a God of grace, not an "in-itself"—but it is the "in-itself" of God which grace reveals to us. Could not the rupture that has been established in Christendom between God and man be one of the greatest causes of present-day unbelief? Could it not be, asks Father Congar, because one has adored a God without man and without the world, that man has received an answer from man and a world without God? Thus the diagnosis encountered

127

earlier when speaking of the inquiry conducted by *La Vie Intellectuelle* is strengthened and broadened. The Bible knows no
other theology than that for man and the world; even more,
perhaps it is above all an anthropology for God. Let me deal
successively with the problem of the knowledge of God and the
knowledge of man.

(A) GOD IN CHRIST

Who Is the Living God?

Who is the living God, our God, the God of Israel, the Father of
our Lord Jesus Christ?

> The living God of rich biblical monotheism is posited as being
> the source and measure of all goodness, of all truth, of all authen-
> tic existence. The God of biblical monotheism is something other
> and more than the great clock-maker or great architect of the the-
> ists who posit him only as the Creator of the world; after this ini-
> tial act the world and man have no longer any rapport with any-
> thing but themselves and their own nature. The living God is
> affirmed by the Bible as sovereign source and measure, to which
> man and all things must unceasingly be referred and must con-
> form so that one does not just exist but exists *truly*, realizing the
> meaning, the fullness of one's existence. God is affirmed as the
> unique, sovereign Subject, who unceasingly makes the world ac-
> cording to a plan which, viewed from its final end, is single, but
> is twofold from the viewpoint of the energies involved and the
> initiatives taken (Creation, Revelation, and Redemptive Incar-
> nation).[1]

The essential note in the experience we have of this God in
salvation history is that he is both transcendent and near; there
is never one without the other. In a retreat preached at the Saulchoir in December, 1961, Father Congar dwelt at length on this
dialectic. God is the Holy One, the Separated One, Holiness
is his proper order of existence. In the New Testament he is
ho Theos, the Father whom no one has ever seen, the absolutely
first principle, not only of the world but of divinity itself, the

---

[1]Conference published in *Socialization et personne humaine,* Semaine
Sociale de Grenoble (Lyons, 1960).

very source of the whole Trinity. Yet he is at the same time near. In the Bible there is never an affirmation of God's holiness without an accompanying affirmation that God comes "toward us," without an insistence on his nearness. The two make but one single affirmation. Likewise, if God is Father, that means that he is bending over us. There is no Father who does not bend over a weakness. God is near. But God is God; I never have the advantage over him.

God Become Visible in Jesus Christ

Known in his Word, known in his striking deeds for Israel, God has never been so well known in this proximity and transcendence as in Jesus Christ, revelation of God, and first of all in the very fact of the Incarnation, of the "descent." This is the theme of an admirable study, "Dum visibiliter Deum cognoscimus."[2] In spite of its erudite notes this article is less a work of patristic science (on this score there are certain reservations) than a profound and rich evangelical and traditional meditation. Here is the God who spoke through the prophets:

> The entire movement of the plan of God was toward this perfection of the communication of himself. The specific note of the new and eternal Covenant consists precisely in this passage from the simple gifts of God to the gift of God himself, ". . . of the God who speaks, to the God made man," as Louis Bouyer expressed it.

Jesus Christ, the last revelation, saves us first by making us know God. As St. Leo said: "God, invisible in his nature, became visible in ours. The supreme and completely true revealer, Christ, reveals at least *ex parte* the depths of the mystery of God." But, "this revelation is not only contained in his teaching, it is also (perhaps one should even say *above all*) in what he has done . . . the descent of the Word into our flesh, the assuming by God of the condition of servant, the washing of feet, the

---

[2]In *Jésus-Christ* (Paris: Editions du Cerf, 1964), pp. 7-38. See Chap. 1, above, footnote 23.

obedience of love even to death on the Cross. All of that realizes a value of revelation, and of the revelation *of God*— 'Philip, he who has seen me has seen the Father.' "

When God became man something that was already true in the previous stages of salvation history reached its highest degree: man resembles God and therefore, in a totally transcendent way, God resembles man. God who created man in his image tells us something essential about himself when his word expresses itself to his own subject as if to the image of man. Such is the meaning of the anthropomorphisms of the Bible:

> God is unceasingly represented as having senses, performing actions, experiencing feelings analogous to the senses, the actions, the feelings of men. These images have served to remove from minds a naturalistic representation of God, but they also had a positive aim and content: they are linked with the development of God's revelation as moral.[3]

But how much truer is this when God becomes man!

> The most astonishing thing is not that Jesus Christ is God but that God is Jesus Christ. Therefore there is something in him which permits him to be so, and not only his omnipotence which of itself is only infinite possibility; not only the liberty of his grace which permits him being so high to bend so low, but something which positively led him so to condescend and to become man.[4]

Here we are at the heart of our reflection—not only have we been led to see that our knowledge of God is inseparable from our knowledge of man and that in the last analysis we do not truly know God except in Jesus Christ, but we are at the point where we can ask ourselves: What is it in God that makes him act and love in this way?

> Evidently the God "for us" is the God of the "economy," and all the acts of salvation economy are free and pleasing. As such

---

[3]*Loc. cit.*
[4]*Loc. cit.*

they do not belong to the necessary mystery of God. They do, however, presuppose and reveal something of his nature. Christmas, which includes the entire paschal mystery . . . and which is the materialization of all the communications interspersed throughout the entire course of sacred history, reveals that the Absolute is not only for itself and in itself but that it is the Love-Gift, that is, *agape*. There is no Absolute which is not at the same time Love, no "Great God" who is not good God, God toward us and for us. . . . There is no "He is, he was" which is not at the same time "He is coming."[5]

To Surrender Oneself to the Living God

If this is true, the way for man to rejoin God, to imitate God in order to be God, will be for him to understand in the light of these same perspectives. In the retreat at the Saulchoir of which I spoke, Father Congar was insistent on this point. Actually, one could be deceived. One could believe that God is automatically the affirmation of isolation and that to go to him one must purify oneself, flee alone to the Alone. Now Paul tells us: "Have within yourself the same mind which was in Christ Jesus," that is, being of a divine nature he humiliated himself even to the death of the Cross. Adam thought that to be like God it was necessary to be independent, self-sufficient. Now the truth revealed in Jesus is the contrary; the true nature of God is not a proud ascent toward an independent exaltation, it is a way of abasement, of humility. The way to ascend is to descend, along the path of love, of service. In the Gospel the true disciple is the one who serves. These are the depths reached by the idea of the hierarchy as service—that to realize the true religious relationship, to know God, is essentially to live in a relationship of service.

This leads to an important point in the domain of prayer and to a criticism of the debatable opposition that has been set up between "contemplation" and "action." Prayer is a personal dialogue with the living God which can only lead the believer to insert himself by this very fact into the movement of love which

---

[5]*Loc. cit.*

comes from God, and to go toward the world of men. Father Congar explains this in an unpublished letter on the Order of Friars Preachers which he sent to Father Régamey:

> Only one thing is true and beautiful—to surrender oneself to God. He wants us, either cooperating with his plan in a hidden way or cooperating with his plan of salvation by an outward expression and by attacking anything that resists him. But it is a question only of surrendering oneself to God. The division of life into "active," "contemplative," and "mixed," comes from the false idea that God is in his heaven as immobile and sovereign as a satrap on his throne, and that the action would be undertaken *by men*—completed by God, rectified, what you will, but by men. Now, such is not the case. . . . If my God is the biblical God, the living God, "I am, I was, I am coming," he is inseparable from the world and from men, and these are true, are saved only if they realize their relation to him. My relation to God is not that of a cult which ascends from me to him, but of faith by which I surrender to his action of the Living God, communicating himself to the world and to men according to his plan. I have only to place myself faithfully and to offer the fullness of my being and of my resources in order to be, as he expects me to be, the relay of God's action. For me there is no difference between offering myself to God (contemplation) and being the minister of the *Sequentia Sancti Evangelii* . . . of the manifestation of God in Jesus Christ.

(B)   CHRISTIAN ANTHROPOLOGY

In Jesus Christ God Has a History

So here we are brought back to man. That God became man tells us something not only about God but about man also. There is an implied anthropology in salvation history. And the first thing that revelation teaches us is the way that God conceives man in his truth and the relation of his creature with himself. Here shall again be found, under another aspect, certain analyses that have already been presented in the ecumenical study. In an exposé (which is to appear in an Italian encyclopedia) entitled "God, Man, and Universe—Answers Demanded of Theology by Contemporary Atheism," Father Congar gives us the essentials of his thought on this point:

In Jesus Christ the transcendent and immutable God has become the subject of a history. But what interests us most here is that in Jesus Christ God has definitively united himself to our humanity and our world—directly to our humanity, but with it to our world also. . . . As incredible as this might appear to anyone who has some glimpse of the absolute God, of his perfection which transcends all representation, God has united himself to our humanity and our world in a *definitive* fashion. Could the adventure of the world fail totally? Such a thing seems dogmatically unthinkable, since God is not content just to have a plan for the world, but he wishes to realize it by uniting himself closely to the world through the humanity which he himself assumes and which is concretely woven into the texture of the world. . . . Under these conditions one understands equally well that he ought not to admit any opposition or disjunction between the glory of God, which is the ultimate end of everything, and the happiness of man or the completion of the world.

The basis for this anthropology is certainly the biblical idea of the image of God, largely developed through tradition, and susceptible of two broad lines of theological exploitation, one more familiar to the Latin Fathers, starting from the spirit of man, the other developed by certain Greek Fathers, starting from man as a collaborator in creation. For Father Congar, a real theological anthropology ought to pick up this trail and transfer it Christologically into a historical perspective. Let me make the observation that this does not necessarily imply an option in favor of a theology systematically Christocentric as some modern authors have proposed. It should be established that, from the "economic" point of view, God desires a world completed by Christ, and this fact must effectively impregnate all theology, not just figure in it accidentally. But this world and this history certainly have God as end and as a permanent center of reference and understanding.

Christ in His Encounter with Man

Father Congar conceives this Christological transfer of which I spoke as developing out of the idea of messianism. Christ responds to man's expectations by the great values which he incarnates. King, Priest, Prophet, he comes to encounter man who is in search of truth, efficacy, purity and integrity, communion, and reconciliation of all things. What he establishes is a messianic people in whom is accomplished the aim of the creation. Here is found a conception of salvation and of the relations between nature and grace of which I shall speak a little later. Let me simply say that, in this perspective, the Church appears as the sign that God is committed to the success of the human effort which we put forth. That is why the category, *People of God*, is the one that has the most promise (being completed of course by *Body of Christ* and *Temple of the Holy Spirit*), for according to the theologian it is the category which best responds to the restoration of creation and best exorcises a clerical or narrowly sacramental vision. It is undoubtedly clearer now where the basis for an ecclesiology should be sought. Like the ecclesiology of the Fathers, it would be essentially anthropological: an ecclesiology of the baptized man living in the Spirit, an ecclesiology of the image of God become God's humanity in Jesus, the first-born of many brothers.

More precisely, what is the view of man which this relation to God in Jesus Christ and salvation history presuppose? What is the anthropology with which Christianity is pregnant? To see what man is, one would have to start with Christian actions, with Christian life—sharing, prayer, thanksgiving, spiritual combat, life in the city of men, poverty. And above all one must not forget to consider these in the plural, for Christian man is a man jointly responsible with others in a community. One of the articles edited by Father Congar in a volume on poverty[6] develops at length this principle of the transference to the Church of the great Christian themes. Thus one would come to a view of man which started from man made for God, with the full dimension of the "natural desire" to know and love completely. It would integrate this collaboration to its own salvation to which God invites man,

---

[6]*Eglise et pauvreté*, in *Unam Sanctam* (Paris: Editions du Cerf, 1965), LVII. See Chapter 1, above, footnote 19.

trusting him to be a mediator of grace. It would make room for the corporeity, temporality, and historicity of the world. It would synthesize the dialectics of society and person, of accomplished fact and doing, etc.

A Humanity of Communion

Rather than skim over all these subjects let me give two examples. To start let us see the Christian contribution in the dialectic of personal and collective life as Congar developed it at the Semaine Sociale, Grenoble, 1963. Even in the plan of the Old Testament, the person confronting God the Creator, who makes a world using secondary agents (in man's case this necessarily involves his consciousness and freedom), "is defined not in opposition to the group but as the individual subject, conscious and free, who in the world and for the fulfillment of its destiny, in the social group and for its salvation, bears a singular vocation."

> In the realm of religious relationship which makes him exist with respect to the Living God, to the God of the Covenant, [man] is constituted a person by his vocation and by the fidelity he gives to it. . . . This way of characterizing person permits the affirmation both of the reality of his freedom, his full value as a creature, and the insertion of this person into the collectivity. There is, in fact, even a mutual interpenetration of person and collectivity. There was this personal vocation even in Israel where election was offered to the people as such. For the Word of God wills a reply from man. . . . [But] in the Bible, the attitude of the person before God, his fidelity, is shown as influencing the fate of the collectivities. These are borne along to a blessing or condemnation by the personal action of one of its members.

And Father Congar concludes this paragraph by saying:

> The human person is characterized precisely by the communicability of the values which it creates. Each human person can introduce into the historical development of the people of men some new principle, some new interpretation of ideas, examples, questions or attitudes, which will henceforth enter into the texture of a great number of personalities, will nourish and specify them.

Having developed a converging theme, that of the *pars pro toto* or of the "corporative personality" in the Bible, which gives evidence of this complementarity of the personal and of community, the theologian moves on to the New Testament. Beginning with the Trinitarian revelation and the relations in God of nature and persons, he proposes a view of human nature which (while not entirely personalized in each human person as in God) keeps nonetheless "the order to the totality that it bears of itself. In virtue of this common element in himself every man tends to this totality, on the one hand through generation, on the other through social life, the framework of civilization." This is accomplished in a history that men make. Thus "each human person can develop for others values of humanity which actualize the virtualities of a nature common to them and transmitted to them to be cultivated." By performing actions which are inalienably theirs, persons are creative of determinations which are a common heritage of humanity. For Father Congar it is in this dialectical "person-nature" that the dialectical "personal life-collective life" finds its true synthesis. And this becomes still more true when, in virtue of the principle of the *pars pro toto* (Jesus Christ having been constituted Head of the Mystical Body or the new human race, thus raising our nature to its state of eschatological perfection), we must personalize in ourselves "the renewed humanity which is communion." (Father Congar then proceeds to develop his analysis by disengaging from what has been said an adequate concept of person and a view of the relationship between person and world.)

To Let God Be God in Us

A morality that is not a moralizing is another consequence of our religious relationship with the living God. He gives us salvation but not without our working for it in time in such a way that *man* will be produced only when all human beings can say *Our Father* together. This is a theological ethics that consists in our being the living and free relays of God's action. But that action passes through Christ, that is, henceforth it will always take on in us the colors, the characteristics that it had in Christ: Cross, love, *agape*, service. Such a perspective completely unifies the moral life at its spiritual height giving it an entirely theological aspect. It does not, however, telescope the human element, nor misjudge the stability of our nature which is precisely in the image of God. Thus our action is a being of God, inscribed into our human texture. Inversely, to sin is to resist God's being God in us as he is in himself. And all this is accomplished in Christ; the morality of the New Testament is always "an imperative coming from an indicative": do this because Christ did it. It is the imitation of Jesus, but an imitation that is not moralistic, narrowly individualistic, and pessimistic. It is theological, historical, cosmic; coming from God it goes toward men through us.

For Father Congar the absolutely decisive importance of this Christian anthropology is due to the already mentioned fact that modern man's rejection of God comes in good measure from his conviction that religion can be nothing but the impoverishment, the destruction, the subservience of humanity. The reply could only be a demonstration of the contrary truth, not by an apologetical argument but by perfecting a reflection on man beginning with God's plan, and correlatively by putting into evidence a Christian man who is both truly man and truly Christian. On these two points the past centuries have left us a heavy enough heritage. In the study previously referred to, "God, Man, and the Universe," Father Congar draws up a balance sheet of these former spiritualities which developed in answer to questions posed by an emerging era (political Augustinianism, monastic ideology, spirituality of the *Imitation,* religion of the age of Louis XIV). He then develops the theoretical considerations on the monotheism of the living God and Christian anthropology which I just exposed, and other thoughts on salvation and the dialectical "faith-religion" which I shall investigate. In such a realm, however, theory is not enough and one can readily understand how attentive Father Congar is to any sign in the Church of the appearance of a type of Christian man who might express this anthropological renewal before God, within the Church, and in the world.

The "Rediscovery of Christian Man"

The following excerpt, which I give at length, can make us aware of the importance of a text from "L'avenir de l'Eglise" for an understanding of Father Congar's thought.

> For about ten years I have been struck by one fact: the re-discovery of Christian man. This statement demands an explanation. There have always been true Christians. There have been previously men who forced themselves to remodel their entire personality according to the spirit of the Gospel. This effort also extended to questions of politics and social action. It seems, however, that these were exceptional personalities or men representing the *longa manus* (extension) of the Church in its temporal structures. What is striking today is the number of men and women, often couples, who being fully *of* the world, seek in the lay authenticity of their temporal engagements to be Christian, and to live their very commitment in an evangelical way in the fabric of this world. The movement appears to me twofold: on the one hand, in the midst of men somewhat worldly and pagan in their humanity but subject to the laws of the Church are found men who want to have a Christian bearing even in the ordinary run of their earthly life. On the other hand these men live their Christian lives as a response to the requests of the world and life, requests which take their inspiration from the Gospel. For them existence is evangelical responsibility for everything in such a way that they live their experiences of Christian life not according to fixed laws laid down once for all in the Church and exterior to their own conscience, but according to what life, events, circumstances reveal to them as requisite or as appeals to the light of the Gospel. The "revision of life" (of which it was written that it was "perhaps the first in history in the spiritual order," i.e., as an original creation coming from the laity, born outside of monasteries and ecclesiastical circles) is characteristic of what I have been trying to explain. Even the idea of holding things in common is not lacking, but is one of the characteristics of this life. The "revision of life," whether systematized or not, is both the fruit and the sign of the restoration of Christian man.

Perhaps one of the essential points of this text appears somewhat abstract: to wish to be Christian in all one's human fibers, in the very activities of the world, without any question of acting within a specific religion or of positing a neo-Christianity. To clarify this let me quote from a conference given by Father Congar at Grenoble in 1963[7] where he develops this precise point.

I am going to start with a banal example, although in its tragic aspect it is very beautiful. I recall that a few years ago, at the height of the Algerian war, I met a French woman who had been in Algeria and had been accused of helping the National Liberation Front. She had done nothing in the political area and even less in the military one. She had simply helped people in distress. Yet she was arrested and severely tortured. In the interrogation she was asked: "You are a communist?"—"Indeed not." "A Union member?"—"No." "Then what are you?" And she replied, "I am a Christian." Thus the quality of Christian became descriptive of an attitude taken at the human level; its action was not political but it touched a situation committed to the war effort. That is what I understand by a Christian—one who tries to carry out to the very end certain imperatives from the Gospel. The one too whose thinking comes from conscience. No one dictated it. What priest, what bishop could have prompted this? It was simply an action of personal conscience performed less from observing the precise rules of the Church than from a study of the Gospel. Of such a life I shall say that one cannot lead it alone, although in the last stages one is often left alone.

The Christian man is also one who thinks that the Gospel makes certain demands within the realms of family, social, and civic conduct, not only in the actions endorsed in the theological treatises (for example the problems of family "planning"), but in the human dignity of the home. The Christian man shares—he takes into his home the children of a neighboring family when it is in trouble. He is a man who does not hesitate to talk about matters of his soul, whereas the man of thirty or forty years ago would never have done so. This fact responds to the necessity of a Christian action beyond the action of the Church, beyond the zone truly controlled directly by the Church, one which is called for by the situation of the world.

---

[7]Published in *Lettre intérieure aux membres des Equipes Saint-Dominique.*

2. SALVATION AND ITS HISTORY
(A) WHAT IS SALVATION?

What goes on between God and man and is thus forever correlative of one another is the drama of salvation. But few theological notions have been as disfigured to such an extent that it is rendered totally unintelligible and unacceptable to most men of good will. Individualism, radical pessimism, or exaggeration of "original sin," false spiritualism, the addition to "nature" of a supernatural stage, even a "supernature," ruinous opposition between nature and grace, creation and redemption—all this and more have contributed to its deterioration.

Salvation Represents a Plenitude of Being

To put salvation in its proper setting we must, according to Father Congar, substitute for these views a more traditional perspective of the unity of creation and Redemption by including the first in the second, a unified perspective of nature and the supernatural. "Supernatural" signifies a retaking and elevation of nature along the line of its natural desire for infinite happiness and truth, which it must long for with all its strength but which it cannot bestow upon itself of its own power. Nature and grace must be distinguished—there is the gratuitous, a "beyond" (nothing less than the friendship of God) which human forces could not attain under any hypothesis. There is also an aspect of healing, especially in the order of knowledge; but this must not be overestimated along the lines of an aggravated Augustinianism. Here the Orthodox criticism, rooted in a very different tradition, proves a precious corrective. Above all, there is finally a *man saved*. But then, in this perspective, what does *salvation* mean?

In a brief synthesis entitled "Perspectives chrétiennes sur la vie personnelle et la vie collective,"[8] Father Congar gives the meaning. In what concerns man God acts with salvation in mind.

---

[8]Conference published in *Socialization et personne humaine, op. cit.*

This means that the human or even cosmic creature is not lost forever but gets the *meaning* of its existence as God wills it for each, and that in some way it carries this vocation within itself. Father Congar takes up this notion more fully and precisely in "Dieu, l'homme et l'univers—Réponses demandées à la théologie par l'athéisme contemporain":

> Salvation must not be imagined as a completely external rescue, accidental to the things themselves and to their internal perfection. It is the realization of their meaning, of what they were made for. It represents for them, therefore, an increase of being beyond their bare existence, a completed, perfect existence, a true and complete being. To miss one's salvation is to keep existence without having this plenitude: hell is the continuance in existence of a being who has failed to attain its end, who knows it and suffers bitterly from this knowledge.

But one must not speculate too much on hell and on those who might be condemned to it. The idea that God would have created beings to deliver them over to the devil is profoundly shocking for the Christian conscience, imbued with the revelation of God's universal love. In *Vaste monde, ma paroisse* (with the telling subtitle *Vérité et dimensions du salut*), one can read beautiful pages on the meaning of hell ("the absolute being and the finite being, each taken very seriously"), and on its nature ("the suffering of being no longer able to love").

"To Have a Destiny Hereafter"

But if one examines this work one discovers before the study on hell a chapter entitled "What is salvation?" This chapter provides some notions which seem to round off nicely the presentation I have just made of the ideas culled from Father Congar's soteriology. What precisely does salvation imply? First of all it implies "a hope for the hereafter. After what? After what is *seen*, objects experienced by our senses and measured by our instruments. The insufficiency of this life. . . ." But one must not believe that this hope of an afterlife is egotistical, that it expresses "the individualism of: I have only one soul and I want to save it. Unceasingly, in one way or another, the haunting thought comes back of a total, a cosmic, salvation, the joint responsibility of *all* in salvation." One must not think either that this hope projects an afterlife which would belittle our present existence:

> Salvation comes down to this, the giving of a meaning to our present life in view of this hope for a hereafter, and of the One who reveals and consummates it; it comes down, too, to trying to anticipate, in the world itself, inasmuch as we can fashion and orientate it, something which, in joining it to Christ, might engage it in this destiny which the Lord offers it.

This mention of Christ brings us to another aspect of salvation: "Salvation, in fact, depends essentially on another since it consists in transcending myself, my possibilities, my present life. It is in the power not of man nor of the world, but of the Lord." Finally, like any transcendence which, as such, has both positive and negative value, "the idea of salvation can likewise be conceived under the aspect of a peril, the possibility of losing everything, even life; one can be saved from a cruel, oppressive, destructive enemy. It can also be viewed under an aspect of life, of joy, of the plenitude to which this rescue restores us and the possibilities of which our Savior opens to us." Thus one can summarize these pages of *Vaste monde, ma paroisse* by saying: to be saved is to have a destiny *hereafter*, thanks to Christ and in him, by the victory over sin and by giving "such a meaning to our life that it is assured its full significance not only here below, where we are only in passing, but there where we are called to remain forever."

Christian Conversion

The decisive act by which man receives this salvation, opens himself to it, accepts it freely, responds to it by adhering with a lively and loving faith, is Christian conversion. Father Congar has consecrated to it a brief, but precise and documented, study:

"La conversion, étude théologique et psychologique."[9] After a delineation of the subject, an analysis of vocabulary, a biblical theology, a phenomenological characterization of the different types of conversion, a critique of the rationalistic attempts at "explanation," Father Congar arrives at the theological exposé which interests us here and which is followed by a reflection on the meaning and value of "confessional conversions."

Two elements should be retained fundamentally. First of all the sovereign and gracious act of God which, without any corresponding human element, produces justification. But, "in fact, what is ordinarily called conversion is produced in the conscious life of an adult, and generally involves a whole process of preparations and progressive approaches. It is rare that it is absolutely instantaneous and coincides with justification." The second element, much harder to establish in its true relationship to the first, is the one which man's response introduces. "If theology affirms unambiguously the first and decisive role of a force from God, namely, grace, which predisposes man without merit on his part and in such a way that even the beginning of conversion is the fruit of the grace, it affirms no less vigorously the reality and the role of human liberty." But it is not easy to scrutinize "this alternating play of grace and liberty," or better, this interpenetration according to which "the God of grace and the liberty of man approach each other in a kind of dialogue and reciprocal conditioning. . . . Biblical religion, the religion of the Covenant, is of a dialoguing structure."

But this new relationship which the personal intervention of the God of the Covenant into the history and world of men establishes between God and man (a divine engagement to which nothing but the homage of the entire human life can reply), represents something very original in regard to the multiple religions of humanity. Something so original that one is led to

---

[9]Reprinted in *Sacerdoce et laïcat*, in coll. *Cogitatio Fidei* (Paris: Editions du Cerf, 1962), IV. See Chap. 1, above, footnote 14.

wonder if it is still necessary to speak of "religion," and if the economy of *faith* is not different enough from the economy of "cult" and of the "sacred" so that it is necessary to mark the rupture strongly even by a change in vocabulary. One recognizes here the present-day problematic opposing "faith and religion." As I shall point out, Father Congar has committed himself strongly along these lines, but with a number of delicate nuances which an occasional sermon or controversial articles undoubtedly do not equally respect. First he observes that one can discuss indefinitely the opportunity of using the words *faith* and *religion* to get the debate going: the essential is not there, for "definitions are free, as the ancients said; it is only necessary to argue coherently on their content. One may challenge the attribution we make of these labels—what is important is the reality we designate by them."[10]

Next it should be remarked that this debate should not be carried to an absurd extreme. The dialogue between man and his Creator, the relationship of Covenant, is indeed "religious relationship." But whether or not one uses the term *religion* to speak of the *economy of faith* (and Father Congar like everyone else uses it from time to time), the whole question is to know what specifically characterizes this economy in order not to dissolve it in a general concept to the detriment of its essential notes. This is the problem as Father Congar sees it.

Faith Replies to the God of Salvation

A first application of this dialectic concerns the decision to set forth what is original in the Judaeo-Christian concept as compared with paganism. In a retreat preached at the Saulchoir in 1961, Father Congar expressed his thought:

> The pagan had nature as a means to go to God. The needs were natural needs (health, fecundity, victory), and men gave themselves divinities by projecting their human needs into mys-

---

[10]From "Dieu, l'homme et l'univers."

terious powers they called their gods . . . a religion therefore founded on the exploitation of man's natural resources including the most interior instincts, such as contemplation, in order to reach God. The God of the Bible is completely different. He is not sought first as a force responding to needs. God is first *the God of salvation history.* And if God is the author of nature it is because he is the author of salvation history. . . . The first chapter of Genesis is the first chapter of faith. . . . One can oppose, by attentive consideration, "religion" as the pagan way of going to God, and "faith" in the Living God who enters into our life as a requirement and asks questions of us. Faith arises when the soul gives itself to God's initiative in its life.

But this dialectic can still serve to oppose two ways of conceiving and of presenting Christianity itself, which is only in part another problem. In fact, if there were excellent Christians in past centuries, Father Congar tells us in "Dieu, l'homme et l'univers," the question is to know if the religious relationship was presented to them principally along the lines of "religion" or along the lines of "faith." What does this mean? In the seventeenth century, in fact, God was often presented as "presiding in the highest heaven like a distant monarch to whom men owe the homage of their adoration and obedience. In behalf of this celestial monarch one celebrates the omnipotence, the greatness, and the glory, in a cult which mounts from men toward him, somewhat the way one would speak at Versailles to God's representative on earth. That is what we call religion." It is opposed, word for word, to faith, for:

> The man of religion is not like the man of faith, the one that God fashions in order that with all his energies he might accomplish, in the place given him, God's plan in the world, or better, God's design on the world. Faith is an act of man, but one by which this man opens himself and offers himself to the action that God wants to accomplish in and by him. Compared to this, religion is static. It can wish to consecrate the world; it does not undertake to act in it. It realizes a movement of adoration and offering which goes from below to above, from man to God. Within its own limits it is not active in history.

It does not seem to me that Father Congar means here that every ascending movement should be excluded from the religious relationship established in faith, but that every offering has, in Christianity, the value of a response to divine initiative. Moreover, it is situated at the term of an effort which prolonged God's movement of descent into the world to restore and fulfill it. I have shown the anthropological consequences of this attitude and finally of the "religious" alienation (Father Congar does not use the word). He himself continues this dialectic in a concise fashion in *L'avenir de l'Eglise*: "Religion renders its duties to God; faith consecrates all its life to his reign. Religion is an ordering of activities on the side, faith transfigures all activity and knows nothing 'profane' except what sin profanes by placing it outside the offering of everything to God."

God's Sacredness and Ours

If faith can "consecrate" everything to God it is because its proper realm of sacred things is of a completely different order from the material sacral realm of religions, which separates the sacred from the "profane." But then, does this original, interpersonal sacredness, linked to the personal relationship with God, exclude all exterior things from the sacral in the classical sense? Is the Christian cult entirely interior? What are the "sacraments" of faith? Father Congar's conviction is that the original sacredness of faith supposes, at its service and to express it, a minimum of external and material things that have to be unceasingly purified and referred back to faith again.

Historically the development started with Constantine and in the climate of the Christian empire and of nascent Christendom in an esthetically admirable way, which however was not without its dangers. Father Congar analyzes this process in "Titres et honneurs dans l'église."[11]

---

[11]In *Pour une Eglise servante et pauvre* (Paris: Editions du Cerf, 1963). See Chap. 4, above, footnote 4.

The liturgy, sober and functional until then, contenting itself with expressing the spiritual cult of faith with its gestures of welcome to the gift of God and of thanksgiving, begins to display in everything a ceremonial, many of the elements of which were borrowed from court ceremonial: processions, sumptuous vestments, furniture and vases of gold, ostentatious display of liturgical ceremonies. . . . Thus was added to God's sacredness (which consists in the active realities of salvation history which men receive and use), a sacredness of ceremonial character, extremely beautiful moreover, full of symbols which the contemplative soul, to its joy, would never cease to value and to explore . . . with a whole ritualization and a whole sacralization of *things* in which the sanctification of the *Ecclesia* by a lively faith is somewhat drowned.

Several times, in speaking thus about salvation, I have been led to recall its collective dimensions and especially to use the term *salvation history,* history God has made for and with men. It is on this aspect of the divine work that I must now reflect with Father Congar. First let me indicate the methodological presuppositions of such a study.

(B)   To Study the History of God with Men

"An Irresistible Liking for History"

It would undoubtedly be useful to recall here that, at the root of the attention Father Congar accords history, there is his fundamental realism, his love of real life in the concrete that the study of St. Thomas' thought as practiced at the Saulchoir could only reinforce. St. Thomas, in fact, is a master of realism; this is one of his most decisive options in philosophy as well as in theology. Undoubtedly his theological realism lacks something of the historical dimension of things, but this had no negative effect on Father Congar. On the contrary, the way of conceiving the study of St. Thomas at Kain, placed in his own time, and enlightened by it, impelled Father Congar toward the historical approach. A genuine talent flourished under the aegis of Father Chenu: "There has always been in me an irresistible liking for history . . . not for history as erudition: with me this fact was only the consequence of a more profound penchant, the feeling that besides the purely speculative and dialectic there was another intelligibility," Congar wrote in his notebook.

But here I am speaking of sacred history. For Father Congar to interest himself actively in biblical salvation history, for him to invest all his historical sense into this reflection, for him to extend this concept to post-biblical sacred history, he needed to come into contact with modern Protestant theology. I said that the eschatological perspectives which Father Allo's splendid commentary emphasized had prepared him for it. But the most decisive influence was, without question, Vischer's and his analysis of the *pars pro toto*.

To Know the History of the People of God

At a moment when Pope Paul VI (echoing a preoccupation prevalent in the Church) several times showed his interest in the perspective of salvation history, it is worth while to take into account a report that two professors of theology, Fathers Congar and Féret (who drew it up), presented in 1946 to a high ecclesiastical authority who had asked them for it. Analyzing with great insight the inefficacy of clerical formation, the authors of this report try to show the causes of this inefficacy by pointing out some characteristic traits of the mentality of contemporary man. The two principal novelties seem to them to be the following: "The priority of *collective values* over individual values," and "The priority accorded to the concrete, immediate experience over abstract thought and theoretical values." The solution that they recommend was "to develop, first among the clergy and then among the faithful, the knowledge of the history of the People of God." In fact, there is no reason to refuse the modern attitude or not to try to respond to it by a renewed pastoral. It must even be said that the nature of the message that one wants to transmit argues in its favor.

Neither in its content nor its progressive proposition in the course of the centuries did God's revelation present itself to men as an abstract, theoretical system. It inserted itself into the history of a People chosen by God, the Jewish people in the Old Testament, the Church in the New. It is in the history of his People, or as we say, in sacred history, that God gave us his revelation.

At the center of this history is the mystery of Jesus. One cannot reject, then, the quest for historicity and concreteness; one must show that the quest is satisfied in Christianity. An a fortiori argument shows us the extension that the concept of sacred history had for these authors:

> If it is true that God's Providence very especially conducts the march of his Church as it conducted the People of Israel in the Old Testament, still more may we think that even the dispositions of the minds of this era, in what they have to offer that is legitimate, far from being independent of this providential guidance, are rather the effect of it.

But how can one show that salvation history responds exactly to the aspirations of contemporary man?

> [On one side] they incline to envisage the problems of human life in terms of the groups to which they belong and of the history of these collectivities. What history is more ancient and what collectivity more admirable than those of the People of God, from Abraham to our days? The Fathers knew this well. Spontaneously, and prolonging most of the time the manner of the Apostles themselves, they envisaged all Christian truth according to its three great historical moments: that of preparations in the Old Testament; that of manifestation and plenitude in the life and mystery of Jesus Christ; that of the uninterrupted and progressive transmission in the Church. In this way, their faithful always lived in the very keen awareness of belonging to the chosen collectivity of the People of God and of being attached, by their slightest beliefs and rites, to the great past of the Church and of Israel. This history of the people of God still offers the spirits of this time the incomparable advantage of putting them in contact with concrete religious experiences which are here of an incomparable quality: those of the great patriarchs and prophets of the Old Testament, of the Apostles and disciples of the New, and of the great saints of the history of the Church.

And the authors of the report conclude by proposing practical measures: to intensify the teaching of the biblical disciplines and of the history of the Church, and in order to attain this end to promote a closer collaboration among all those who teach these subjects. In fact, study ought to be adapted to the desired end. For example, a critical analysis of certain texts is not enough for a study of Holy Scripture, but one must have "the concern to disengage above and beyond these analyses the great lines of the history of Israel and of the development of Revelation."

Without teaching the history of the Church or biblical theology professionally, Father Congar had occasion a number of times in the following years to show the global significance and the great themes of salvation history according to the method that this new program recommended.

(C) THE ECONOMY OF SALVATION

Today the chief criticism that Father Congar makes of his article "Théologie" in the *Dictionnaire de théologie catholique,* written before 1939, is that it is not thought in a biblical enough fashion, not conceived sufficiently in terms of salvation history. Like Father Féret, to whom he owes much on this point, he has been led to attach more and more importance to the framework for the exposition of the work of salvation even while having some reservations (as does Father Féret also) about the expression "salvation history" itself. In a Catholic perspective, in any case, salvation history begins with Adam, although by salvation history Oscar Cullmann, who contributed so much to spread the term, understands the history of Revelation. "Salvation economy" or "the economy of salvation" is undoubtedly a better term because it includes everything: preparations (which are not only in the Old Testament) and decisive actions, prophetic enunciations and realization. Whatever the influences might be, there is also at the root of the insistence on salvation history a fundamental spiritual experience. Father Congar, when he looks back on the decisive converging orientations of the years 1942-1943, is convinced that one can and ought to read in the events a mission of the Holy Spirit to direct minds toward all the themes which are fruitful today. That is what expresses the time of the Church as salvation history; a time measured by the divine missions creating spiritual events in the Church. This perception, and that of "sacramental time," with which it is interrelated, constitute the essential notes of the very important analysis of the Church as original time. It is this that Father Congar treats in the second volume of *La Tradition et les Traditions.*

Sacred History Is Given by God

Historicity is an attribute of man in the sense that "man lives in time, he needs time, his acquisitions are dated, successive, situated in a continuum where they occupy a place defined by a before and an after." Then too, "man is not only situated in time, affected by temporality—*he has a history.* Every man has a history and humanity has a history. . . . Because he transcends time, what he does in time not only can survive time . . . but is collected and permits a progress. All the communicable acquisitions can be integrated into the realization of a destiny which has a meaning." This is true both for salvation and for the Church. But when it is a question of the Church, there is this particularity —the more decisive partner is God who establishes it in a supernatural way. As a result it will have a proper type of duration and history: "Established and being constructed on earth, the Church of God exists in earthly time . . . created once and unceasingly by the gracious initiative *of God,* the Church has for its proper time the time of sacred history." What does this mean?

Sacred history is at one and the same time given by God and made by us. Given by God, it is so at two successive moments. One is the progressive constitution of the Covenant culminating in Jesus Christ who accomplishes the preceding revelations and establishes the definitive religious relationships in such a way that "the initiatives taken by God to establish the religious relationship in Jesus Christ remain not only as a truth and a memory but as an operating dynamism." There is also the moment of men's entrance into the Covenant according as they are born and live in history, inscribing to their benefit what it offers them of salvific truth and virtue. When that happens, a moment of salvation is accomplished. Thus:

> Sacred history, where the design of God is accomplished by the power of God, combines a triple presence, that of the salvific acts posited once for all, which operate, not by a simple memory or recollection but by an actually operating power; that of the end which is intended, and again, not only as a thought and a desire, but as a fruit present in the seed; that of the union actually realized at one and the same time as the fruit of what establishes it, as the seed of what it will procure, and as the reality actually lived.

This is what could be called the sacramental nature of the time of the Church by analogy with the sacramental theology of a St. Thomas Aquinas. It is the Holy Spirit who effects this communication through time, but his role does not stop there.

Sacred History Is "Made" by Us

In fact, sacred history is also made by man who must commit his liberty, reply to the call and initiatives of God, confront the demands of the times beginning with the unique gift of truth and grace which has been given us: "The time demands, of the faithful, responses of thought and witness arising from faith, and responses of service, of commitment, of a true community of goods arising from charity." But of every human response to God, whether interior and secret, or inscribed into the history of the world, it can be said that "each of the supernatural actions of every man involves an act of God. It is even posited by us only because God has first aroused and worked it in us." Here again is found the immediacy of God: "Sacred history, the history of the Church as the Church *of God* is thus made from the series of God's comings, thanks to which men produce these responses of faith and love by which the City of God is constructed." Sacramental time, time animated by the missions of the Holy Spirit in dependence on the sacred humanity of Jesus, is that time of the Church "which arouses in us holy responses in the order of truth and love . . . from visits by which the 'I am, I was, I am coming,' accomplishes the religious relationship of Covenant, revealed and posited once for all. Each moment of this time is both actuality of the religious relationship, the active presence of that which established it once for all, and the beginning of its final consummation."

What a far cry this is from the completely doctrinal view of Christianity in which history and reality are there only to furnish arguments for non-temporal theses, or are even considered almost embarrassing, as for example the Incarnation. This was the perspective of the intellectual circles in Paris which Father Congar frequented in the 1920's. Underlying it there was a philosophy according to which the highest activity of the mind was to contemplate being and the principle of identity. Unfortunate the man who "fell into facts"! Perhaps this contrast between two problematics was influential at the Council in evoking certain discussions on the schema *De Revelatione*. But another characteristic of this speculative position was its refusal to pay attention to the requests and actualities of human history. By contrast, one of Father Congar's greatest concerns was to show how this sacred history answers the longing, the desires of the history of men. He does it especially in *The Wide World, My Parish*, in the part entitled "Heaven, Salvation, and World History":

> This history strives for two things. First to restore to man an integrity which many evils and limitations have wounded in him; to bring to him the perfection of what he bears within him, if not its possibility at least the desire. . . . At its extreme, this desire is to conquer death and everything which opens ways to it and does its work . . . finally to conquer the many oppositions which make us suffer and which fetter us, which make men and things strange and inimical to us, whereas we are made to love and be loved; we are made for harmony, unity, peace, communion.

Therefore, history tries to overcome anything that limits and wounds us and to surmount divisions and oppositions. Now the history of God with men comes to accomplish precisely that. The definitive kingdom "when it comes will crown and assume all of man's worthwhile efforts to conquer misery and the opposition from which he suffers, for consciously or not these efforts work for God's plan."

The Constants in God's Design

If, as Father Congar invites us to do in the article "Histoire" in the encyclopedia *Catholicisme*, we were to seek "in Scripture and the life of the Church, what one could call if not the *laws* at least the *constants* of God's action, the *ways* of Revelation and God's action," the great axes of the history of salvation, what material would we find in the work of the Dominican theologian? Let me enumerate certain paths already indicated and others that will seem new:

1. In God's work everything, proceeding from a seed, tends toward an end (*Vraie et fausse réforme, La Tradition et la vie de l'Eglise*).

2. This development is accomplished along lines of interiorization (*Vraie et fausse réforme, Le Mystére du Temple*).

3. At this time it is accomplished in the sense of an intensification of the presence of God (*Le Mystére du Temple*).

4. Thus, at a certain moment, everything is *already* given although not yet realized, a perspective parallel to Oscar Cullman's research which Father Congar grasped on his own ("Histoire" in *Catholicisme*).

5. This therefore implies a maturing, some delays, and finally —patience; but once the seed is planted the contradictions are negligible (*Vraie et fausse réforme*, Preface to *Chrétiens en dialogue*).

6. The contradiction can go even as far as the Cross, whose fecundity is a profound law in the economy of salvation—success contained in failure (*Dum visibilitier . . .*).

7. There is no opposition between Creation and Redemption. Together with their totality of active energies and gifts, they

make the one single Lordship of Christ, one single dispensation, and are applied to one single subject: man redeemed (articles and conferences cited at the beginning of this chapter).

8. One constant principle rules the dispensation: that of the *pars pro toto,* the election of some for the salvation of many (*Vaste monde, ma paroisse*).

9. But no substitution can dispense man from his free response: history is the arena of liberty, that is, of the free response of faith and of Christian liberty in the Church: law of divine interpellation and of human response (*La tradition et les traditions,* "La Conversion").

It is quite clear that this list is not exhaustive. To close, let me cite some beautiful and significant texts on some of these great "constants in God's plan." The reader will thus come into contact with the living thought of the author.

"Everything Begins with a Seed"

First of all there is "germination."[12]

> There is a discovery to be made, but once made, it is so illuminating, so exalting that every page of the Bible cries out its truth—every work of God is a history and a development. This is true not only of the work of creation, where it is so manifest, but of the work of grace and salvation. God did not accomplish it in a non-temporal heaven of ideas, but he inserted it into our history, thus manifesting that time itself had a meaning and a value. Everything, in God's plan, begins with a seed, develops by stages, and reaches its fulfillment.

What is true in nature and in human history is just as true when it is a question of salvation history.

> From beginning to end God's gifts are first given in a seed. From the beginning this seed contains, although enclosed and hidden, the plenitude to which it is ordained. But it develops this content only by stages, progressively and always imperfectly. It

---

[12]*Vraie et fausse réforme,* in *Unam Sanctam* (Paris: Editions du Cerf, 1950), XX, pp. 132-35.

is not only the Bible that begins with a Genesis and ends with an Apocalypse, that is, with a disclosing; all are gifts—the very work of God. From one end to the other there is promise, then fulfillment of the promise, but a fulfillment that is only partial and that cries out for completion. From one end to the other everything takes its meaning from the final plenitude.

Then there is a progressive interiorization which is accompanied by a gradual intensification of the divine presence.

> One can characterize God's plan (as biblical Revelation makes it known to us) as a process going from the exterior to the interior, from sensible forms and means to a reality found in man himself. . . . St. Augustine saw the whole dispensation of salvation not only in individual lives but in a great collective movement coming from Abraham, even from Adam, to the heavenly city, ascending by stages to the point where everything would be consummated— the perfect interiority of men to each other, through the unity of all in one, that of God becoming truly all in all.[13]

In this text it can be clearly seen how, to the growing personalization of the religious relationship there corresponds an increased and renewed presence of God.

A *Presence Which Moves by Intensifying Itself*

There is the major theme of the *Mystère du Temple,* a passage from which follows. The passage is taken from the conclusion, which has the significant title: "The Economy of Providence and God's Presence in the World." If the Bible says little of God's presence in the temple of nature, his Creation, it does show the progress of this presence in history.

> First God arrives unexpectedly; he intervenes in the life of the Patriarchs by a kind of transitory contact or encounter. Then as soon as he constitutes a people who are *his* people he exists for them as being particularly *their* God. He establishes his presence in the midst of them as being the one who reveals, guides, listens and judges, aids or chastises.

---

[13]*Ibid.,* pp. 136-41.

There is the Ark, there is the Temple, but that is not the truest presence. The prophets "do not cease to preach that, beyond even the moral and spiritual demands of Temple worship, there is the truth of the presence linked to the effective reign of God in the hearts of men. God does not dwell materially in a place, he dwells spiritually in a faithful people." But here it is that:

> The Incarnation of the Word of God in the womb of the Virgin Mary establishes an entirely new stage in the history of the Presence of God—a new stage, but a definitive one too, for what more could be given to the world? The religious and above all sacrificial institutions of the Mosaic cult disappeared in the sacrifice of Christ, as the light of a candle melts away into the light of the sun when it appears. There is henceforth only one Temple in which we can validly adore, pray, and offer sacrifice, and where we truly encounter God: the Body of Christ. In him the sacrifice becomes entirely spiritual at the same time that it becomes real: not only in the sense that it originates in us from the spirit of God which has been given us . . . beginning with Jesus, the Spirit of God is truly given. He is, in the faithful, a water gushing up into eternal life; he makes them sons of God and capable of truly laying hold of him by knowledge and love. It is no longer just a question of *presence*, but of the *indwelling* of God in the faithful. Each one personally and all of them together in their very unity are the Temple of God, because they are the Body of Christ, animated and united by his Spirit. Such then is the Temple of God in messianic times.

In it, however, there is still something carnal, but "when everything will have been purified, when everything is grace, when God's part will be so victorious that 'God will be all in all,' when everything proceeds from his Spirit, then the Body of Christ will be established forever with its Head in the house *of God.*"

The Time of the Church

Two dialectical notions mark in a decisive way this development of the seed and this process of interiorization and of intensified presence: first that of the small number as compared with the whole, and secondly that of the already given and the not yet accomplished. The first idea is presented in the article, "A Little Church in the Vast World."[14]

> [In the Bible the] totality is considered as represented in a portion of itself which, according to God's plan, bears the destiny of the whole. Biblical studies such as that of Wilhelm Vischer's *La loi ou les cinq livres de Moïse* have shown that this dynamic and progressive plan was imbued with the idea of *pars pro toto*— mankind is chosen for the world to render to God the praise of creation; Israel is chosen for mankind to be God's witness and priest among men. . . . But for us Israel is now the Church; we must apply to our Christianity the same notion of being this representative and dynamic minority, spiritually responsible for the final destiny of all.

Moreover, "even within Israel a part often represented the whole," and the idea of the representative remnant was to dominate the thought of the prophets. But "finally, it is not in a collective remnant that the new Israel is represented and has its points of departure but in one person alone, the Son of Man who bears within himself all the Holy People of the Most High." Therefore, at each moment of God's design "a great number are seen by God and included in his plan in a little group or in a single individual who providentially bears the good destined for all."

But between this mercy which is shown to us all in Christ and the full manifestation of our salvation, the time of the Church "is essentially an in-between time."

> It is defined by its relationship to the two comings of Christ— the first in humility, salvation, and grace; the second in majesty and glory, justice, and power. The first is his Alpha from which everything comes; the second will be his Omega toward which everything tends. Thus this time is described as an "already and not yet"; already a certain presence of heavenly favors, but they are as a pledge, *in mysterioso*, concealed under signs. There is a

---

[14]In *Vaste monde, ma paroisse* (Paris, 1959). See Chap. 1, above, footnote 16.

lack of evidence and a weakness; man is still tempted; Satan, although already chained, is still active and can "bite through to the length of his leash," the cockle is still mixed with the wheat and we possess the Spirit under the conditions of the flesh.

It is the time of salvation, of mission, and of the apostolate.[15]

In this time of the Church the major acts of its life are events of salvation history. Especially so are the great moments of reform, of a crisis of self-awareness, of conversion to God, of the elucidation of his presence in the world. So it was that, on the eve of the first session of Vatican II, the Council could be defined by a theologian as this council which is both God's and man's, a privileged moment in the Church's own life, as a "fact both human and divine. *It is the place of Jesus Christ's action in history.* The communion of bishops is the public sign of this action." And so I am quite naturally led to speak of the Council in order to describe the role that Father Congar played in it, to recall some of his reactions to the principal events of the conciliar development, and his interpretations of some of the difficult problems that were threshed out.

[15]Extract from "Histoire" in *Catholicisme.*

CHAPTER SIX

At the Service of the Council

1. THE WORK OF A THEOLOGIAN

I will be very discreet in discussing the role of Father Congar at the Council. This discretion does not come from a superstitious respect for keeping things secret (such a practice in Church matters is more than questionable), but from a very natural concern about anything that pertains to actions and proceedings not in the public domain. Those who have had anything to do with teamwork know how fallacious it can be to calculate the importance of any one individual contribution. Yet it is no secret that Father Congar played a considerable role at the Council and even in its preparation. This contribution can be seen in what he gave to a goodly number of bishops and theologians who were to work at the Council, in his competence and his labors in the different commissions where his cooperation was requested, in his reaction when confronted by such or such a question under discussion, in the numerous conferences given by him in Rome in the course of the four sessions, in this radiance or communication by osmosis of which I spoke, and last but not least in the confidence of the two popes who presided at the Council. Even certain of his past difficulties contributed to his prestige.

An Active Collaboration

In fact I have already shown that he had elaborated and put forth all the great themes which were to interest the Council: ecclesiology, ecumenism, the laity, the priesthood, missiology, tradition. I shall not refer again to the influence of his work, but let me say just a few words about what he did during the four sessions of the Council. John XXIII himself named him consultant to the preparatory commission along with Father de Lubac, but he could not do much that was useful. In principle, the theologians could speak only if questioned. It was possible of course to arrange to be questioned by a friendly bishop, but Father Congar is a relatively shy man and to put himself forward in such a way was distasteful to him. Besides, he had hesitated to accept and remained very perplexed about the outcome of the work. Or perhaps I should say that hope and scepticism predominated alternately in his spirit.

A few days after John XXIII's announcement of the Council, Father Congar, in a conference at the Saulchoir, remarked that this convoking (there was still the idea that all separated Christians would be invited to participate) could make sense only in faith. "It has been without reflection—and then what a catastrophe!—or it is the work of the Holy Spirit, in which case everything is possible!" He added, "I believe it is the Holy Spirit." On his return from the first session he was to say, "Now I no longer believe it, I know it."

Father Congar had practically nothing to do with the prepared texts. At the beginning he had not always been summoned to some of the important meetings. After some protest, and especially thanks to the loyal and open way that the president of the *De Ecclesia* Commission conducted the meetings, he was led to participate more actively in that sub-commission. But the structure did not allow much leeway—to a text drawn up according to the great encyclicals only a few modifications could be proposed. Father Congar suggested some on collegiality and ecumenism—which hardly helped much.

After the Council got off to an unbelievably good start, the climate of opinion of the theological commission was entirely different. At the beginning the 198 experts were not attached to any particular commission. Actually, they distributed themselves very quickly. Except in a rare case each one went just to one commission, Father Congar being called to the theological commission. Obviously to work within the structure of the plenary sessions of these commissions was not easy. Here again the experts had to wait for questions to be put to them or ask for recognition which was not always granted. But the real work was done in sub-committees where bishops and experts worked together. These men, reserved with each other and even opposed in thought at the start, learned to know and respect each other after frequent meetings and much work in common. The climate of opinion consequently was far different from the one I described in speaking of the pre-conciliar period. That of the Council itself greatly helped in this evolution. The work consisted chiefly in the elaboration, editing, and revision of the text. Then once this was presented to the Council it was a question of devoting oneself to the cataloguing of the *desiderata* and to the modification or recasting of the schema. Such was the work Father Congar did on *De Ecclesia* (especially on the *De Populo Dei,* and also on the Mystical Body and images of the Church), on *De Revelatione* (tradition), on *De Presbyteriis,* and especially on *De Missionibus.* He had collaborated on the first draft of schema XVII (later XIII), then on the so-called Malines' edition, although less actively on the later text. I mentioned earlier his role in the revision of the text on religious liberty. The reader will understand if I do not enter more into detail.

Theologians and Pastors

During all this time there was the added burden of editing texts for bishops, and the continuing obligations of conferences for clubs and seminaries. There was no letup in spite of the fact that Father Congar was ill and harassed. Yet this activity played a very important role on numerous decisive points, especially at the first session. The confidence that the conciliar Fathers had in certain theologians (Congar, Rahner, Häring, Philips, to name a few) and of course in John XXIII and Cardinal Bea, was of primary importance. Thus theologians succeeded in playing a very great role at the Council—undoubtedly more than at any previous council. This was so because of the difficulty, the multiplicity, and the technicality of the questions brought up. Anything lacking careful theological preparation could not be realized successfully. In a subtle and humorous way Father Chenu, in his affectionate homage to Father Congar in 1963, brought up the question of the theologian's role:

> I think that the role of theology at the Council is very great. . . . A council is a council of bishops. Some, who do not feel too kindly toward this council of bishops, wished to vent their feelings against the theologians. In a way it is true that this council is a council of theologians. This is quite curious, because it is a council of pastors, and God knows if this has been noticed. But it is also a council of theologians. And here we have, in a concrete experience, this kind of mutual exchange of roles between the theologian and the pastor. Bishops tease me, saying they couldn't extricate themselves from their difficulties if it weren't for the theologians. But the theologians reply that if it weren't for the bishops the theologians would remain in their school.

And we must insist on the type of theology which permits such work and such collaboration, a theology that "might be a Word of God in ferment in a continuous tradition." But it is not from the theologians that decisions come, nor authority. The divine guarantee was not promised to them. This collaboration between bishops and theologians should not cease with the Council. In his notes for November 15, 1965, commenting on the *Decree on the Bishops' Pastoral Office in the Church* and remarking that its third chapter formulates a program for a true renewal of the conciliar life of the Church, Father Congar states:

> The place of theologians and investigators must not be forgotten here. Without them Vatican II would not have been what it was. Their collaboration must continue in activities of a conciliar type, the benefits of which we wish to keep. . . . A sharp division between research or thought and pastoral guidance would be unhealthy. In our opinion, the fecundity of a renewed conciliar life in the Church will largely depend on such collaboration. The requirements for it on both sides must be examined.

2. THE COUNCIL AS SEEN BY FATHER CONGAR

I plan to conclude this book by presenting from Father Congar's notes some excerpts that seem most significant for the history of the Council and for a knowledge of the thought of their author, whose reactions are always profoundly personal. However, I shall not return to the theological discussions. To do so would be a repetition of the work of the three preceding chapters.

(A)   FIRST SESSION: BIRTH OF A CONCILIAR SPIRIT

The First Conciliar Act

The Council opened October 11, 1962, with an elaborate ceremony which is eclipsed in memory by the unforgettable countenance of John XXIII, already emaciated, suffering, completely absorbed by prayer, by an intense emotion. His opening discourse, the importance and consequence of which have not yet been completely understood, set the tone so decisively that as early as October 13 Cardinal Liénart's intervention, proposing (with Cardinal Frings' support) that the elections of the members of the conciliar commissions be put off until later and prepared by the episcopal conferences, was accepted unhesitatingly. Here is Father Congar's entry on this for October 18:

> The action of Cardinal Liénart was of great significance and will largely determine the future development of the Council. *It was the first conciliar act*—not in the unacceptable and condemned sense of conciliarism, but in the sense of an act of an assembly deliberating and deciding freely. It marked the general desire of the bishops to examine, to treat, and to decide for themselves, putting aside even the suggestion of the pre-determined or discreetly manipulated. Such is, without a doubt, the spirit of the Holy Father who, though not physically present, is present in soul and in heart at all the proceedings.

October 21 was to see the very beautiful *Message to the World* drawn up, with the approval of John XXIII, by four French bishops (including Cardinal Liénart and Bishop Guerry) from a project proposed by a number of theologians, among whom were Fathers Congar and Chenu.

"With Tears in My Eyes . . . They Are Here!"

Another striking fact from the beginning of the first session was the presence of the observers who had been received by the Pope on October 13. Father Congar wrote (still in his October 18 entry):

> There were tears in my eyes when I met the observers for the first time here! Of course their presence still has to bear fruit; everything is still to be done. Of course they will experience moments of boredom, of emptiness, of exasperation. But the essential has been accomplished—they are here. The program drawn up for them is broad and generous. Like the "experts," they assist at the general meetings where the bishops express their reactions, and if invited or authorized by the president, at the work sessions of the commissions. They do not have speaking privileges but can submit written observations and are free to keep their constituents informed. This juridical framework is already indicative of a certain spirit, but the effective role of the delegated or invited observers will be what they themselves make it. . . . Who can estimate the influence that private conversations, both frank and loyal, might have on the outcome of certain debates?

As early as December 2 he could write:

> The presence of the thirty-seven observers of the non-Catholic Christian communities is one of the major elements of the conciliar meeting. The question usually asked about them is desperately banal: Are they satisfied? They themselves reply without the slightest hesitation: Yes. The welcome, or rather the confidence shown them will be more efficacious than a hundred apologetical treatises for dissolving the complex of distrust which often weighs more than real reasons—or which in any case gives to the reasons for refusal the weight of an insurmountable difficulty.

The Spirit of John XXIII

The discussions on the schema prepared by the Commission on the Sacred Liturgy had begun October 21. Considering these debates and without minimizing the tensions which had begun to be evident, Father Congar, on November 2, described the atmosphere of the Council in a very positive way:

The conciliar climate reflects the spirit of John XXIII, which
is a spirit of confidence and supernatural optimism, of pastoral
candor and humility, of kindliness and peace. This climate has thus
far been unquestionably well preserved. Everything must be done
to prevent its deterioration, which would set in if the normal
and invigorating tensions resulted in parties with their sterile cold
(or even lukewarm) war. . . . The Council also represents in its
way a "milieu" which has its own reactions and influence. Classical
theology perhaps did not take note of the concrete importance of
what it said when it distinguished between the bishops gathered
together at the Council and the bishops dispersed throughout
the world. It is the same college but in two different states.
The assembly as such has its power and develops its singular
possibilities. It permits a broad development, spontaneous and
relaxed, of the dialoguing nature of the spirit, which wishes to be
enriched by its contact and exchange with others. . . . By itself
the Council is a kind of Agora or Forum of the spiritual Christian
Republic. Its climate is that of the free expression of thought by
any one who thinks he has something to say. This freedom is paid
for by the length of the sessions, wherein one after the other
thirty or forty members speak. . . . This handicap in the workings
of the Assembly must be accepted. Freedom is always costly but
its price is always relative, and thus always less than its value
which, in its order, is absolute.

Father Congar concludes his chronicle by showing that the
problem unceasingly on the horizon is the one which will be the
problem of the Council: the episcopacy.

What is Doctrine?

After the approval of the general principles of the schema on
the liturgy, the Council, on November 14, passed to the study
of the text on "The Sources of Revelation." The discussion of
this text brought out more clearly the differences between the
two groups at the Assembly. On November 21, the Pope decided
to send the text back to a mixed commission to recast it. I shall
not enter into the heart of the problem itself (which however
Father Congar describes very succinctly in his notes), but I
shall cite instead a passage where the theologian reflects on the
idea, expressed by the partisans of the official schema, which
was that "to teach doctrine" was the first duty of the pastor and

the most necessary ecumenical presupposition. The argument did not convince those who rejected the schema, precisely in the name of pastoral duty and ecumenism, and from an indubitable doctrinal concern.

> The partisans of the schema seemed to understand by doctrine a certain number of statements, fixed and as it were expressed in standard formulas, placed like objects or things before the mind. Above all it was necessary to guard these formulas, to exhibit them, even to brandish them the way one takes out and brandishes an article of the code. Those who were not satisfied by the challenged schema do not separate "doctrine" from the activity of the spirit which professes it. As a result, they included, in the most profound fidelity to this doctrine, a perpetual activity of *research.*

And Father Congar shows the forms which this activity takes in the pastoral domain, interest in men's problems, and in the ecumenical field a desire to overcome present opposition by the purity and depth of a return to the sources. On December 8, 1962, telling his readers that the opening date for the second session had been put off until September 8, 1963, Father Congar speculates on the chances of accomplishing some fruitful work between the two sessions, but he concludes:

> A shadow hovers over these optimistic views—that of the health of the Holy Father. At the end of this first session uneasiness overwhelms the spirits animated by a respectful affection unanimously felt by all. At the very moment the Fathers are going back to their dioceses, the Holy Father will perhaps have to undergo an operation, made even more serious by reason of his age. May God spare us this man who united us into a fraternal assembly of the greatest Council of all time. But should he will to take him from us let him give us in place of Elias an Eliseus who, having received his mantle and office, might also have received his spirit!

The Episcopacy Found Itself

Meanwhile, the schema on the unity of the Church drawn up by the Commission for the Oriental Churches had been presented to the Council. On December 1, the Fathers demanded that it be recast with the schema on ecumenism, prepared by the Secretariat for Christian Unity. The same day the schema on the Church was introduced; it was to have a fate similar to that of the text on Revelation. December 8 marked the close of the session. December 18, back at Strasbourg, Father Congar took inventory. He concluded that the advantages were less in the order of decisions than in that of vital experience and of a certain spirit. Even were the Council not to arrive at any precise text "a result of incalculable importance was had from this moment on. Something irrevocable had been produced and affirmed in the Church." What was this? It can be described thus:

> The episcopacy has found itself. It has seen itself. It has become aware of itself. Henceforth formulas will be found; they will come of themselves, given an opportunity. We have already said (having like so many others experienced it very strongly), what an original and irreplaceable "fact" the Assembly as such represented. By it each of the participants becomes, under many aspects, another man—he sees things differently. Tendencies which were somnolent in him take on all their vivacity, whereas others which dominated in him are discreetly held in reserve. He finds himself uplifted by his participation with other human beings, by his exposure to other horizons. At last he realizes fully the world-wide solidarity and responsibility of the episcopacy. The trite images of a bishop in his bishopric, alone at the head of a diocese whose daily problems sometimes appear petty, tend to fade away. Each bishop feels himself a member of a body limited by neither cantons nor years—the body of the apostolic pastorate of which Jesus Christ is the invisible Head, he whose universal pastorate is reflected visibly in that of Peter's successor.

(B) SECOND SESSION—ANOTHER IDEA OF THE CHURCH

That God Might Give Us an Eliseus

An article in *Le Monde* for June 22, 1963, and one of the first entries in Father Congar's chronicle for the second session were to give an answer to the questions asked by Father Congar in his notes of December 8, 1962: Would John XXIII live to the end of "his" Council?

The period between the sessions was marked by an event of great importance, the death of good Pope John XXIII. It was extraordinary. By the hundreds and from all sides testimonies piled upon testimonies showing how deeply humanity had been touched. John XXIII was a universal Father, an ecumenical pope —in a way that overwhelmed the whole world when it realized (at the very moment of losing him) how deeply and truly he had been just that.

In particular, he was the instrument of bringing together Catholics and members of the non-Roman Church: "For the first time in history," said Pastors Charles Westphal and Georges Casalis, "Protestants mourn a pope." Would his successor be of the same mind? Commenting on Paul VI's speech for the opening of the Council, Father Congar writes in his notes for October 4, 1963:

> The Holy Father, while pronouncing each word with great emphasis, experienced moments of intense emotion in speaking of Jesus Christ, in speaking of divided brethren. Three features struck us at the time: the very strong Christological affirmation, the insistence on the bishops, and, let us add, on episcopal solidarity and fraternity, and a lengthy development of the theme of "openness" toward others. No one can doubt any longer that the evolution promoted by John XXIII and the Council is henceforth ratified and irreversible.

The Light from the East

The Council, in its new structure (the real role of the president was henceforth assumed by the four "moderators"), had first to take up the study of seventeen schemas that were to be reduced to thirteen. The Council opened September 29, the Pope giving the discourse of which we spoke. Immediately afterwards discussion was started on *De Ecclesia*. I have said enough about the thought of Father Congar on these themes, even though the importance of the debates was considerable. Let me simply note, under the date of October 17, this observation:

> It is evident [besides other defects of the schema, judged good however by Father Congar] that the light of the East, that

the meaning of things kept in the admirable Eastern tradition are sadly neglected in the proposed texts. This lack, deplored by the small number of men capable of realizing it, indicates clearly how necessary it is for the East to correct in us what is excessively Cartesian, juridical, and analytical. But who, with one stroke, can make the Eastern Church speak up in a place that she has been absent from for centuries? How indeed open another path to so many men of good faith who believe that their Latinism is Catholicism?

In his own notes for November 16 through November 18, Father Congar brings out one point in the answer:

The day before Cardinal Frings' speech to which I just referred, His Beatitude Maximos IV had given a wonderful address. The speaker is one of the outstanding members of the Council. An old man, he is an example of a spirit young in heart and an intelligence preserved intact, combined at an age where, having nothing more to expect from the world, a man, if he has kept his strength, enjoys the freedom to serve the great causes to which he has devoted his life.

For him, there was question of only one cause:

To upset the customs and the contrary habits accumulated over a thousand years, to make possible, some day, the re-establishment of communion between the Christian East and the Roman West. . . . He demanded for the universal Church, made up of the Churches of different peoples, a kind of life based on this ecclesial reality itself, and not on the local Church of Rome alone, of which the Cardinals are, in the last analysis, members and in which the Curia is nothing but the court of the bishop of Rome.

The Exercise of Primacy

What should one think of this last affirmation? Father Congar tells us in the same entry which must be situated in its proper place in the development of the second session. Discussion was going on about the text on the Church; the liturgical schema was voted on; Paul VI received the observers, exchanging very important remarks with their representative K.E. Skydsgaard, and named several lay auditors. Father Congar commented on all these happenings, analyzing too the significance of the insertion of the text on the Virgin Mary into the *De Ecclesia*. He also wished that one would single out intra-ecclesial problems by having witnesses come before the assembly and set before them an honest "balance sheet" showing the condition of the world before any discussion on Schema XIII. On November 5, there was discussion of the schema on bishops and the government of dioceses, which appeared immediately as "in little harmony with the trend so clearly manifested by the voting on October 30 in regard to the basis of the authority of the bishops and collegiality." It was at this point that Cardinal Frings intervened on the point of Curial reform and Maximos IV on the participation of the episcopacy in the central government of the Church, other speakers insisting on the role of episcopal conferences. But Maximos IV terminated his speech by pronouncing a judgment on the government of the universal Church and on the role of the Curia. To this the members of the Curia replied that it is only a service of the pontifical office of the universal government of the Church, by virtue of its primacy; to attack it is to attack the Holy Father himself. Such is not the opinion of Father Congar. He writes:

> It seems to us that in all good faith one combines or even identifies here two things which are really distinct: the primacy, which is of divine institution, and a certain form of exercising it, which is an ecclesiastical creation. Historical knowledge or sociological analysis enables us to judge the decisive part of the human element in it. Papal primacy has been exercised under more than one form.

Many concrete forms of exercising it, many interventions of the pope in the universal Church and in its service, for which he utilizes the services of the Curia, are made possible to him through the primacy, but do not involve it to such a point that it would be the least bit lessened if they were suppressed. The pope can use the service of the Curia, but is in no way obliged to do so, and he can decide today to decentralize the government of the Church, or even to associate to the central government his brother bishops of the entire world without losing one iota of his primacy.

Ecumenism Is Not Easy

On November 16, discussion on this text ceased. On November 14, the schema on the means of social communication, and on November 18, the liturgical schema, had also been approved, chapter by chapter. This same day the schema on Ecumenism had been introduced. In his last bulletin, dated December 5, and drawn up at Rome, Father Congar observed that, "On the whole, the Catholic Church has carried on its ecumenical conversation at the highest level without drama and without ostentation. The Catholic Church and the entire Christian people have, in fact, lived a historical moment comparable to the greatest." It is well known that "ecumenism is not easy. It demands patience. Generations are needed, so that little by little the blocked roads are cleared, attitudes adopted and become habits. Even evidence must open up, and the share of truth held by others must be acknowledged." With restrained enthusiasm Father Congar then shows the importance and the beauty of the text on the liturgy and its profound harmony with ecclesiological renewal (community and sacrament). He further observes that it is because it "takes over what has been adopted by the proponents of the liturgical movement and approves their research that it was considered satisfactory from the outset, whereas other texts, foreign to the development of ideas, were severely criticized and rejected." On December 4, there was a speech by the Holy Father. Once the prepared text was finished, Paul VI announced his intention to go as a pilgrim to the Holy Land. After this announcement the session closed.

(C) THIRD SESSION: AN ARDUOUS TASK—THE DIFFICULTY
OF OPENING UP TO THE WORLD

The Church, a Communion

The third session began September 9 in St. Peter's Basilica. On September 15, Father Congar stated forcefully in an article that appeared in *Informations Catholiques Internationales* (but which had been written before the opening of the session) that the true significance of the Council would depend on the passing from declarations, texts, and *symbolic* actions (like those of Pope Paul VI) to *real* action. "Such options involve intellectual and practical implications before which one must not draw back, but must approach them seriously with all the fidelity and patience which accompany a real feeling of responsibility in great matters. One cannot remain at the level of good intentions."

But the reality fell far short of the ideal since all the great texts had already been promulgated. Before commenting on the discussion of *De Ecclesia* in his notes for October 1, Father Congar says a word about the concelebration during the opening ceremony and the intense participation of the assembly, so different from the icy pomp of 1962 with its polyphonic modulations of the Sistine choir and the princely elegance of the pontifical court. And this difference goes very far:

> At the beginning of a session which, one hopes, is going to be dedicated to a [traditional] theology of episcopal collegiality, the celebration manifested the profound nature of the Church as a priestly body called, in solidarity, to praise God and to give witness to his coming to us. The Church showed itself as Communion, the unity of the priesthood was affirmed, the assembly revealed its profound nature—a wholly priestly people, united to the one, who at its head represents Jesus Christ sacerdotally inasmuch as he is the supreme and invisible Head of the whole Body.

To Declericalize the Idea of the Church

In these same notes Father Congar mentions the mediocrity of the debates over the texts concerning the Mother of God. Previously (November 1, 1963) he had written that the opposition on this subject came "from the gulf which presently exists between the 'back-to-sources' Catholicism (a Catholicism which is centered on Christ and is at the same time biblical, liturgical, paschal, community-centered, ecumenical, and missionary), and a 'non-source' Catholicism, within which some specialized teams are devoted to obtaining the maximum 'development' of certain mariological propositions." Remarking that there is a very positive common doctrine, he comes back to this thought in 1964 and insists on the fact that "some have a very keen awareness of the unity of revelation and theology centered on the Christian mystery, and are reluctant to particularize one article or another, or to develop propositions indefinitely by means of argumentation, thus getting too far away from the central affirmations which have scriptural and traditional support." This absolute Christocentricity and reference to the judgment of the Word of God seem less carefully safeguarded by those who develop for themselves the aspects of the Marian doctrine without a firm biblical basis, by an "analogical" transposition of what properly belongs to Christ.

While voting on *De Ecclesia* the Fathers discussed the schema on the pastoral function of bishops, then (from September 24 on), the texts on religious liberty and on the Jews. These two topics, like Schema XIII itself, were to provoke heated discussions which by their very obstinacy were highly significant of the great difficulty the Church was having in trying to situate herself clearly in the world. On October 15, Father Congar explained the doctrine of episcopal collegiality and insisted equally on the importance of the restoration of the diaconate, introduced on September 28. A renewed diaconate would have good practical consequences, but would also possess a great ecclesiological significance, conferred as it can be on married men, exercising or having exercised a profession among their fellow citizens. "This involves a development of the notion of 'minister.' Instead of being purely clerical or sacerdotal, concretely linked to the cassock, to Latin, to celibacy, to clericalism, the ministry expressly becomes an act which all baptized men can, to some degree, perform." This has already been the case, in fact, for many catechists, leaders of the liturgical movements and others, but it is important that it be henceforth held in honor in order "to declericalize the notion we have of the Church."

Human Liberty and God's Right

On October 15, Father Congar described the debate on religious liberty to the readers of his chronicles. He indicated clearly where the difficulty lay. At the practical level everyone agrees to accept religious liberty, but disagreement arises as soon as one tries to establish it as a right. If one were contented with the given proposition, that of staying at the practical aspect of things, one would not encounter the oppositions raised by the project of the Secretariat for Unity which establishes religious liberty in "the right of the human person not to be constrained in a matter of conscience by any created power." This is indispensable, moreover, notes the theologian, for the Catholic Church has been intolerant and has even made a theory of intolerance; if today we change only in practice, how shall we avoid the fear of a return the day the Church again finds a temporal power docile to it? Certain Fathers feared that, in thus insisting on the right of consciences not to be constrained, one might slight another principle—the objective right of revealed truth to make itself accepted by minds, and "since this truth is found in the Church of Jesus Christ, which is the Catholic Church, this would logically and practically result in claiming for the Catholic Church a specific right . . . to be recognized and favored in a privileged way." Other religions should enjoy only a tolerance. How can one reply to this? I give Father Congar's position in an analysis where his principles outlined above in speaking of Christ's Lordship will be recognized. (It is only fitting to recall here that Jacques Maritain was the first to enunciate them in *Humanisme intégral* in 1936.)

God and the absolute truth of his Word have rights but according to their mode. This notion of rights can be applied to them but only in a way that is fitting to their transcendence, analogically. . . . God is transcendent and at the same time immanent to each human conscience. His authority is *sui generis*. It does not impose itself in the same way that a human power does, but proposes itself as truth. . . . Hence one cannot translate God's original and transcendent right as such into rights of a political nature.

Thus the theology of religious liberty involves, besides the doctrine of liberty of conscience and of an act of faith, a whole view on the relation between the Church and the City of Men.

To Keep a Calm Judgment

While the assembly was voting on *De Oecumenismo,* it discussed the new text of *De Revelatione,* the schema on the apostolate of the laity and the project concerning priests. Beginning October 21, Schema XIII was to be discussed and a vote taken on the text of interest to the Uniate Churches. On November 15, Father Congar explained the difficulties encountered in the editing of the schema of the Church in the world—what literary genre should be adopted? To whom should it be addressed? The decision was made to address Christians, hoping through them to reach all men of good faith. But this option presupposed a more biblical, a more theological, text than the first draft. Many debates and votings took place between November 4, when voting began on the text of the pastoral function of bishops, and November 21, when the session closed with the promulgation by the Pope of *De Ecclesia,* of *De Oecumenismo,* and of the text on the Oriental Catholic Churches.

Meanwhile there were some unfortunate incidents: the *nota praevia* on collegiality, the last-minute revision of the text on ecumenism, and the postponement of the schema on religious liberty until the next session. These incidents troubled not only the Fathers (who were already tired and overworked), but the observers as well. In fact the whole of public opinion was aroused.

Father Congar explained these incidents and gave his reactions. Whatever maneuvering there might have been, the events themselves must be judged objectively and calmly. The *nota praevia* does no more than express the conception the theological commission has of its own text, and casts aside unjustified fears. Father Congar had expressed several times in the past his regret that the reporters of the commissions could not come to the tribune, as at Vatican I, to explain the text and the intentions of those who drew it up. The corrections of *De Oecumenismo* came so late only because the text had not been presented to the Pope until the last minute. This fact is more widely known today than it was at the time Father Congar wrote these lines. But even then he noted that the corrections were quite minimal and their bad effects were more from psychological reactions than anything else. Just the fact of going backward even ever so little was a risk—this will be seen again in the text on the Jews. Finally it was quite normal to postpone for a more careful study the adoption of a text on religious liberty which had been considerably revised. But, asked Father Congar, could not this have been done without such administrative highhandedness? Could not the satisfaction of an indicative vote have been given? Here again, from a distance we can better measure the wisdom of the appeal to prudence which concludes these reflections of Father Congar's —the text of 1965 is better than the one that would have been adopted at the close of the session.

(D) FOURTH SESSION: FINAL HARVEST

He Is Not a Prince but a Pastor

In his chronicles for the third session, commenting (December 1, 1964) on the gesture of Paul VI in laying aside his tiara and placing it on the altar as a symbol of giving it to the world's poor, Father Congar asked the following question:

> Is it simply *one* tiara that the Pope has just placed on the altar—the one that the people of Milan gave him, which is especially dear to him, or is it *the* tiara insofar as it is historically the

symbol of a pretension to a temporal power and to a certain world empire (Boniface VIII)? How, after giving his tiara to the poor, could Paul VI still wear one? And if it is *the* tiara, this gesture should be the beginning of a process by which the Church will rid itself of its temporal and lordly external trappings in order to be a better sign of the Gospel in the midst of the world, especially the world of the poor.

These questions were answered by the description the same chronicler gave of the opening ceremony of the fourth session.

> The Holy Father, preceded by the cardinals, enters on foot. He refuses the sedia, for both the processional and recessional. No tiara, no flabella, no military escort or court, simply the ecclesiastical functionaries of the Vatican. A mitre on his head, the pope who has never had a crozier, holds in his left hand (like a pastoral baton) a silver crucifix. It is not a prince but a pastor, a priest, who approaches the altar.

Father Congar then commented on the discourse of the Holy Father and analyzed the discussion on religious liberty, the meaning of which he again explained in more detail.

On October 3, there was the indicative vote on this schema, the acceptance of the texts on the apostolate of the laity, the pastoral duty of the bishops, and Revelation which engaged Father Congar's interest. He then commented on the section on the Jews, finally inserted into the declaration on the non-Christian religions. We know the enormous difficulties that this provoked and the disappointment that certain changes caused. These changes were doctrinally of little importance, but the psychological reaction was that they revealed a lack of decision and courage. In spite of this reaction, the text firmly opposed antisemitism. Why had the condemnation of the accusation of deicide disappeared? "For our part we do not regret it," wrote Father Congar. "It is a vulgar expression and has been the source of grave misunderstandings. The essential is that the text *really* proclaims that what happened at the time of the passion of the

Savior can be imputed neither to all the Jews then living nor to the Jews of today." Finally, some reflections on Schema XIII complete this chronicle. The three following were devoted to a rapid presentation of the different texts discussed or promulgated.

To Keep the Spirit of the Council

On November 18, Father Congar for the first time wonders what the post-conciliar era will be like:

> A new work will begin. In one way, everything remains to be done. In fact it is necessary that the conciliar decisions be progressively carried out. This will again demand everyone's co-operation, an effort of diffusion and explanation, the courage to carry out, prudently, the *aggiornamento* already begun. The entire body of the Church will be involved, from the periphery to the center. Many things will depend on the reform of the Curia, on the new synod of bishops, and on post-conciliar commissions. Two of these have already been established: the liturgical *consilium* which works methodically and effectively and the commission on the revision of the code of canon law, whose notebook of duties and whose files are quickly filled with the promulgation of each new conciliar document. The spirit of the Council must be faithfully kept. The episcopal conferences are concerned with this. Evidently there are many human reasons for fearing that at the end of two or three years memory becomes blurred, attention is relaxed, routines once broken again take over in the offices. The strength of these routines is in tradition; it resists innovation. It is not easy, we ourselves know, to think henceforth of everything in the light of the renewed vision which the Council has given to the function of episcopal collegiality, of a catholicity in which the East regains its original place, of a theology returned to its sources, of a laity fully integrated into the life of the People of God, etc., etc.
>
> We have already spoken of the indispensable role theologians will have to take in the process of carrying out Council decrees. They in their proper place with the bishops largely made the Council. Our conviction is that the post-conciliar era will not continue along conciliar lines unless theologians are utilized in the work to be done. Means and, where needed, necessary structures will have to be found. This is demanded by the new awareness (become a living experience at the Council) of the fact that the Church is constructed by the effort of all the charisms and ministries existing in the People of God and not only by a vertical

hierarchical communication—the chain and the web of which we spoke in *Jalons pour une théologie du laïcat*.[1]

To Draw Up a Balance Sheet of the World

In these same bulletins Father Congar regretted that so much time was given to a discussion on indulgences. The discussions, in the presence of somewhat shocked observers, were without any particular merit. On this subject he offered an interesting suggestion:

> If it was a question of using up time which discussions no longer filled one could have found something else. One could have heard informative reports on the great actual questions of exegesis, science, or philosophy. One could have heard conferences from the bishops on how they conceive the post-conciliar era. One could have drawn up a *balance sheet of the world,* or made an inventory of the apostolic fields of labor on the different continents. But on the other hand one must appreciate the frankness with which the Catholic Church acknowledges its difficulties and refuses to treat them as trifles. For our part, while we see the positive in such conduct, we also estimate as well the conditions which its full success would involve.[2]

The Church Declares That It Believes in Man

On December 4, Father Congar sought to clarify the major significance of Schema XIII which had just been voted on in the aula. He wrote:

> A fatal divorce between man, or the world, and God has too often prevailed. A certain theology, a certain representation and presentation of things is partly responsible for this. Too often Christianity has been limited to a purely religious cult, to an affirmation of God without man or a world. To such an affirmation different philosophies have replied by affirming man and the world without God. Contemporary atheism is often an affirmation first of man and his project in the world and only by way of consequence a denial of God whose existence, it is thought, would make man's freedom and initiative impossible. Schema XIII was

---

[1] *Le Concile au jour le jour,* Session IV, pp. 81-82.
[2] *Ibid.,* p. 84.

to reply to this frightful and disastrous mistake. It does so in the first part, entitled "The Church and Man's Calling." In it is found an anthropology—that is, a vision of man seen in his dignity as a person. In it too is found a theology of man's work in the universe, what is sometimes called a theology of terrestrial realities and work. There is, finally, a precise exposition of what the Church is aware of being and owing in regard to all this. Perhaps anthropology *thus* formulated is imperfect; such is our thought. Anthropology *ought* to be the field of research in the years to come. The Council has treated classical theses rather than opening up new perspectives. However, it has opened up some, and very important ones they are.

Some eighteen months ago we asked a young engineer engaged in atomic research what he expected of Schema XIII. He replied, "Let the Church announce that it believes in man!" This has been done. The Church accepts modern man and speaks to him in the name of Jesus Christ, who is the eschatological, that is, the final man, to whom the world must tend.

In Jesus Christ the Church knows the depths of man and also the extent to which man is a sinner. The text is *not* silent—on the contrary it forcefully exposes sin and the need for God's pardon and help to which it reduces us. The text shows sin at work in man's enterprises and offers the remedy—Jesus Christ. It also denounces an ignorance of God and speaks of contemporary atheism, seeing it as one of the essential characteristics of the contemporary world.[3]

A Plebiscite for Union

In his following bulletin, the chronicler-theologian described the closing ceremonies of the Council. First there was the farewell to the observers at St. Paul's Outside the Walls on December 4. December 7 saw the promulgation of the last texts and, the same day, the solemn abolition of the reciprocal excommunications of 1054 between Rome and Constantinople. The symbolic value of this act can be grasped and the joy which this event must have brought to Father Congar is easily understood. He adds:

At the moment the text was read [in French] at Rome, it was also proclaimed at Constantinople where there was a Catholic delegation led by Cardinal Shehan. At St. Peter's in Rome it was

---

[3]*Ibid.*, pp. 101-2.

the Metropolitan Meliton of Tyre. He stood near the Pope, before the altar, facing the immense assembly. The accolade of Jerusalem was publicly renewed. An extraordinary ovation, intense and prolonged, expressed the sentiment of the Catholic episcopacy and people—it was a plebiscite for union! The future is open for an advance to new stages. The Lord who has begun this great work will know how to complete it.

In closing, Father Congar describes the great public ceremony which took place December 8 in St. Peter's Square.

Do Not Betray the Aggiornamento

Following these chronicles Father Congar published a whole series of balance sheets, written after his return to Strasbourg. From one of these, dated December 13, let me pick out a short passage to serve as a conclusion to this chapter.

The danger is that one will not *seek* any more, but will simply exploit the inexhaustible warehouse of Vatican II. Then a post-Vatican era would open up in the way a post-Tridentine era existed. It would be a betrayal of the *aggiornamento* if we thought it could be fixed once for all in the texts of Vatican II.

From Beginning to Beginning

I return to an older text to conclude this book, which as I have already said does not need a real conclusion since it is about a living subject. In Father Congar's Council chronicles from November 18, 1963, are the following lines which describe the action of a Council. They show the influence of a work like their author's, and include an entire conception of the divine plan which should already be familiar to us.

> November 3 and 4 saw the celebration of the fourth centenary of the Council of Trent with special reference to the institution of seminaries. In reality, although the Council itself had the benefit of various experiments and although several foundations followed fairly rapidly, it needed almost a century for the institution to take shape in the form now familiar to us. That is an example of the way in which councils work and act. They bring together preliminary attempts which have reached a certain point of maturity and, by making some kind of decision, they establish something new in the Church to which they communicate the strength which comes from a common conscience and a unanimous agreement. Then, by the work of men, the planted seed bears fruit. The effects of their action are felt long afterwards; in fact, almost indefinitely. Time collaborates with what is confided to it, just as it collaborates with all seeds to bring them to harvest. Fundamentally, councils are major events in the age-old course of salvation history which, in St. Gregory of Nyssa's wonderful phrase, "goes from beginning to beginning, by beginnings which have no end."[*]

---

[*]*Le Concile au jour le jour,* Session IV, pp. 125-26.

PIETRO QUATTROCCHI

General Bibliography of Yves Congar

INTRODUCTION

It is perhaps still too soon to write the religious history of contemporary France; besides, some essential points are still lacking. It is time, however, considering the speed with which present-day events occur, to begin to gather the documents which will be indispensable in writing such a history. This writing will be the work of men who themselves experienced the events and who, while recognizing some failures, nevertheless will transmit to us a faithful witness of the ideal they desired to actualize.

This will also be the work of a young generation who, looking over a recent past, will discover inspirations that might sustain their intellectual endeavors or orientate their commitment in the practical order.

It is with this in mind that I have endeavored to draw up a bibliography of Father Yves Congar's works. I hope that it will be a useful tool for consultation and that in its modest way it will contribute to the history of ecclesiology. Titles are given without any commentary or any particular explanation in a simple chronological succession of works and articles. In general however, books have been placed at the end of each annual list.

Not all of Father Congar's editorials (often unsigned and impossible to locate[1]), appear in this bibliography. Several translations and reproductions of articles, especially those done in other countries,

---

[1] These editorials can be found especially in the *Revue des Sciences philosophiques et théologiques* (Father Congar was responsible for the "Chroniques" from July 1932 to July 1939); the *Bulletin thomiste* (see the table of contents); *La Vie Spirituelle;* the *Revue des Sciences religieuses* (from 1957 on); and the *Polybiblion* (from 1932 on).

have likewise escaped my notice, but I can safely say that nothing noteworthy has been omitted.

Everything contained herein has been established from Father Congar's personal notes or by research in such collections as the encyclopedia *Catholicisme; la Revue des Sciences philosophiques et théologiques;* the table of contents of *La Vie Intellectuelle; La Vie Spirituelle;* etc. At the beginning there is a list of abbreviations and at the end a list (drawn up by Father Congar himself) of works which are to appear soon.

Pietro Quattrocchi
Strasbourg, November 1, 1966

ABBREVIATIONS
Books by Father Congar

AOe	Aspects de l'Ecuménisme.
CED	Chrétiens en dialogue.
CME	Le Christ, Marie et l'Eglise.
EME	Esquisses du mystère de l'Eglise.
SE	Sainte Eglise.
SL	Sacerdoce et laïcat.
VDV	Les Voies du Dieu Vivant.
VMM	Vaste monde, ma paroisse.

Magazines and Collected Works

ADom	Année dominicaine.
Bl	Blackfriars.
BT	Bulletin thomiste, Le Saulchoir, Etiolles.
DC	Documentation catholique, Paris.
ICI	Informations catholiques internationales, Paris.
Ir	Irenikon, Amay, Chevetogne.
LTK	Lexikon für Theologie und Kirche, Fribourg (1930-1938).
LV	Lumière et Vie, Lyon.
MD	Maison-Dieu, Paris.
MO	Masses ouvrières, Paris.
MSR	Mélanges de Sciences religieuses, Lille.
NRT	Nouvelle Revue théologique, Tournai, Louvain, Paris.
OR	Osservatore Romano.
PM	Parole et Mission, Paris.
REA	Revue des études augustiniennes, Paris.
RJ	Revue des Jeunes, Paris.
RN	Revue Nouvelle, Tournai.
RevSR	Revue des Sciences religieuses, Strasbourg.
RSPT	Revue des Sciences philosophiques et théologiques, Paris.
RThom	Revue thomiste, Paris.
SVS	Supplément de la Vie spirituelle.
TC	Témoignage chrétien, Paris.
TTZ	Trierer theologische Zeitschrift, Trèves.
UDE	Unité de l'Eglise.
VI	Vie intellectuelle, Paris.
VS	Vie Spirituelle, Paris.
VUC	Vers l'unité chrétienne.

Cities Where Published

Ba	Barcelona.
D	Düsseldorf.
Fr	Freiburg im Breisgau.
Fri	Fribourg, Switzerland.
Ly	Lyon.
Ma	Madrid.
Mi	Milan.
NY	New York.
P	Paris.
Pa	Paderborn.
R	Rome.
St	Stuttgart.
Str	Strasbourg.
T	Turin.
Tou	Tournai.

THE BIBLIOGRAPHY[2]

1924

1. *Pourquoi la philosophie de Saint Thomas est-elle la philosophie officielle de l'Eglise?* Bulletin del'Institut de Paris, 2nd series (March 25, 1924), n. 3, 91-100.

2. *Réflexions sur la jeunesse d'âme.* La Croix, July 24, 1924; signed Leclerc.

1930

3. *Face au casque d'acier.* VI, November, 1930, 283-286.

1931

4. *Les fêtes du B. Albert le Grand en Allemagne.* ADom (1931), 49-51.

5. *Une volonté de "catholicité évangélique" en Allemagne: la Haute Eglise luthérienne.* UDE, January-February, 1931, 398-403.

6. *Deux gestes de deux grands saints. Le devoir d'état.* ADom (1931), 65-67; reprinted in VDV, 306-308.

7. *Conversion d'Erik Peterson.* VI, 12 (1931), 211-212.

8. *Les Conférences théologiques entre Orientaux et Occidentaux.* UDE, September-October, 1931, 513-515.

9. *Théologiens orthodoxes et protestants.* VI, 13 (1931), 212-214.

10. *Grandeurs et souffrances d'une vocation intellectuelle.* Bull. de Sainte-Geneviève, P, November, 1931, 20-24.

11. *La question du ministère ecclésiastique des femmes.* Les documents de la VI, December 20, 1931, 381-408.

12. *Essai de statistique des Confessions chrétiennes.* UDE, 1931, 530-534.

13. *Essai de bibliographie albertinienne;* in collaboration with M.H. Laurent. RThom, 1931, 422-468.

14. *Bulletin d'histoire des doctrines chrétiennes.* RSPT, 20 (1931), 591-596; 600-618; 631-633.

15. *Bulletin d'histoire de la philosophie du Moyen Age.* RSPT, 20 (1931), 718-744.

---

[2]The titles of Father Congar's articles and studies are in italic, as are the books into which they have been collected. The titles of books are given chronologically and have been set in small capitals. References to magazines, reviews, places of publication, dates, etc., are in roman type.

1932

16. *Parallèle entre le coq et le prédicateur.* ADom (1932), 18.

17. *Sainte Elisabeth. La charité de la croix.* VS, 30 (1932), 51-73; Italian trans. in Collectanea Franciscana, 1934, 668 ff.

18. *Le "Je vous salue Marie" de saint Albert le Grand.* ADom (1932), 36-41.

19. *En marge de quelques études sur l'Eglise.* VI, 15 (1932), 18-29.

20. *Pierre pasteur des brebis de Jésus.* VS, 31 (1932), 250-256; reprinted in VDV, 238-242.

21. *Prières de saint Albert le Grand* (trans.). ADom (1932), 301-303.

22. *Bulletin d'histoire des doctrines.* RSPT, 31 (1932), 478-485; 493-500.

23. *Bulletin de théologie.* RSPT, 31 (1932), 680-686.

1933

24. *Ordre et juridiction dans l'Eglise.* Ir, 10 (1933), 22-31; 99-110; 243-252; 401-408; reprinted in SE, 203-237.

25. *Albert le Grand, théologien de la grâce sanctifiante.* VS, 34 (1933), 109-140.

26. *Pensées choisies de saint Albert le Grand.* VS, 34 (1933), 171-184.

27. *Une fidélité dominicaine. La doctrine de l'Eglise, Corps mystique de Jésus-Christ.* ADom (1933), 239-245.

28. *Sur les saints Anges.* VS, 37 (1933), 18-28; reprinted in VDV, 227-235.

29. *Le Verbe s'est fait chair.* L'Unité dans la Lumière, 53 (1933), 397-402; reprinted in RJ, 28 (1937), January.

30. *Bulletin d'histoire des doctrines chrétiennes.* RSPT, 22 (1933), 525-538; 545-552.

31. *Bulletin d'histoire de la philosophie.* RSPT, 22 (1933), 696-718.

32. *Bulletin de théologie.* RSPT, 22 (1933), 747-750; reprinted in SE, 463-466.

33. *Compte rendu de H. Lang: Die Lehre des hl. Thomas von Aquin von der Gewissheit des übernatürlichen Glaubens historisch untersucht und systematisch dargestellt.* BT, III, 1 (1933), 40-47.

34. *Bibliographie critique.* BT, III, 1 (1933), 229-231; 266-267; 268-273; 299-313.

35. *Bibliographie critique.* BT, III, 2 (1933), 744-746; 948-958; rep. SE, 466-473.

1934

36. *Dogme et vie spirituelle.* RJ (1934), 149-161; 298-306; 458-467.

37. *Martyre de saint Pierre.* RJ (1934), 739-741; reprinted in VDV, 243-246.

38. *Pensée orthodoxe sur l'unité de l'Eglise.* VI, 29 (1934), 394-414.

39. *Protestantisme français.* Bull. du Groupe saint André, Le Havre, n. 13 (1934), 21-23.

40. *Cajetan et la dévotion à la compassion de Marie. L'opuscule "De Spasmo".* SVS, 38 (1934), March, 142-160.

41. *Deux textes de saint Albert le Grand sur le Cœur eucharistique de Jésus.* ADom (1934), 169-170.

42. *Récit de la mort du cardinal Cajetan* (trans.). ADom (1934), 335-337.

43. *La date de la mort du cardinal Cajetan.* Angelicum, Annus XI (1934), 603-608.

44. *Faut-il des dogmes a la religion?* (on the occasion of the centenary of Schleiermacher). Nova et Vetera, April-June, 1934, 113-130.

45. *Le maréchal Fabert et le retour des calvinistes à l'unité.* UDE, May-June, 1934, 257-265.

46. *Actualité de Kierkegaard.* VI, 32 (1934), 9-36; reprinted in part in Foi et Vie, August-September, 1934, 712-717.

47. *Réunion de tous les Chrétiens?* Bulletin du Groupe saint André, Le Havre, n. 16, 1934, 22-26.

48. *Anxiété des catholiques allemands.* Sept, September 8, 1934, p. 7; September 15, 1934, pp. 6-7; under the name of Ober.

49. *Lettre collective des évêques allemands* (translation, extracts). VI, September 10, 1934, 384-388.

50. *Je crois à la communion des saints.* L'Unité dans la Lumière, n. 62 (1934), 678-689.

51. *Praedeterminare et praedeterminatio chez saint Thomas.* RSPT, 23 (1934), 363-371.

52. *Bulletin de l'histoire des doctrines chrétiennes.* RSPT, 23 (1934), 474-483; 491-494; 510-513.

53. *Bulletin d'histoire de la philosophie médiévale.* RSPT, 23 (1934), 637-653.

54. *Bulletin de théologie.* RSPT, 23 (1934), 680-687.

1935

55. *De la communication des biens spirituels.* VS, 42 (1935), 5-17; reprinted in VDV, 347-356.

56. *Déficit de la théologie.* Sept, January 18, 1935, 6.

57. *La Jeunesse d'âme.* RJ (1935), 9-21; reprinted in VDV, 381-390.

58. *De la rue.* RJ, February 15, 1935, 147-149.

59. *Les protestants et nous.* VI, 33 (1935), 357-366; reprinted in Cahiers pour le protestantisme, 1, 1-10 and CED, 357-364.

60. *La déification dans la tradition spirituelle de l'Orient d'après une étude récente.* SVS, 43 (1935), May, 91-107; reprinted in CED, 257-272.

61. *Une conclusion théologique à l'Enquête sur les raisons actuelles de l'incroyance.* VI, 37 (1935), 214-249; English trans. in Integration, August, 1938, 13-21; December, 1938, 10-26.

62. *La pensée de Möhler et l'ecclésiologie orthodoxe.* Ir, 12 (1935), 321-329.

63. *D'abord comprendre.* VI, 38 (1935), 6-8; signed Christianus; reprinted CED, 365-368.

64. *"Nunc et in hora mortis nostrae." Réflexions sur le sens chrétien de la mort.* VS, 45 (1935), 113-125; reprinted in VDV, 435-444.

65. *De consensu ecclesiarum* (une réponse inédite de Mgr. Dechamps à Mgr. Ketteler). RSPT, 24 (1935), 296-299; reprinted in SE, 351-355.

66. *Bio-bibliographie de Cajétan.* RThom, special number on Cajetan, 1935, 3-49.

67. *Le rôle des images dans l'abstraction intellectuelle selon Cajetan.* RThom, 1935, 225-245.

68. *Bulletin d'histoire des doctrines chrétiennes.* RSPT, 24 (1935), 357-369; 379-385.

69. *Bulletin de théologie.* RSPT, 24 (1935), 707-734.

70. *Bibliographie critique.* BT, IV, 1 (1934-1935), 272-277; 343-346.

71. *Bibliographie critique.* BT, IV, 2 (1935-1936), 740-742; 749-752; 766-772.

1936

72. *Pour l'unité de tous les chrétiens.* Sept, January 17, 1936, 13.

73. *L'esprit du III*e *Reich.* Sept, February 14, 1936, 21.

74. *Pour l'unité du monde chrétien.* VS, 46 (1936), 304-311; reprinted in Le Semeur, April, 1936.

75. *Pour une théologie du vêtement* (trans. by Erik Peterson). SVS, 46 (1936), March, 168-179 (cf. n. 151).

76. *Réponse à W. Monod.* VI, 41 (1936), 363-365.

77. *Chronique catholique.* Oecumenica, 3 (April, 1936), 63-68.

78. *L'octave de prière pour l'unité du monde chrétien.* Unitas, March-May, 1936, 23-24.

79. *L'Eglise selon M. Georges Bernanos.* VI, 43 (1936), 387-390 (cf. n. 282).

80. *Le point de vue d'un théologien. Questions, explications et principes au sujet des groupes d'Oxford.* VI, 44 (1936), 30-66; followed by a French bibliography on the groups, 66-68; extracted and published separately: C. Vignon, E. Brunne, M.-J. Congar, *Les groupes d'Oxford,* Ed. du Cerf, Juvisy (S. et O.), 1936.

81. *Réflexions sur le Tiers Ordre et l'apostolat auprès des non-catholiques.* ADom, July, 1936, 248-253.

82. *Tendenzen und Bewegungen der katholischen Theologie im heutigen Frankreich.* Geistige Arbeit, July 5, 1936, 3. Jhg., n. 13, 3-4.

83. *Chronique catholique.* Oecumenica, 3, July, 1936, 181-186.

84. *Peuples, races et cultures.* Sept, July 31, 1936, 10.

85. *The origins of the Anglican Ministry.* Bl, 17 (1936), 699-703.

86. *Bulletin d'histoire de philosophie médiévale.* RSPT, 25 (1936), 152-168.

87. *Sur l'inclusion de l'humanité dans le Christ.* RSPT, 25 (1936), 489-495.

88. *Bulletin de théologie spéculative.* RSPT, 25 (1936), 747-773.

89. *Faut-il désirer que les dissidents tombent dans l'indifférence religieuse?* SVS, 49 (1936), October, 172-178.

90. *Chronique catholique.* Oecumenica, 3, October, 1936, 253-261.

91. *Meetings between Catholics and Orthodox: Some Possibilities.* The Eastern Churches Quarterly, October 4, 1936, 131-135.

92. *Chronique ouverte.* Sept, December 4, 1936, 20.

1937

93. *Chronique catholique.* Oecumenica, 3, January, 1937, 363-367.

94. *Les chrétiens dissidents dans notre prière catholique.* SVS, 50 (1937), 74-85.

95. *Une théologie de la mystique.* SVS, 50 (1937), January, 46-50.

96. *Le Corps mystique du Christ.* SVS, 50 (1937), 113-138; reprinted in Etudes religieuses, Liège, March 15, 1937, 405, and in EME 93-115.

97. *Catholicism and Protestantism.* The Student World, 2 (1937), 142-149; French text: Dogmes protestants et dogmes catholiques comparés, RSPT, 26 (1937), 499-509, and in Foi et Vie.

98. *Saint Thomas serviteur de la vérité.* SVS, 50 (1937), 259-279, reprinted in VDV, 289-306.

99. *Le sens religieux de l'encyclique sur le communisme.* VI, 48 (1937), 359-361.

100. *Ecclesia de Trinitate.* Ir, 14 (1937), 131-146.

101. *La Croix de Jésus du P. Chardon.* SVS, 51 (1937), April, 42-57; reprinted in VDV, 129-141.

102. *Chronique.* OEcumenica, 4 (April, 1937), 445-450.

103. *La catholicité de l'Eglise.* Russie et Chrétienté, April, 1937, 139-164.

104. *France, nation chrétienne.* Sept, May 27, 1937, 6-7.

105. *La condition chrétienne.* VI, 50 (1937), 356-358.

106. *Pour une théologie de l'Eglise.* SVS, 52 (1937), 97-99.

107. *L'unité de l'Eglise et sa dialectique interne.* SVS, 52 (1937), July, 9-29.

108. *Qu'est-ce que l'homme?* (trans. by Erik Peterson). VI, 51 (1937), 9-22.

109. *Il faut que Chrétienté continue.* VI, 51 (1937), 162-164; signed Christianus.

110. *Chronique catholique.* Oecumenica, July 4, 1937, 564-567.

111. *Les grandes Conférences oecuméniques et l'abstention de l'Eglise catholique.* VI, 51 (1937), 182-189; reprinted in Cahiers pour le Protestantisme, 2, 35-52; English trans.: *Rome, Oxford and Edinburgh,* BL, September, 1937.

112. *La crédibilité des révélations privées.* SVS, 53 (1937), October, 29-48; reprinted in SE, 375-392, with supplementary documentary notes.

113. *Bulletin de théologie.* RSPT, 26 (1937), 779-782; 785-794.

114. *Loyauté et correction fraternelle.* VI, 52 (1937), 9-17; reprinted in Cahiers pour le protestantisme, 2, 1-9, and CED, 369-376.

115. *Chronique documentaire des Conférences œcuméniques d'Oxford et d'Edimbourg.* VI, 52 (1937), 31-50; reprinted in Cahiers pour le Protestantisme, 2, 53-72.

116. *Lettre sur Sept.* La Revue catholique des idées et des faits, December 3, 1937, 14-15.

117. CHRETIENS DESUNIS. PRINCIPES D'UN "OECUMENISME" CATHOLIQUE. Cerf, P, 1937. XIX + 403 pp. "Unam Sanctam," 1; English trans.: *Divided Christendom*, London, 1939. French reproduction with no change, Ed. du Cerf, P. 1965.

1938

118. *Chronique catholique.* Oecumenica, January 4, 1938, 726-740.

119. *L'état présent de l'effort catéchistique.* VS, 54 (1938), 89-95.

120. *Pour l'unité de tous les chrétiens.* Cité Nouvelle, Bruxelles, January, 1938; reprinted in Italian in La Roca, January 15, 1948; in Jeunesse et Vie, Bruxelles, January, 1949, 7; in Cahiers de l'Aumonerie Catholique, December, 1950; in Ecclesia, January, 1952; in Bulletin des Officiers d'active, January, 1952.

121. *Pour une étude de la sensibilité protestante.* VI, 55 (1938), 165-172; reprinted in Cahiers pour le protestantisme, 3, 1-12; reprinted in CED, 377-383.

122. *Sur le grand choral de Luther: "C'est un rempart que notre Dieu."* VI, 55 (1938), 195-197; reprinted in Cahiers pour le protestantisme, 3, 59-61.

123. *La signification œcuménique de l'œuvre de Möhler.* Ir, 15 (1938), 113-130.

124. *Note sur l'évolution et l'interprétation de la pensée de Möhler.* RSPT, 27 (1938), 205-212.

125. *L'esprit des Pères d'après Möhler.* SVS, 55 (1938), April, 1-25; reprinted in EME, 1st ed. 1941, 129-148.

126. *Chronique catholique.* Oecumenica, April, 1938, 63-65, 75-76.

127. *L'apolégétique et l'initiative chrétienne.* VI, 57 (1938), 29-36.

128. *Chronique.* Oecumenica, July, 1938, 145-158.

129. *The Reasons for the Unbelief of Our Time.* Integration, II, n. 1, August-September, 1938; n. 3, December, 1938-January, 1939, 10-26 (cf. n. 61).

130. *Chronique catholique.* Oecumenica, October, 1938, 253-258.

131. *Vie de l'Eglise et conscience de la catholicité.* Bull. des Missions, 18 (1938), 153-160; reprinted in EME, 118-127; German trans.: *Das Leben der Kirche und das Bewusstsein ihrer Katholizität*, Catholica, 1938, 1-9.

132. *Je crois en la sainte Eglise.* RJ, 1938, 85-92; reprinted in SE, 9-17.

133. *Bulletin d'histoire des doctrines chrétiennes.* RSPT, 27 (1938), 291-300; 320-322; 332-335.

134. *Bulletin de théologie.* RSPT, 27 (1938), 639-661.

1939

135. *Chronique.* Oecumenica, January, 1939, 342-349.

136. *L'Eglise et l'unité du monde.* RJ, 1939, 6-18.

137. *Autour du renouveau de l'ecclésiologie: la collection "Unam Sanctam."* VI, 61 (1939), 9-32; reprinted in Cahiers pour le protestantisme, 4, 74-99; reprinted in SE, 513-528.

138. *"Frères séparés."* VI, 64 (1939), 162-165.

139. *Chronique.* Oecumenica, April, 1939, 78-83.

140. *Una seria di publicazioni sulla Chiesa: la collezione Unam Sanctam.* OR, July 7, 1939, 2.

141. *The Idea of the Church in St. Thomas Aquinas.* The Thomist, October, 1939, 331-359; French text: *L'idée de l'Eglise chez saint Thomas,* RSPT, 29 (1940), 31-58; EME, 59-91.

142. *Vigilance de Pie XII.* VI + RJ, série de guerre, I, n. 2, November 25, 1939, 166-177.

143. *Schisme.* DTC, 14, 1286-1312.

144. *L'hérésie, déchirement de l'unité,* in *L'Eglise est une. Hommage à Möhler,* P, 1939, 255-269; German trans.: *Die Häresie, der Riss durch die Einheit* in *Die Eine Kirche,* Pa, 1939, 283-301.

145. *Bibliographie critique.* BT, V (1937-1939), 490-505; 523-524; 528-533; 541-542; 745-748.

1940

146. *Der mystische Leib Christi und seine sichtbare Manifestation,* in *Die Kirche Christi,* hrsg. v.O. Iserland, Einsiedeln-Köln, 13-59.

1941

147. *L'Eglise Corps mystique du Christ.* VS, 64 (1941), 242-254.

148. ESQUISSES DU MYSTERE DE L'EGLISE. Ed. du Cerf, P, 1941, 168 pp., "Unam Sanctam," 8; 2nd ed. 1953; 3rd ed. 1963; pocket edition, coll. "Foi Vivante," 18, Ed. du Cerf, P, 1966; English trans.: *The Mystery of the Church,* London, 1960, 1965; Spanish trans.: *Ensayos sobre el misterio della Chiesa,* Vicenza, 1961; Portuguese trans.: *Introdução ao mistério da Igreja;* Sâo Paulo, 1966.

1942

149. *Bulletin d'histoire des doctrines chrétiennes.* RSPT, 30 (1941-1942), 460-464.

1943

150. *Théologie.* DTC, 15, 341-502.

151. *Pour une théologie du vêtement* (trans. from Erik Peterson). Ed. de l'Abeille, Ly, 1943, 23 pp. (cf. n. 75).

1945

152. *Qui est mon prochain?* TC, November 16, 1945.

153. *Prix Nobel.* TC, November 23, 1945.

154. *Vous m'avez recontré chaque jour.* TC, December 7, 1945.

155. *La fête de la vie.* TC (Christmas Number), December 21, 1945.

156. *Simples notes sur la notion catholique de liberté.* Cahiers de la Paroisse universitaire, December, 1945, 43-54; reprinted in SL, 447-457.

1946

157. *Sur le problème de l'acte de foi.* VI, 14 (1946), 44-46.

158. *L'œuvre posthume du P. Mersch.* VS, 74 (1946), 117-124; reprinted in SE, 528-534.

159. *L'Eglise et les Nations.* TC, January 3, 1946.

160. *Lettre à un ami orthodoxe.* TC, January 11, 1946.

161. *Prions pour l'Unité.* TC, January 18, 1946.

162. *Nous répudions la violence.* TC, January 25, 1946.

163. *Retournons-nous au ghetto?* TC, February 8, 1946.

164. *A propos de l'unité chrétienne.* Réforme, n. 47, February 9, 1946, 2.

165. *Dans la nouvelle Constitution, n'oublions pas la famille et les syndicats.* TC, February 15, 1946.

166. *Au-delà des techniques.* TC, February 22, 1946.

167. *Réflexions sur prosélytisme et évangélisation.* Rythmes du Monde, 2, 1946, 58-68; reprinted in SL, 51-64.

168. *A propos du "Journal d'un Pêtre."* VS, 74 (1946), 439-449.

169. *La tentation.* TC, March 8, 1946.

170. *Tuer Tartuffe.* TC, March 15, 1946.

171. *Vraie et fausse sincérité.* TC, March 22, 1946.

172. *Les "Juifs" et les "Trusts."* TC, March 29, 1946.

173. *Rythmes de l'Eglise et du Monde.* VI, 14 (1946) 6-22; German trans. in Universität, 1947.

174. *Le Grand Retour.* TC, April 5, 1946.

175. *Pour un esprit public.* TC, April 12, 1946.

176. *Ce qui s'est passé à Jérusalem.* TC, April 19, 1946.

177. *Jours de communion.* TC, April 26, 1946.

178. *La famille, école de respect.* TC, May 3, 1946.

179. *Civilisation chrétienne.* TC, May 10, 1946.

180. *Les laïcs dans l'Eglise.* TC, May 17, 1946.

181. *Pacifisme.* TC, June 28, 1946.

182. *Rayés de la vie.* TC, July 6, 1946.

183. *Le Problème oecuménique.* Lumières d'Assise, nn. 2-3, 1946, 99-107; reprinted in CED, 79-88; German trans.: *Das ökumenische Problem* in *Wort und Wahrheit*, n. 9, 357-363; Italian trans. in Il Regno, 9, 1946, 16-19; reproduced in part in Missions Populaires diocésaines, Chéry-les-Puilly (Aisne), January, 1964.

184. *La Saint-Barthélemy.* TC, August 23, 1946.

185. *L'Eglise existe.* TC, September 13, 1946.

186. *A ceux qui en veulent encore.* TC, October 11, 1946.

187. *Conversions forcées.* TC, November 8, 1946.

188. *Sacerdoce et laïcat dans l'Eglise.* VI, 14 (1946), 6-39; MO, 18 (1946), 19-56; reprinted in *Problèmes du Clergé diocésain*, n. 2, 1947, Ed. du Vitrail, P, 7-38; German trans.: *Priester und Laie in der Kirche. Um eine "Laikologie,"* in Documente, n. 7, 1947, 390-402; n. 8, 1947, 509-519; Dutch trans.: *Priester en Leek in de Kerk*, Anvers, 1950.

189. *Voici nos armes.* TC, December 6, 1946.

190. *Noël, un beau conte.* Fêtes et Saisons, December, 1946, 4.

191. *Bibliographie critique.* BT, VII (1943-1946), 454-457; 603-613; 638-641.

1947

192. *Bulletin d'ecclésiologie.* RSPT, 31 (1947), 78-96; 272-296; reprinted in SE, 549-592.

193. *Propos d'Epiphanie.* TC, January 3, 1947.

194. *Encore l'Argentine.* TC, January 10, 1947.

195. *Grandeur et tragédie de Luther.* TC, January 24, 1947; German trans. in Dokumente, 3, 1947, 327 ff.

196. *Jésus-Christ, Agneau de Dieu.* Cahiers bibliques de Foi et Vie, January-February, 1947, 46-67; reprinted in VDV, 109-128.

197. *Ökumenische Probleme.* Universitas, 2, 1947, 1269-1272.

198. *Amitié partout.* TC, May 16, 1947.

199. *Trois livres de Pentecôte.* VI, 15 (1947), 37-43; reprinted in SE, 535-541.

200. *Diagnostic.* TC, June 6, 1947.

201. *Cent pour cent chrétiens.* TC, June 20, 1947.

202. *Initiative laïque.* TC, June 27, 1947.

203. *Consciences chrétiennes.* TC, July 4, 1947.

204. *Vacances sans Dieu.* TC, August 1, 1947.

205. *Lettre sur la Saint-Barthélemy.* TC, August 24, 1947.

206. *Théologie de l'Eglise, maison du peuple de Dieu.* Art Sacré, August-September, 1947, 205-220.

207. *Réponse à une enquête sur l'Orient russe.* Humanitas, August-September, 1947, Italie.

208. *Sur la délation.* TC, October 17, 1947.

209. *Sainteté et péché dans l'Eglise.* VI, 15 (1947), 6-40; German trans.: *Heiligkeit und Sünde in der Kirche,* in Dokumente, n. 7 (1948), 531-544.

210. *Notre charité à l'échelle du monde.* TC, November 21, 1947.

211. *Responsables de l'Eglise.* Anneau d'Or, 18 (1947), 13-15.

212. *Noël: une promesse.* TC, December 25, 1947.

1948

213. *Pour une théologie du laïcat.* Etudes, January, 1948, 42-54; February, 1948, 194-218.

214. *Pour les protestants d'Espagne, nous demandons.* TC, January 23, 1948.

215. *Le drame de l'unité chrétienne.* TC, January 23, 1948.

216. *Unité dans la transcendance de la foi.* VI, 15 (1948), 36-38; reprinted in SL, 437-440.

217. *Chronique.* BT, VII (1943-1946), 605-613 (drafted in February, 1948); reprinted in SE, 542-549.

218. *Tendances actuelles de la pensée religieuse en France.* Cahiers du monde nouveau, (1948), 33-50; adapted in German: *Vor einem veitalter der Mission,* in Wort und Wahrheit, August,

1948, 561-579; reprinted with modifications in **Dokumente** (1949), 2, 120-132, and 3, 245-255, under the title: *Entwicklungen in religiösen Denken des heutigen Frankreich.*

219. *Etre du monde sans en être.* TC, March 5, 1948.

220. *Et si nous parlions de Dieu?* TC, March 26, 1948.

221. *Conditions d'un vrai renouvellement.* Jeunesse de l'Eglise, n. 8 (1948), 154-164.

222. *Les chrétiens à la recherche de l'unité.* La femme, la vie, le monde, Bruxelles (1948), 15.

223. *Ma paroisse.* TC, April 9, 1948.

224. *Dimanche se meurt.* TC, April 30, 1948.

225. *Interview.* TC, May 14, 1948.

226. *Les Eglises séparées.* Ecclesia, Encyclopédie populaire des connaissances religieuses, 934-950; reprinted with clarification in Ecclesia, January, 1962, 19-29, 77-85.

227. *Parole de Dieu et inspiration.* Fiches de l'ACJF, nn. 4, 5, 1948.

228. *La femme et la sexualité dans le plan de Dieu.* Fiches de l'ACJF, n. 7, 1948.

229. *Assez de sang.* TC, May 21, 1948.

230. *Lettre sur la liberté religieuse à propos de la situation des protestants d'Espagne.* RN, 7-15 May, 1948, 449-466; reprinted in CED, 387-407.

231. *Présentation simple de l'idée essentielle du dimanche.* MD, 13 (1948), 133-135.

232. *Die Katholiken und die christliche Einheit.* Der Ueberblick, 10 (1948), 13 ff.

233. *A propos des saints canonisés dans les Eglises orthodoxes.* RevSR, 82 (1948), 249-259; reprinted in CED, 289-311.

234. *La grande angoisse de l'Eglise de France.* TC, June 18, 1948.

235. *Faits, problèmes et réflexions à propos du pouvoir d'ordre et des rapports entre de presbytérat et l'épiscopat.* MD, n. 14 (1948), 107-128; reprinted in SE, 275-302.

236. *L'Eglise catholique et le mouvement œcuménique.* VUC, June-July, 1948, 14.

237. *Le grand enjeu des vacances.* TC, July 22, 1948.

238. *Pour une prédiction et une liturgie réelle.* MD. n. 16 (1948), 75-87; reprinted in SL, 161-173.

239. *Le dialogue avec nos frères séparés est-il un dialogue de sourds?* TC, August 27, 1948.

240. *Le réarmement moral.* TC, September 3, 1948.

241. *Le Vatican et l'œcuménisme.* Le Monde, September 7, 1948.

242. *Le réalisme apostolique de notre père saint Dominique.* France dominicaine, 1, 1948, August, 9-12.

243. *Le Seigneur n'a pas pris de vacances.* TC, October 8, 1948.

244. *Nous n'avons plus le temps d'être bons.* TC, October 29, 1948.

245. *Le semaine de la bonté.* TC, December 17, 1948.

246. *Pourquoi le Peuple de Dieu doit-il sans cesse se réformer?* Ir, 22 (1948), 365-394.

247. *Mission de la Paroisse,* in *Structures sociales et Pastorale paroissiale* (Congrès national de Lille), P, 1948, 48-65; reprinted in L'Union, revue mensuelle du clergé paroissial, May-June, 1948, 27-39; reprinted SL, 175-205.

248. *Een theologie von den leeken stand.* Kathol. Archief., III, 1948, 66-70.

249. *La théologie du dimanche,* in *Le Jour du Seigneur,* Ed. Laffont, P, 1948, 131-180.

250. *Prèface à E. Joly : saint Paul et l'Apocalypse,* Ed. Bloud, P. 1948.

251. *Le salut des "Grecs schismatiques" d'après un théologien du XIIIe siécle* (Roger Marston, Quodl. 11, 10). Mémorial Louis Petit, Bucarest, 1948, 51-55.

252. LEUR RESISTANCE. MEMORIAL DES OFFICIERS EVADES, ANCIENS DE COLDITZ ET DE LUBECK. Grand 8º de 164 p., P, 1948.

253. HISTOIRE ILLUSTREE DE L'EGLISE, 2, XVIII : LA CATHOLICITE EN MARCHE. REALISATIONS ET ESPOIRS DE L'EGLISE. (XIXe ET XXe CENTURIES). Genève, 1946-1948, 327-392.

254. *Nous aimerons cette année qui commence.* TC, December 30, 1948.

255. *Trop quelconques.* Nancy. Journal d'information du Congrès eucharistique national, December 31, 1948.
Contributions à: *CATHOLICISME, HIER, AUJOUR-D'HUI, DEMAIN.* Encyclopjédie directed by G. Jasquemet, Letouzey et Ané, P, I, 1948.

256. *Abjuration,* cols. 38-40.

257. *Acéphales,* col. 76.

258. *Adventistes,* cols. 168-169.

259. *Alliance Baptiste Mondiale,* col. 337.

260. *Alliance Evangélique universelle,* cols. 337-338.

261. *Alliance Israélite universelle,* col. 339.

262. *Alliance Presbytérienne,* col. 339.

263. *Alliance universelle pour l'amitié internationale par les Eglises,* col. 340.

264. *Alliance universelle des unions chrétiennes de jeunes gens,– de jeunes filles,* col. 340.

265. *Anabaptistes,* cols. 500-501.

266. *Anglicanisme,* cols. 561-571.

267. *Antinomisme,* col. 647.

268. *Apostolicité,* cols. 728-730.

269. *Armée du Salut,* cols. 841-842.

270. *Arminiens,* col. 845.

271. *Arminius,* cols. 845-846.

272. *Arndt (Ernest-Maurice),* col. 852.

273. *Arndt (Jean),* cols. 852-853.

274. *Articles fondamentaux,* cols. 882-883.

275. *Autocéphales (Eglises),* cols. 1088-1089.

276. *Autonomes (Eglises),* col. 1093.

277. *Baptême chez les dissidents,* cols. 1229-1231.

278. *Baptistes,* cols. 1236-1237.

279. *Barth (Karl),* cols. 1267-1268.

1949

280. *Le rôle des hérésies dans l'histoire de l'Eglise.* JECF de l'enseignement libre, January 18, 1949, 6.

281. *Obstacles et progrès au royaume de la vérité.* TC, January 14, 1949.

282. *Bernanos romancier de la grâce et théologien de l'Eglise.* La Nef, January, 1949, 44-48; reprinted in *Georges Bernanos, Les Cahiers du Rhône,* 1949, 89-98. (cf. n. 79).

283. *Sur deux aspects du travail apostolique : le prêtre, chef de peuple et apôtre.* Prêtres diocésains, February, 1949, 81-89; reprinted in SL, 207-216.

284. *Les images pour le peuple de Dieu.* TC, February 18, 1949.

285. *Les bourreaux sont toujours vaincus.* TC, February 25, 1949.

286. *L'homme de Dieu et l'homme de l'homme.* TC, March 4, 1949.

287. *Les faux prophètes.* TC, March 13, 1949.

288. *Commencement d'un nouveau dialogue.* Réforme, n. 214, April 23, 1949: réponse au pasteur Finet à propos de l'article "Au Père Congar."

289. *Les trois niveaux de notre fidélité.* TC, June 17, 1949.

290. *La frauternité universelle.* Le Messager du Sacré-Cœur, July-August, 1949, 249-253; reprinted in SL, 441-446.

291. *Lire la Bible "dans 'Eglise."* TC, August 5, 1949.

292. *Le prophète Péguy.* TC, August 26, 1949.

293. *Que pouvons-nous trouver dans les Ecritures?* VS, 81 (1949), 227-231; reprinted in Integrity, N.Y., February, 1954, 9-10; reprinted in VDV, 11-15.

294. *Faim et soif de justice.* TC, September 16, 1949.

295. *L'Ancien Testament, témoin du Christ.* VI, 1949, II, 335-343; reprinted in VDV, 17-24.

296. *T.C. et l'objection de conscience.* TC, October 21, 1949.

297. *Que votre règne arrive.* TC, November 4, 1949.

298. *De Josué à Samuel.* Fiches de l'ACJF, n. 17, 1949.

299. *David et Salomon.* Fiches de l'ACJF, n. 18, 1949.

300. *Les prophètes.* Fiches de l'ACJF, nn. 19-20, 1949.

301. *L'Eglise a toute sa jeunesse devant elle.* TC, December 2, 1949.

302. *Attendons-nous encore le Christ?* VS, 81 (1949), 451-455 (talk given on Radio Luxembourg, December 7, 1947); reprinted in Ecclesia, November, 1950, 119-121; in VDV, 143-147.

303. *Les directives du Saint-Siège en matiére d'œcumènisme.* VUC, 1949, 2-5.

304. *Bulletin d'apologétique.* RSPT, 33 (1949), 68-75.

305. *Bulletin d'histoire des doctrines chrétiennes.* RSPT, 33 (1949), 215-222; 241-243; 250-253.

306. *Bulletin de théologie dogmatique.* RSPT, 33 (1949), 450-454; 456-464.
Contributions à : *CATHOLICISME, HIER, AUJOUR-D'HUI, DEMAIN,* Encyclopédie directed by G. Jacquemet, Letouzey et Ané, P, II, 1949.

307. *Bibliques (sociétés) Protestantes,* cols. 26-29.

308. *Bishop (Edmund),* col. 71.

309. *Blanchard (Pierre-Louis),* col. 73.

310. *Bohèmes (Les Frères),* cols. 109-111.

311. *Bolsec (Jérôme-Hermès),* cols. 117-118.

312. *Bordas-Demoulin (Jean-Baptiste),* col. 161.

347. *Christianisme au XXᵉ siècle*, col. 1090.

348. *Cluny (Communauté protestante de)*, cols. 1271-1272.

349. *Cocceius (Jean Koch)*, col. 1274.

350. *Communion ecclésiastique*, col. 1375.

351. *Concile*, cols. 1439-1443.

352. *Confession (communauté religieuse)*, cols. 1504-1505.

353. *Confession (Profession de foi)*, cols. 1507-1508.

354. *Confirmation (chez les protestants)*, cols. 1520-1521.

1950

355. *L'appel œcuménique et l'œuvre du Saint-Esprit.* VS, 82 (1950), 5-12; reprinted in CED, 71-78.

356. *Note sur les mots "Confession," "Eglise," "Communion."* Ir, 1950, 3-36; reprinted in CED, 211-242.

357. *Pour que tous ceux qui sont du Christ soient réunis dans la maison de la lumière.* TC, January 20, 1950.

358. *Culpabilité et responsobilité collectives.* VI, 1950, I, 259-284; 387-407.

359. *Mentalité "de droite" et intégrisme.* VI, 1950, II, 644-666.

360. *Luther vu par les catholiques, ou de l'utilité de faire l'histoire de l'histoire.* RSPT, 34 (1950), 507-518; Swedish trans. in Credo, Stockholm, 1953, 219-221: *Luther sedd med Katolska ögon;* German trans. in Evangelische-Lutherische Kirchenzeitung, September, 1951; reprinted in VUC, March, 1950, 3-6; reprinted in CED, 437-451.

361. *Ecuménisme et fidélité catholique.* TC, March 17, 1950.

362. *De la guerre à la paix.* TC, April 21, 1950.

363. *L'Eucharistie et l'Eglise de la Nouvelle Alliance.* VS, 82 (1950), 347-372; reprinted in VDV, 185-206.

364. *Position des Orthodoxes et des Anglicans en regard d'une position "protestante" en ecclésiologie.* IR, 1950, 298-308.

365. *Incidence ecclésiologique d'un thème de dévotion mariale.* MSR, 1950, 277-292.

366. *Il faut construire l'Eglise en nous.* TC, July 7, 1950.

367. *Ordre temporel et vérité religieuse.* Intervention au débat des Intellectuals français du mars 1950 sur la Tolérance, appeared in Supplément Sciences religieuses de Recherches et Débats, July, 1950, n. 10; reprinted in SL, 458-470; reprinted in DC, June 15, 1952, 729-738; Spanish trans. in Documentos, n. 10, 1952, 39-50.

368. *Le nouveau dogme.* TC, November 3, 1950.

369. *Un journaliste suisse a présenté en février un projet semblable au nouveau plan Schuman.* TC, November 3, 1950.

370. *Mission du prêtre dans l'évolution du monde actuel.* Les Cahiers du Clergé rural, November, 1950, 385-393; reprinted in SL, 227-241.

371. *Qu'est-ce qu'un laïc?* SVS, 4 (1950) November, 363-392; résumé in Theology Digest, 1953, 8-12; Spanish trans.: *Que es un laico?* Cuandernos Heroica, Buenos Aires, 1960.

372. VRAIE ET FAUSSE REFORME DANS L'EGLISE. Ed du Cerf, P, 1950, 648 P., "Unam Sanctam," 20; Spanish trans. *Falsas y verdaderas Reformas en la Iglesia,* May, 1954.

373. *Préface à F. Dvornik : Le schisme dè Photius.* Ed. du Cerf, P, 1950, "Unam Sanctam," 19, 7-21.

374. *Pour le dialogue avec le mouvement œcuménique.* Verbum Caro, 4 (1950), 111-123.

375. *Bulletin de l'histoire des doctrines chrétiennes.* RSPT, 34 (1950), 391-392; 396-399.

376. *Bulletin de théologie dogmatique.* RSPT, 34 (1950), 636-637; 640; 648-655; reprinted in SE, 601-609.

377. *Le Congrès généal des religieux n'a pas été un "coup de théâre."* TC, December 1, 1950.

378. *Un Seigneur, une Eglise, un salut* (trans. by A.-M. Hunter: *The Unity of New Testament,* London, 1944). Delachaux et Niestlé, December 12, 1950.

379. *Pour l'unité de tous les chrétiens.* Cahiers de l'aumôneirie catholique, n. 9, 1950, 261-263.

380. *Rapprochements entre chrétiens: redécouverte protestante.* VUC, n. 27, 1950, 5-7.

1951

381. *Semaine de l'Unité 1951.* TC, January 19, 1951.

382. *Structure du sacerdoce chrétien.* MD, n. 27 (1951), 51-85; reprinted in SE, 239-273; Spanish trans. (extracts) in Selecciones de Teologia, 13 (1965), 89-97.

383. *Notes théologiques à propos de l'Assomption.* L'Amitié, January, 1951, 6-15; reprinted in Dieu Vivant, n. 18 (1951), 107-112; reprinted in VDV, 219-226.

384. *Rapproachements entre chrétiens: redécouverte catholique.* VUC, January 29, 1951, 2-5.

385. *Considérations sur le schisme d'Israël dans la perspective des divisions chrétiennes.* Proche-Orient chrétien, 1 (1951), 169-191; reprinted in CED, 165-210.

386. *Wahre und falsche Reform in der Kirche.* Una Sancta Rundbriefe, n. 2 (1951), 1-4.

387. *La participacion de los laicos en el gobierno de la Iglesia.* Revista de Estudios Politicos, 39 (1951), 27-56.

388. *Une réponse fraternelle aux difficultés protestantes sur le dogme de l'Assumption.* VUC, February 30, 1951, 8-10.

389. *Examen de conscience d'un archevêque* (trans. from Cardinal Manning). MO, 62 (March, 1951), 20-44.

390. *A propos du catéchisme.* MO, 62 (March, 1951), 67-68.

391. *The Ecumenical Movement.* Pax Romana, March-April, 1951, 7.

392. *Lendemain de Pâques.* TC, April 6, 1951.

393. *Catholiques et protestants devant l'incarnation du Christ.* Cahiers de Neuilly, April, 1951, 12-40.

394. *Un essai de théologie sur le sacerdoce catholique. La thèse de l'abbé Long-Hasselmans: introduction et remarques critiques.* RevSR, 25 (1951), n. 2, 187-188; n. 3, 288-304.

395. *Le peuple fidèle et la fonction prophétique de l'Eglise.* Ir, 1951, 289-312; 440-466.

396. *"Dieu a besoin des hommes": propos d'un théologien.* VI, 1951, II, 4-22.

397. *Hors de l'Eglise, pas de salut.* Ecclesia, June, 1951, 34-39.

398. *Espérance et libération du mal.* Intervention à la Semaine des Intellectuels catholiques: *Espoir humain et espérance chrétienne,* P, 1951, 65-75.

399. *A Budapest. Plan bleu ou témoins de la liberté de l'Evangile.* TC, July 6, 1951.

400. *Pourquoi nous combattons. Partir des faits.* TC, July 6, 1951.

401. *Royaume, Eglise et Monde.* Recherches et Débats, nn. 15-16, July, 1951, 2-42.

402. *A propos du Directoire des évêques. Les laïcs font aussi l'œuvre de l'Eglise.* TC, August 24, 1951.

403. *Marie, l'Eglise et le Christ. Pour une célébration œcuménique du concile de Chalcédoine.* VI, 1951, II, 6-22; 67-88; reprinted in CME, 9-53.

404. *L'Unité chrétienne au congrès de l'apostolat des laïcs: Rome 7-14 octobre 1951.* VUC, November, 1951.

405. *Le gout du merveilleux n'est pas la foi.* TC, November 9, 1951.

406. *Le purgatoire*, in *Le mystère de la mort et sa célébration*, Ed. du Cerf, P, 1951, "Lex Orandi," 12, 279-336.

407. *Bulletin d'histoire des doctrines chétiennes*. RSPT, 35 (1951), 331-334; 340-345; 363-365.

408. *Bulletin de théologie dogmatique*. RSPT, 35 (1951), 591-603; 616-638; reprinted in part (sacraments, 629-636) in SE, 609-618.

409. *Une fois de plus Noël*. Ecclesia, December, 1951, 3-6; Spanish trans.: *Natividad, ha venido una persona*, in Criterio, December 1, 1953, 947-948.

410. *La vocation du chrétien est-elle paradoxale?* TC, December 28, 1951.

1952

411. *L'Eglise travaille-t-elle pour la paix?* Jeunesse et Vie, Bruxelles, January, 1952, 10-11; reprinted in L'aimitié internationale, n. 17, March, 1952, and in Le Nouvel Alascien, February 18, 1962.

412. *A propos d'une excommunication. Je crois à l'Eglise Une, sainte* . . . TC, January 11, 1952.

413. *Brisure entre l'Orient et l'Occident*. TC, January 18, 1952; in La Vie Catholique illustrée et l'Echo illustré de Genève.

414. *Nos fréres protestants*. TC, January 18, 1952; reprinted in La Vie Catholique Illustrée et l'Echo illustré de Genève.

415. *Dieu écrit droti avec des lignes courbes. 1952 Ecuménique*. TC, January 25, 1952.

416. *Au monde et pas du monde*. SVS, 6 (1952), 5-47.

417. *Cephas, Céphalè, caput*. Rev. du Moyen Age Latin, January-March, 1952, 5-42.

418. LE CHRIST, MARIE ET L'EGLISE. Ed. Desclée de Brouwer, P, 1952, 109 pp.; German trans.: *Christus, Maria, Kirche*. Mainz, 1959; English trans.: *Christ, our Lady and the Church*, London, 1957; Italian trans. *Il Cristo, Maria e la Chiesa*, T, 1964; Catalan trans.

419. *Position de l'Eglises: dualité et unité*. Forma gregis (1952), April-May; reprinted in SE, 45-67.

420. *Amica contestatio*, in *Intercommunion*, edited by D. Baillie et J. Marsch. London, 1952, 141-151; reprinted CED, 243-254.

421. *La personne et la liberté humaine dans l'anthropologie orientale*. Recherches et Débats, May, 1952, 99-111; reprinted in CED, 273-288.

422. *Bulletin d'histoire des Institutions*. RSPT, 36 (1952), 250-253.

423. *Bulletin d'histoire des doctrines chrétiennes.* RSPT, 36 (1952), 551-560; 573-575; 578-582.

424. *Le Saint-Esprit et le Corps apostolique, réalisateurs de l'œuvre du Christ.* RSPT, 36 (1952), 613-625; reprinted in EME, 2e éd., 129-179 (cf. n. 463).

425. *El problema actual de una teologia del laicado.* Criterio, 25 (July, 1952), 1513-1516.

426. *Compte rendu de Ch. Journet: L'Eglise du Verbe Incarné.* BT, VIII (1947-1953), 746-756; reprinted in SE, 659-669.

427. *Ecclesia ab Abel,* in *Abhandlugen über Theologie und Kirche. Festschrift für Karl Adam.* Patmos-Verlag, D, 1952, 79-108.

428. *Le christianisme doctrine de la liberté,* in *L'Eglise et la liberté, Semaine des Intellectuels catholiques,* P, 1952, 16-32; English trans.: *Christianity and Freedom. A Symposium.*

429. *Mammon n'est pas le Dieu du christianisme.* TC, August 1, 1952.

430. *Le superflu appartient à tous les hommes.* TC, August 8, 1952.

431. *L'espérance de ceux qui ont faim gronde comme untonnere.* TC, August 15, 1952.

432. *Le chanoine Albert Gratieux* (1874-1951). VUC, 45 (1952), 4-8; reprinted in Semaine religieuse du diocèse de Châlons-sur-Marne, August 22, 1952, 380-388.

433. *De la responsabilité comme valeur fondamentale d'une spiritualité des laïcs.* Présence, September-October, 1952, 9-15; German trans.: *Verantwortung als Seelsorglicher Grundwert der "Laienfrömmigkeit,"* in Anima, Vierteljahrschrift für praktische Seelsorge, 1952, n. 2, 148-154.

434. *Marie et l'Eglise chez les protestants.* Etudes Mariales, Bull. de la Société Française d'Etudes mariales, 10 (1952), 87-106; reprinted in CED, 431-518.

435. *Het priesterschap van alle gelovigen.* Actio catholica, Jààrgang 15 (1952), 337-360.

436. *Les conditions théologiques d'un pluralisme,* in *Tolérance et communauté humaine: chrétiens dans un monde divisé.* Cahiers de l'Actualité religieuse, Casterman, P, 1952, 191-223; reprinted in SL, 401-435; English trans. in *Tolerance and the Catholic,* NY, 1955: *The Theological conditions of any Pluralism,* 166-199.

437. *Le Christ-Roi.* TC, October 24, 1952; Dutch trans. in De Bazuin, October 25, 1952.

438. *Préface à: G. van Ackeren: Sacra doctrina, the subject of the first question of the Summa.* R, 1952, 13-18.

439. *Marie et l'Eglise dans la pensée protestante*. VUC, December, 1952, 4-6.

440. *A propos des vestigia Ecclesiae*. VUC, 39 (1952), 3-5.

1953

441. *Le pharisaïsme des publicains*. TC, January 9, 1953.

442. *Témoignage sur l'Una Sancta*. VS, 88 (1953), 54-67.

443. *Efficacité temporelle et message évangélique*. RN, January 15, 1953, 32-49; reprinted in SL, 357-377; reprinted in Documentos, 11-12, 61-80.

444. *OEcuménisme et polémique confessionnelle*. RSPT, 37 (1953), 203-207.

445. *"L'affaire Finaly" et la conscience chrétienne*. TC, February 20, 1953.

446. *Baptêmes d'enfants et liberté de la foi*. TC, February 27, 1953.

447. *Du nouveau sur la question de Pierre? Le Saint-Pierre de M. O. Cullmann*. VI, I, February, 1953, 17-43.

448. *Conception chrétienne de l'histoire*. Bulletin de la Communauté Saint-Séverin, 21 (March, 1953), 11-17; reprinted in SL, 305-313.

449. *La participation des fidèles à l'Eucharistie d'après la Tradition et le Magistère catholique*. LV, n. 7, 1953, 54-72 (dated December, 1952).

450. *Le mystère du Temple de Dieu et l'économie de sa présence dans le monde*. L'Année théologique augustinienne, 4, (1953), fasc. 1-2, 1-12.

451. *Notes sur notre sacerdoce*. Cahiers de l'Aumônerie catholique, n. 21, May, 1953, 7-13; reprinted in SL, 109-122.

452. L'EGLISE CATHOLIQUE DEVANT LA QUESTION RACIALE. Unesco, P, 1953; 63 pp.; German trans.: *Die katholische Kirche und die Rassenfrage*, Recklinghausen, 1961; English trans.: *The Catholic Church and the Race question*, P, 1953; Spanish trans.: *La Iglesia católica y la cuestión racial*, Unesco, P, 1953.

453. *Dimensions de la foi*. VI, I, June, 1953, 114-121.

454. *L'Esprit-Saint dans l'Eglise*. LV, n. 10, June, 1953, 51-74; reprinted in VDV, 165-184.

455. *Les attitudes de l'Eglise en face des faits de race*. Recherches et Débats, 6 (1953), 51-63.

456. *Palestine, patrie de notre être spirituel*. TC, August 21, 1953.

457. *L'Eglise et les races*. Le Courrier de l'Unesco, August-September, 1953, 6; French, English, Spanish versions.

458. *Quand Israël redevient un peuple.* TC, September 4, 1953.

459. *Quand Israël répudie l'argent.* TC, September 18, 1953.

460. *Réflexions sur Israël. Menace d'embourgeoisement. Point de vue arabe.* TC, September 25, 1953.

461. *L'avenir des prêtres-ouvriers.* TC, September 25, 1953.

462. JALONS POUR UNE THEOLOGIE DU LAICAT. Ed. du Cerf, P, 1953, 685 pp., "Unam Sanctam," 23; 2nd ed. 1954; 3rd ed. 1964, with appendix: revision of the first two editions, 647-669; German trans.: *Der Laie,* St, 1957; English trans.: *Lay People in the Church,* London, 1957, 1965; extracts in Downside Review, Winter, 1955-1956, 17-37; Spanish trans.: *Jalones para una Teologia del Laicado,* Ba, 1961; Italian trans.: *Per una Teologia del Laicato,* Brescia, 1966; Portuguese trans.: *Os leigos na Igreja,* Herder, Sâo Paulo, 1966.

463. *Le Saint-Esprit et le Corps apostolique, realisateurs de l'œuvre du Christ.* RSPT, 37 (1953), 24-48 (for continuation and conclusion see n. 424); reprinted in EME, 129-179.

464. *Bulletin d'histoire des doctrines chrétiennes.* RSPT, 37 (1953), 499-502; 549-565; 570-573.

465. *Bulletin de théologie.* RSPT, 37 (1953), 733-737; 748-769; reprinted in SE, 618-640.

466. *Bibliographie critique.* BT, VIII, 2 (1947-1953), 746-756; 783-785; 786-794; 814-815; 975-977; 1051; 1211-1232: reprinted in SE, 640-658.

467. *Le problème du mal* in *Essai sur Dieu, l'homme et l'univers,* Ed. Casterman, P, 1953, 551-594; Italian trans.: *Il problema del Male,* in *Dio, l'Uomo e l'Universo,* Ed. Marietti, T, 1953, 537-580; 611-612; English trans.: *The Problem of Evil,* in *God, man and the universe,* 1954, 393-421; German trans.: *Das Problem des Uebels,* in *Gott, Mensch, Universum,* Koln-Graz, 1964, chap. XVII, 711-759; Portuguese trans., Porto, 1956, 683-736.

468. *Considération sur l'objection de conscience.* Teaching teams, 3rd trimester 1952-1953, 80-86; reprinted in *l'Armée et la Vie nationale,* Ly, 1962.

469. *Laïcat.* Teaching teams, first trimester, 1953-1954.

470. *The race question in catholic Tradition.* The Sword, November-December, 1953, 18-22.

471. *Un livre important pour étudier la Parole de Dieu.* TC, December 18, 1953.

472. *Avertissement à A. Gratieux: Le mouvement slavophile à la veille de la Révolution,* Ed. du Cerf, P, 1953, "Unam Sanctam," 25, 7-17.

473. *Groupes sociaux humains et laïcat d'Eglise.* MO, December, 1953, 25-40; reprinted in SL, 315-328.

474. *Moral Dilemmas. Spiritual Maturity.* Bl, 24 (1953), December, 528-535.

475. *Hors de l'Eglise pas de salut. Destin et sens d'une formule.* VUC, December, 1953, 3-5; reprinted in *Oekumenische Centrale Materialdienst,* 1956: *Ausserhalb der Kirche kein Heil;* Swedish trans.: *Utanför Kyrkan ingen frälsning,* in Lumen, 1, 1. Argang, October, 1957, 5-22.

476. *Jalons pour une théologie du laïcat d'Eglise.* MO, n. 92 (December, 1953), 25-40.

477. *L'ecclésiologie de saint Bernard. Saint Bernard théologien.* Analecta Sacri Ordinis Cisterciensis, 1953, 136-190; German trans. abridged in Bernhard von Clairvaux, Mönch und Mystiker, Wiesbaden, 1955, 76-119.

1954

478. *Le Saint Sépulcre ne doit pas rester comme il est actuellement un symbole de la désunion des chrétiens.* TC, January 15, 1954.

479. *Enotès kai Oikoumenismos enopion tès christianikès Suneideseos.* Katholike, Athens, February 5-12, 1954; appeared in French in AOe, *Le problème de l'union et de l'œcuménisme devant la conscience chrétienne,* 27-38.

480. *Après neuf cents ans: juillet 1054-janvier 1954.* Proche-Orient chrétien, January, 1954.

481. *Marie et l'Eglise dans la pensée patristique.* RSPT, 38 (1954), 3-38.

482. *Jésus-Christ en France.* VI, I, February, 1954, 113-130; reprinted in SL, 243-256.

483. *Le Christ, l'Eglise et la grâce dans l'économie de l'espérance chrétienne.* Istina, April, 1954, 132-158; English trans. distributed at Evanston, 1964.

484. *Bulletin d'histoire des institutions chrétiennes.* RSPT, 38 (1954), 715-731.

485. *Bulletin de théologie.* RSPT, 38 (1954), 736-739; reprinted in SE, 669-672.

486. *David et Salomon, types du Christ en ses deux avènements.* VS, 91 (1954), 323-340; reprinted in VDV, 149-164.

487. *Dogme christologique et ecclésiologie. Vérité et limites d'un parallèle,* in Grillmeier-Bacht: *Das Konzil von Chalkedon,* t. III, Würzburg, 1954, 239-263; reprinted SE, 69-104.

488. *Regards et réflexions sur la christologie de Luther,* in Grillmeier-Bacht: *Das Konzil von Chalkedon,* t. III, Würzburg, 1954, 457-486; reprinted CED, 453-489.

489. *Neuf cents après. Notes sur le "Schisme Oriental,"* 1054-1954, in *L'Eglise et les Eglises,* studies in honor of Dom Lambert Beauduin, Chevetogne, 1954, 1, 3-95; published separately, 102 pp.; German trans.: *Zerrissene Christenheit,* Wien, 1959; English trans.: *After Nine Hundred Years,* NY, 1959; Spanish trans.: *Christianos ortodoxos,* Ba, 1963.

Contributions to: *CATHOLICISME, HIER, AUJOURD'HUI, DEMAIN,* encyclopedia directed by G. Jacquemet, Letouzey et Ané, P, III, 1954.

490. *Congrégationalistes,* cols. 10-12.

491. *Conseil œcuménique des Eglises,* col. 75.

492. *Constant (Gustave-Léon-Marie-Joseph),* cols. 93-94.

493. *Controverse,* cols. 154-156.

494. *Corps mystique (Vocabulaire),* cols. 212-213.

495. *Cosin (John),* col. 226.

496. *Court (Antoine),* col. 248.

497. *Cowley-Fathers,* col. 266.

498. *Croix-Bleue (La),* cols. 342-343.

499. *Crypto-calvinistes,* col. 357.

500. *Darby, Darbysme,* cols. 467-468.

501. *Dénomination,* col. 612.

502. *Diaconesses,* cols. 719-721.

503. *Dialectique (Théologie protestante),* cols. 738-739.

504. *Disciples du Christ,* col. 879.

505. *Dissident,* col. 895.

506. *Dogmatique,* cols. 949-951.

507. *Döllinger,* cols. 972-974.

508. *Dominis (Marc-Antoine de),* cols. 1005-1006.

509. *Dordrecht (Synode de),* col. 1036.

510. *Drey (Jean-Sébastien),* cols. 1085-1086.

511. *Dvornik (François),* cols. 1213-1214.

512. *Ecclésial,* cols. 1239-1240.

513. *Economie (Dans la théologie orientale),* cols. 1305-1307.

514. *Ecosse (Protestantisme),* cols. 1311-1313.

515. *Eglise (vocabulaire)*, cols. 1407-1408.

516. *Eglise et Etat*, cols. 1430-1441.

1955

517. *Les trois âges de la vie spirituelle*. VS, 92 (1955), 115-129; reprinted in VDV, 367-379.

518. *Eglise orthodoxe et unité*. Recherches et Débats, May 1, 1955.

519. *Réponse*. La Pensée catholique, 39 (1955), 51-54.

520. *Le saint engagé dans le monde*. Bucéphale, special number for Chartres, 1955, 8-10; reprinted in VS, 96 (1957), 401-408; reprinted in VDV, 359-366; English trans.: *In the World and not of the World*, in Scripture, n. 9, April, 1957, 53-59.

521. *Les souvenirs de Godefroy de Bouillon à Jérusalem*. Etudes ardennaises, n. 3 (1955), 7-20; n. 5 (1956), 16-24.

522. *Das Priestertum aller Glaübigen und die Pfarrei*. Anima, 10, 1955, 207 ff.

523. *Bulletin d'histoire des doctrines chrétiennes*. RSPT, 39 (1955), 318-320.

524. *Bulletin d'histoire des doctrines médiévales*. RSPT, 39 (1955), 432-449.

525. *Marie et l'Eglise: perspectives médiévales*. RSPT, 39 (1955), 408-412; reprinted in SE, 682-686.

526. *Préface à H. Rahner: Marie et l'Eglise*, Ed. du Cerf, P, 1955, "Unam Sanctam," 29, 7-10.

1956

527. LA PENTECOTE—CHARTRES 1956. Ed. du Cerf, P, 1956, 115 pp.; English trans.: *The Church and Pentecost*, in *The Mystery of the Temple*, London, 1960, 1965; Castillian trans.: *Pentecostes*, Ba, 1961; Catalan trans.: *Pentecostès*, Ba, 1961; German trans.: *Nun bitten wir den heiligen Geist*, Recklinghausen, 1962; Italian trans.: *Pentecoste*, 1962.

528. *Le Tiers-Ordre dans le service dominicain de l'apostolat catholique*. France dominicaine, April-May, 1956, 126-136.

529. *Il problema delle razze nell'Unione Sud-Africana e la coscienza cristiana*. La Missione, June, 1956, 7-18.

530. *Theology of the Apostolate*. Conference given in English to the students of the "Beaufort Society," May 2, 1956, at Cambridge; published in World Mission, NY, VII, 1956, 283-294; in New Life, London, September-October, 1956, 164-174; in Bulletin d'Orientations œcumeniques, Beyrouth, July-August, 1956, 11-19; reprinted in SL, 11-21.

531. *Notes d'histoire des institutions et des doctrines médiévales.* RSPT, 40 (1956), 754-780.

Contributions to: *CATHOLICISME, HIER, AUJOUR-D'HUI, DEMAIN*, encyclopedia directed by G. Jacquemet, Letouzey et Ané, P, IV, 1956.

532. *Enthousiastes*, cols. 262-263.

533. *Episcopaliens*, cols. 330-331.

534. *Episcopalisme*, cols. 331-335.

535. *Eraste, Erastianisme*, cols. 375-376.

536. *"Etudes théologiques et religieuses,"* col. 623.

537. *Etudiants (Fédération universelle des Associations chrétiennes d')*, cols. 624-625.

538. *Evangélique*, cols. 752-754.

539. *Evangélique (Communauté)*, cols. 754-755.

540. *Evangélisme*, cols. 764-765.

541. *"Evangile et liberté,"* col. 770.

542. *Evêques (en dehors du catholicisme)*, cols. 825-828.

543. *Ex cathedra*, col. 867.

544. *Fait dogmatique et foi ecclésiastique*, cols. 1059-1067.

545. *Fallot (Tommy)*, col. 1070.

546. *Fareinistes ou Flagellants*, col. 1095.

547. *Farel (Guillaume)*, cols. 1095-1096.

548. *Fédérale (Théologie)*, cols. 1132-1133.

549. *Fédération luthérienne universelle*, col. 1134.

550. *Fédération protestante de France*, col. 1138.

551. *Fessler (Joseph)*, cols. 1213-1214.

552. *Fidéisme*, col. 1261.

553. *Fixisme*, col. 1323.

554. *Flacius*, cols. 1324-1325.

555. *Fondamentalisme*, cols. 1413-1414.

556. *Fox (George)*, cols. 1480-1481.

557. *Frank (Sébastien)*, cols. 1530-1531.

558. *Freytag (Alexandre)*, col. 1643.

559. *Froschammer (Jakob)*, cols. 1650-1651.

560. *Gallicanisme*, cols. 1731-1739.

561. *Gardiner (Etienne, Stephen)*, cols. 1757-1758.

562. *Geiger (François)*, col. 1800.

563. *Gerhard (Jean)*, col. 1880.

1957

564. *Une étude sur Alexandre III.* RSPT, 41 (1957), 44-48.

565. *Vie dans le monde et vie dans le Seigneur.* VS, 96 (1957), 401-408; reprinted in VDV, 359-366 (cf. 520).

566. *Préface à Louis Evely: C'est toi cet homme.* P, 1957, 7-14; American trans.: *That man is you,* Westminster, Maryland, 1964, VII-XIV.

567. *Brève histoire des courants de pensée dans l'anglicanisme.* Istina, 4 (1957), 133-164; reprinted in CED, 315-354.

568. *L'organisation interne dans l'Eglise anglicane.* (Trans. from Bishop Bell), Istina, 4 (1957), 165-174.

569. *Quatre questions et trois réponses sur la pluralité des mondes habités.* Petite Revue, Suppl. littéraire du Nouvel Alsacien, May 22, 1957, 1-3.

570. *Les deux formes du Pain de Vie.* Petite Revue, Suppl. littéraire du Nouvel Alsacien, July 10, 1957; Spanish trans.: *Las dos formas del pan de vida* in *Criterio,* Natividad, 1957, 889-891.

571. *Le sacerdoce de l'Evangile, le sacerdoce aaronique et les sacerdoces païens.* Bull. du Cercle Saint-Jean-Baptiste, June-July, 1957, 193-204; reprinted in Evangéliser, Bruxelles, January-February, 1959, 288-304; reprinted in SL, 91-107.

572. *Salvation and the Non-Catholics,* BL, July-August, 1957, 290-300; French text, RevSR, 32 (1958), 53-65 (n. 583); reprinted in SE, 433-444; German trans.: *Das Heil der Nicht-Katholiken,* in *Theologisches Digest,* 1959, 8-16.

573. *Unità dell'Umanità e vocazione dei Popoli.* La Missione, July-September, 1957, 7-17; published in French, SVS, 11 (1958), 70-87; SE, 163-180.

574. *Maître Rufin et son De bono pacis.* RSPT, 41 (1957), 428-444.

575. *Le sens de l' "Economie" salutaire dans la "théologie" de saint Thomas d'Aquin (Somme Théologique).* Festgabe J. Lortz, II, B. Grimm, Baden-Baden, 1957, 73-122.

576. *L'apport du Prof. J. Lortz à la cause de l'unité chrétienne.* Die Warte. Perspectives, Luxembourg, December 11, 1957.

577. *Saint Thomas et les archidiacres.* RThom, 57 (1957), 657-671.

578. *Ecce constitui te super gentes et super regna (Jér. 1, 10)* in *Geschichte und Gegenwart,* in *Theologie in Geschichte und Gegenwart. Michael Schmaus zum sechzigsten Geburtstag,* Munich, 1957, 671-696.

579. *"Civitas Dei" et "Ecclesia" chez saint Augustin. Histoire de la recherche, son état présent.* REA, III-1, 1957, 1-14.

580. *De Civitate Dei XV, 2.* (Trans. from Cranz.) REA, III-1, 1957, 15-27.

581. *The State of Israël in Biblical Perspectives.* Bl, June, 1957, 244-249; German trans.: *Der Staat Israël in biblischer Sicht,* in *Deus lo vult. Ordensbrief des Ritterordens vom Heiligen Grab,* December 11, 1957, 321-323.

1958

582. *Anglikanische Kirche.* LTK, 2nd ed., I, cols. 787-790; reprinted in Theologischer Digest, n. 1, 3-16.

583. *Au sujet des non catholiques.* RevSR (January, 1958), 53-65; reprinted in SE, 433-444 (cf. n. 572).

584. *Unité de l'humanité et vocation des peuples.* SVS, n. 44 (1958/1), 70-87; reprinted in SE, 163-180.

585. *The Idea of Conversion.* Thought, XXIII, Spring, 1958, 5-20; reprinted in The Life of the Spirit: *A Note on Conversion,* August-September, 1959, 62-68; published in French in PM, 11, October, 1960, 493-523: *La conversion, étude théologique;* reprinted in SL, 23-49; text revised and augmented in Swedish trans.: *Sympunkter päomvändelseproblemet,* Lumen, n. 10, October, 1960, 1-22.

586. LE MYSTERE DU TEMPLE OU L'ECONOMIE DE LA PRESENCE DE DIEU A SA CREATURE DE LA GENESE A L'APOCALYPSE. Ed. du Cerf, P, 1958, 347 pp. "Lectio Divina," 22; 2nd ed. 1963; German trans.: *Das Mysterium des Tempels,* Salzburg, 1960; English trans.: *The Mystery of the Temple,* London, 1962; American trans.: *The Mystery of the Temple,* The Newman Press, Westminster, Maryland, 1962; Italian trans.: *Il mistero del Tempio,* T, 1963.

587. *Eucharistie et achèvement du monde en Dieu.* Bible et Terre Sainte, June, 1958, 2-4; reprinted in VDV, 207-216.

588. WENN IHR MEINE ZEUGEN SEID. St, 1958 (cf. n. 624).

589. *Quod omnes tangit, ab omnibus tractari et approbari debet.* Revue historique du droit français et étranger, 1958, 210-259.

590. *L'Etat d'Israel dans le dessein de Dieu.* PM, n. 2, July, 1958, 168-187; Spanish trans.: *El Estado de Israel en los designios de Dios,* in Orbis Catholicus, Herder, Ba, 1958, 30-46; reprinted in CED, 529-547.

591. *Esquisse d'une théologie de l'Action catholique.* Cahiers du clergé rural, August-September, 1958, 387-407; reprinted in SL, 329-356.

592. *Die Kasuistik des hl. Paulus*, in *Verkündigung und Glaube. Festgabe für F.X. Arnold*, St, 1958, 16-41; reprinted in SL, 65-89.

593. *Das oekumenische Anliegen*. Una Sancta, 1958, 213-224; reprinted in CED, 89-105.

594. *Henri de Marcy, abbé de Clairvaux, cardinal-évêque d'Albano et légat pontifical*. Analecta Monastica, Studia Anselmiana, 43 (1958), 1-90.

595. *Action et Foi*. Bulletin FFEC, November, 1958 (conférence donnée aux responsables de la FFEC, Jambeville, October 10, 1958); reprinted in VDV, 391-422.

596. *Konfessionnelle Auseinandersetzung im Zeichen des Oekumenismus*. Catholica, 12 (1958), 81-104 (cf. n. 600).

597. *Chronique ecclésiologique*. MD, 53 (1958), 170-172; reprinted in SE, 687-688.

598. *Tiers-Ordre, vie religieuse et laïcat*. France dominicaine, December, 1958, 289-306 (see July, 1959, 207-210); Dutch trans. in Zwart op wit, April, 1959, 50-68.

1959

599. *Propos sur le travail œcuménique. Point de vue catholique*. ICI, 88, January 15, 1959, 1-2 et 32; reprinted in CED, 141-147.

600. *La rencontre des confessions chrétiennes dans le passé et aujourd'hui*. PM, January, 1959, 103-123; reprinted in CED, 157-184; German trans. in Catholica, 12 (1958), 81-104 (see n 596).

601. *Bibliographie sur le salut des non évangélisés*. PM, January, 1959, 142-146.

602. *Saint-Esprit et esprit de liberté*. RN, 29 (1959) 3-24; reprinted in *Si vous êtes mes témoins*, 9-55.

603. *Les Conciles dans la vie de l'Eglise*. ICI, February 15, 1959, 17-26; German trans.: *Die Konzilien im Leben der Kirche*, Una Sancta, August, 1959, 156-171; reprinted in SE, 303-325.

604. *Conscience ecclésiologique en Orient et en Occident du VI au XI siècle*. Istina, April, 1959, 187-236; English trans. in *The Unity of the Churches of God*, Baltimore and Dublin, 1963, 127-184; Spanish trans.: *La conciencia ecclesiologica en Oriente y en Occidente del siglo VI al XI*, Herder, Ba, 1962.

605. *La Seigneurie du Christ sur l'Eglise et le monde*. Istina, April, 1959, 131-166.

606. *Enige notities aangaande de Derbe Orde, het religieuze leven en het Lekenleven*, Zwart op wit, April, 1959, 50-67.

607. *Ce monde nouveau où nous vivons.* TC, April 10, 1959; reprinted in VMM, 11-17.

608. *Petite Eglise dans le vaste monde.* TC, April 24, 1959; reprinted in VMM, 18-26.

609. *Préface to: M. J. André: Equilibre, fidélité à la nature et à la grâce,* Alsatia, Str, 1959, 9-12.

610. *Por que me hice Sacerdote?* Salamanque, 1959, 77-86; résumé in *Testimonis de Ruta,* Estela, Ba, 1960, 33-40.

611. *L'Eglise chez saint Anselme. Spicilegium Beccense,* 1, P and Le Bec-Hellouin (Actes du IXᵉ centenaire de l'arrivée d'Anselme au Bec-Hellouin), 371-399.

612. *Christianisme et autres religions.* TC, May 8, 1959; reprinted in VMM, 37-42.

613. *Le salut, qu'est-ce que c'est?* TC, May 29, 1959; reprinted in VMM, 43-54.

614. *L'Enfer existe, mais il n'est pas celui des diablotins cornus.* TC, June 19, 1959; reprinted in VMM, 85-90.

615. *Eglise cité de Dieu chez quelques auteurs cisterciens à l'époque des croisades, en particulier dans le "De peregrinante Civitate Dei,"* in *Etudes de philosophie médiévale. Mélanges offerts à Etienne Gilson,* Vrin, P, 1959, 173-202.

616. *Si nous pouvons tout perdre, c'est que nous pouvons tout gagner.* TC, July 10, 1959; reprinted in VMM, 100-108.

617. *Hors de l'Eglise pas de salut, ou l'histoire d'une formule.* TC, July 24, 1959; reprinted in VMM, 109-115.

618. *Toutes les religions sont-elles bonnes?* TC, August 21, 1959; reprinted in VMM, 161-167.

619. *Dieu a-t-il peuplé les astres?* TC, September 25, 1959; reprinted in VMM, 212-217.

620. *Théologie du rôle de la religieuse dans l'Eglise.* SVS, 12 (1959), 315-342; reprinted in *Le rôle de la religieuse dans l'Eglise,* Ed. du Cerf, P, 1960, 29-57; Spanish trans.: *Mision de la religiosa en la Iglesia,* Ma, 1962, 31-60 (cf. n. 646).

621. *Traditions apostoliques non écrites et suffisance de l'Ecriture.* Istina, 59/3 (1959), 279-306.

622. *Un théologien réformé traite de l'Eucharistie.* Bull. ecclésiastique du diocèse de Strasbourg, 43 (1959), 472-479; reprinted in CED, 519-526.

623. *Dum visibiliter Deum cognoscimus... Méditation théologique.* MD, 59 (IV), 1959, 132-161; reprinted in VDV, 79-107, and *Jésus-Christ, notre médiateur, notre sauveur,* 7-48 (cf. n. 877).

624. SI VOUS ETES MES TEMOINS. TROIS CONFERENCES SUR LAICAT, EGLISE ET MONDE. Ed. du Cerf, P, 1959, 128 pp.; German trans.: *Wenn ihr meine Zeugen seid*, St, 1958 (cf. n. 588); English trans.: *Laity, Church and World*, London, 1960; Catalan trans.: *Si sou els meus testimonis*, Ba, 1960; Italian trans.: *Spirito e libertà*, T, 1962; Dutch trans.: *Zo gif mijn Getuige zift*, Anvers, 1960; Castilian trans.: *Si sois mis testigos*, Ba, 1962, 1965.

625. *Geschichtliche Betrachtungen über Glaubensspaltung und Einheitsproblematik*, in *Begegnung der Christen*, Studien evangelischer und Katholischer Theologen, hrsg. von M. Roesle u. O. Cullmann (Festgabe Otto Karrer), St and Einsiedeln, 1959, 405-429; reprinted in CED: *Considérations historiques sur la rupture du XVIe siècle dans ses rapports avec la réalisation catholique de l'unité*, 409-435.

626. *Leben zu lasten Christi*, in *Frömmigkeit in einer weltichen Welt*, hrsg. v. H.J. Schultz, St, 1959, 117-127.

627. *I pagani non vanno all'inferno*. Digest religioso, Autumn, 1959, Pérouse.

628. *Toussaint du ciel et salut du monde*. VS, 101 (1959), 427-444; reprinted in VMM, 55-72.

629. *Je crois à la Résurrection de la chair*. TC, November 6, 1959; reprinted in VMM, 195-199.

630. *"Ariana haeresis" comme désignation du néomanichéisme au XIIe siècle. Contribution à l'histoire d'une typification de l'hérésie au Moyen Age*. RSPT, 43 (1959), 449-461.

631. *La "problématique" actuelle du Conseil œcuménique des Eglises*. Petite Revue, Suppl. littéraire du Nouvel Alsacien, December 2, 1959, 1-2.

632. *Dialogue*. France dominicaine, 1959, 207-210.

633. *Hors de l'Eglise, point de salut*. Ecclesia, 129, December, 1959, 146-151.

634. VASTE MONDE, MA PAROISSE. VERITE ET DIMENSIONS DU SALUT. Ed. TC, P, 1959, 228 pp., collection of articles from TC, 1959; 4th edition revised and augmented, "Foi Vivante," 27, P, 1966; German trans: *Ausser der Kirche kein Heil*, Essen, 1961; English trans.: *The Wide World, My Parish*, London, 1961; Spanish trans.: *Amplio mondo, mi parroquia*, Ba, 1965; Italian trans.: *La mia parrochia vasto mondo*, ed. Paoline, R, 1961.

1960

635. *Sainte Ecriture et sainte Eglise*. RSPT, 44 (1960), 81-88; English trans.: *Holy Writ and Holy Church*, Bl, 41 (1960), 11-19.

636. *L'apostolicité de l'Eglise selon saint Thomas d'Aquin*. RSPT, 44 (1960), 209-224.

637. *Nouvel an œcuménique.* TC, January, 1960; reprinted in CED, 149-153.

638. *Le Concile, l'Eglise et "les Autres."* LV, 45 (1960), 69-92; adapted in German: *Konzil und Oekumenismus,* in TTZ, 1960, 129-147; Italian trans. in *Il Concilia emucenico,* Mi, 1960, 95-124; American trans. in Cross Currents, Summer, 1961, 241-254; reprinted in SE, 327-349.

639. *Pour que l'Eglise soit l'Eglise!* Signes du Temps, 6 (1960), 9-12; German trans.: *Auf dass die Kirche Kirche sei!* in Theologie der Gegenwart, Summer, 1961, 143-147.

640. *Le dialogue entre chrétiens.* Fiches Vérité et Vie, 47, n. 376, Str, 1959-1960, 37-47.

641. *Pédagogie de l'oecuménisme.* Fiches Vérité et Vie, series 49, Str, 1960; German trans.: *Was kann ich als Laie für die Einigung tun?* in Una Sancta, 1960, 107-133; brochure containing a more complete text, Meitingen, 1960; Swedish trans.: *Lekmannens ekumeniska uppift,* in Katolska Smaskrifter, 6, Lund, 1962; reprinted in AOe, 97-123.

642. *Réponses.* TC, June 16, 1960.

643. *The Idea of Reform.* Bl, 41 (1960), 386-391.

644. *Réflexions sur l'aspect spirituel de la construction de la maison de Dieu.* Pêcheurs d'hommes, Montpellier, 46, October, 1960, 10-17; reprinted in SL, 257-264.

645. *Annunciar el Evangelio.* El Ciervo, October, 1960, 1.

646. *Les leçons de la théologie in Le rôle de la religieuse dans l'Eglise,* Ed. du Cerf, P, 1960, 29-57; Spanish trans.: *Las lecciones de la teolgia,* in Mision de la religiosa en la Iglesia, Ma, 1961; Italian trans.: *La missione della religiosa secundo la teologia,* in La missione della religiosa, T, 1962, 33-68 (cf. n. 620).

647. *Interview.* Midi Libre, November 3, 1960.

648. *Questions raciales et théologie.* Revue de l'Action populaire, 142, November, 1960, 1031-1046; German trans.: *Rassenfrage und Theologie* in Dokumente, February, 1961, 13-24; reprinted in SL, 471-490.

649. *Présence du P. Lacordaire.* Le Monde, December, 1960; reprinted in VDV, 317-322.

650. *Noël c'est d'abord Jésus-Christ.* La Croix, December 21, 1960; reprinted in VDV, 75-78.

651. *Tradito und Sacra Doctrina bei Thomas von Aquin,* in Kirche und Ueberlieferung (Festschrift J. R. Geiselmann), Fr, 1960, 170-210; French text in Eglise et Tradition, Mappus, Le Puy-Lyon et P, 1963, 157-194.

222   YVES CONGAR

652. *Théologie de l'Eglise particulière*, in *Mission sans frontières*, Ed. du Cerf, P, 1960, 15-52.

653. *Primauté des premiers conciles œcuméniques*, in *Le Concile et les conciles*, Ed. du Cerf, Chevetogne, 1960, 75-109; Italian trans.: *Il Concilio e i concilii*, Ed. Paoline, R, 1962.

654. *Conclusion*, in *Le Concile et les conciles*, Ed. du Cerf et Chevetogne, 1960, 285-334; Italian trans.: *Il Concilio e i concilii*. Ed. Paoline, R, 1962.

655. *Lettre-Préface à G. Michonneau: Au risque de "rabâcher,"* in *Pas de vie communautaire sans communauté*, Ed. du Cerf, P, 1960, 7-19.

656. *L'ecclésologie de la Révolution française au Concile du Vatican sous le signe de l'affirmation de l'autorité.* RevSR, 2-3-4, 1960, 77-114 (Acts of the ecclesiological colloquium held at Strasbourg in November, 1960: *L'ecclésiologie au XIXᵉ siècle*), and in *L'ecclésiologie au XIXᵉ siècle*, Ed. du Cerf, P, 1961, Unam Sanctam, 34, 77-114.

657. LA TRADITION ET LES TRADITIONS. ESSAI HISTORIQUE. Ed. Fayard, P, 1960, 303 pp.; Italian trans.: *La Tradizione e le tradizioni*, Ed, Paoline, R, 1961; German trans.: *Die Tradition und die Traditionen*, Mainz, 1965; English trans.: *Tradition and traditions*, London, 1966.

1961

658. *Les chrétiens et l'antisémitisme.* Le Courrier de l'Unesco, January, 1961, 31-32.

659. *Orthodoxes.* Echanges, January, 1961, 15-16.

660. *Interview.* Ecclesia, January, 1961, 91-96.

661. *La préparation du Concile.* Cahiers S. Dominique, January, 1961, 29-34.

662. *Au cœur d'une double réalité œcuménique.* La Croix, January 24, 1961.

663. *Inspiration des Ecritures canoniques et apostolicité de l'Eglise.* RSPT, 45 (1961), 32-42; condensed reprint in Selecciones de teologia, 1 (1962), 15-16; reprinted in SE, 187-200.

664. *Perspectives chrétiennes sur la vie personnelle et la vie collective*, in *Socialisation et personne humaine*, compte rendu in extenso de la Semaine sociale de Grenoble 1960, Chronique Sociale, Ly, 1960, 195-223; Spanish trans.: *Perspectivas cristianas sobre la vida personal y la vida colectiva*, in Criterio, February 9, 1961, 88-93, and February 23, 1961, 126-128.

665. *Interview.* La Vanguardia española, April 16, 1961.

666. *Autordid y obediencia.* El Ciervo, May 10, 1961, 8-9.

667. *Interview : Perspectives for the Council.* America, June 3, 1961, 394-398; reprinted in *God and Man in America,* Chicago, 1962, 188-220; *Between two Cities;* reprinted in *The Second Vatican Council,* The American Press, 1962, 25-35.

668. *Interview: Przyszlosc Kosciola.* Tagodnik Powszchna, Kraków, December 17, 1961, 1 et 3.

669. *Au Concile l'Eglise se regardera dans l'Evangile.* TC, July 28, 1961, 2, 4.

670. *Tauler dans son temps et son actualité permanente.* Petite Revue, Suppl. littéraire au Nouvel Alascien, July, 1961, 2, 4; reprinted in VS, 105 (1961), 642-649; reprinted in VDV, 309-316.

671. *Postface à: Ils attendent le Concile.* Cahiers du témoignage chrétien, XLIII, July, 1961, 69-77.

672. *Comment l'Eglise sainte doit se renouveler sans cesse.* Ir, 34 (1961), 322-345; pamphlet, Chevetogne, 1961; 2nd ed. 1963; English trans. in Theology Digest, Autumn, 1962; Spanish trans. in Selecciones de teologia, 4, 1962, 98-104; Italian trans.: *Come la Chiesa deve renovarsi incessantemente,* pamphlet, Mi, 1962; American trans., Paulist Press, 1966.

673. *S. Isidore et la culture antique.* RevSR, 35 (1961), 49-54.

674. *Der Platz des Papstums in der Kirchenfrömmigkeit der Reformer des 11. Jahrhunderts,* in *Sentire Ecclesiam (Festschrift Hugo Rahner),* Ed. Herder, Fr, 1961, 196-217.

675. *Aspects ecclésiologiques de la querelle entre Mendiants et Séculiers dans la seconde moitié du XIIIᵉ siècle et le début du XIVᵉ.* Archives d'histoire doctrinale et littéraire du Moyen Age, 28 (1961), 35-152.

676. *Diversité et divisions,* in *Catholicisme un et divers.* Semaine des Intellectuels catholiques, E. Fayard, P, 1961, 27-43; reprinted in SE, 105-130.

677. *Simples réflexions sur l'originalité de l'entreprise œcuménique,* in *Découverte de l'Ecuménisme.* Cahiers de la Pierre-qui-Vire, Ed. Desclée de Brouwer, P, 1961, 48-64; reprinted in CED, 107-121.

678. *Laie, Laienstand.* LTK, 6 (1961), 733-740.

679. *Peut-on définir l'Eglise? Destin et valeur de quatre notions qui s'offrent à le faire,* in J. Leclercq: *L'homme et ses amis,* Ed. Casterman, P, 1961, 233-254; reprinted in SE, 21-44.

680. *La jeunesse, l'armée et le salut de la nation.* DC, 1359, September 3, 1961, cols. 1109-1134; reprinted in Elan, Str, 1961; in La Revue militaire. Notes et documents, 34, October 15-31, 1961, and 35, November 1-15, 1961; reprinted in *La montée des Jeunes dans la communauté des générations,* Semaine sociale

de Reims, 1961, Chronique Sociale, Ly, 1962, 203-231; Spanish trans. in Questiones de vida cristiana, 16 (1962), Montserrat, 43-70; reprinted in *Armée et vie nationale*, Chronique sociale, Ly, 1962.

681. *1961. Année œcuménique.* Recherches et Débats, 36 (1961), 212-231; reprinted in AOe, 77-95.

682. *De la situation faite à la culture de la foi dans le monde moderne.* Foi et culture. Congrès FFEC, Str, 1961; reprinted in VDV, 423-434.

683. *Le laïcat. Vocavulaire et histoire.* Bull. du Cercle Saint Jean-Baptiste, October-November, 1961, 15-22; December, 1961, 15-26; reprinted in *Les laïcs et la mission de l'Eglise*, Ed. du Centurion, P, 1962, 11-38.

684. *Une, sainte, catholique et apostolique,* in *Un Concile pour notre temps.* Ed. du Cerf, P, 1961, 225-252; Castilian trans.: *Un Concilio para nuestro tiempo*, Ba, 1962; Catalan trans.: *Un concili per al nostre temps*, Ba, 1962; Dutch trans.: *Ein, heilig, katholiek en apostolisch*, in Kerk en Ruimte, Hilversum, 1961, 31-47; Italian trans., 1962.

685. *Pour l'Alsace. Histoire d'un homme, destin d'un peuple.* La Croix, December 13, 1961, 6.

686. *Réponse à l'enquête sur le Concile.* Esprit, December, 1961, 691-700; American trans. in Cross Currents, 12/2, Spring, 1962; *Looking towards the Council*, Italian trans.

1962

687. *Oekumenische Bewegung.* LTK, 7 (1962), 1128-1137; reprinted in CED, 21-35.

688. *Interview.* Le Lien de l'Eglise évangélique libre du canton de Vaud, January 25, 1962, 1, et 4.

689. *The Historical Development of Authority in the Church. Points for Christian Reflexion,* in *Problems of Authority. An Anglo-French Symposium.* Ed. Todd, London, 1962, 119-156; French text in *Problèmes de l'Autorité*, Ed. du Cerf, P, 1962, "Unam Sanctam," 38, 145-181; reprinted in part in *Pour une Eglise servante et pauvre* (cf. n. 751), 39-68.

690. *Les chrétiens séparés d'Orient.* Ecclesia, 154, January, 1962, 19-29.

691. *Les étapes du dialogue oecuménique.* Evangéliser, 16 (1962), January-February, 345-361; Dutch trans. in De Bazuin, April 7, 1962; reprinted in AOe, 7-25.

692. *Le Mystère du Temple.* Le Psautier de Notre-Dame, mensuel du Rosaire, n. 125, February, 1962, 8-10.

693. *Collaboration aux différents thèmes proposés dans le dialogue entre théologiens des confessions chrétiennes* d'où est sorti: *Dialogue œcuménique,* Ed. de Fleurus, P, 1962.

694. *La miséricorde, attribut souverain de Dieu.* VS, 106 (1962), 380-395; reprinted in VDV, 61-74.

695. *L'Eglise ce ne sont pas les murs, mais les fidèles.* MD, 70 (1962), 105-114; reprinted in SL, 295-303.

696. *Sanctification du chrétien et service.* Cahiers de saint Dominique, June, 1962, 15-23 (287-295).

697. *Quelques lois de vérité d'un comportement pastoral.* Prêtres diocésains, n. spécial pour le centenaire, June-July, 1962, 169-180.

698. *Qui peut accueillir la Parole?* PM, n. 18, July, 1962, 357-362.

699. *François de Sales aujourd'hui.* Choisir, n. 33-34, July-August, 1962, 24-26; German trans.:*Franz von Sales,* St, 1962, préface.

700. *L'Episcopat et l'Eglise universelle.* L'Ami du Clergé, August 9, 1962, 508-511; reprinted in SE, 688-696.

701. *L'épiscopat et l'Eglise universelle.* La Croix, August 31, 1962.

702. *Le Concile. Ses préparations, ses espoirs.* Cahiers Lacordaire, 16 (1962). Dijon, renèotypé.

703. *La signification théologique du Concile.* Le Monde, September 6, 1962; Spanish trans. in Ensayos, Loyola, 31, September-October, 1962, 5-9; reprinted in *Vatican II. Le Concile au jour le jour,* Ed. du Cerf, P, 1963, 11-21.

704. *Le thème du don de la Loi dans l'art paléochrétien.* NRT 84 (1962), 915-933.

705. ARMEE ET VIE NATIONALE. La Chronique Sociale, Ly, 1962, 142 pp.; Spanish trans.: *El ejercito, la patria y la conciencia,* Ba, 1966.

706. ASPECTS DE L'OECUMENISME. Ed de la Pensée Catholique, Bruxelles, 1962, 128 pp.; Castilian trans.: *Aspectos del Ecumenismo,* Ba, 1965; Catalan trans.: *Aspectes de l'Ecumenisme,* Ba, 1965; Italian trans.: *Aspetti dell'Ecumenismo,* T, 1965; American trans.: *Ecumenism and the Future of the Church,* The Priory Press, Chicago, 1967, 15-153.

707. *Tradition et vie ecclésiale.* Istina, October, 1962, 411-436.

708. *Le bloc-notes du Pére Congar,* ICI, nn. 179-183, November 1, 1962-January 1, 1963: articles sur la première session du Concile, reprinted in *Vatican II. Le Concile au jour le jour,* Ed. du Cerf, P, 1963 (cf. n. 724); Dutch trans. in De Bazuin, nn. November 13 and 24, December 8 and 15, 1962, and January 12, 1963.

709. *Les deux formes du Pain de Vie dans l'Evangile et dans la Tradition,* in *Parole de Dieu et Sacerdoce,* études prèsentées à

Mgr Weber, ed. Desclée, P, 1962, 21-58; reprinted SL, 123-159; German trans.: *Das Brot des Lebens in seinen beiden Formen,* in Der Christliche Sonntag, December 26, 1965, 413-414.

710. *La hiérarchie comme service selon le Nouveau Testament et les documents de la Tradition,* in *L'épiscopat et l'Eglise universelle,* Ed. du Cerf, P, 1962, "Unam Sanctam," 39, 831 pp., 67-100, and in *Pour une Eglise servante et pauvre;* German trans.: *Das Bischofsamt und die Weltkirche,* Leinen, 1964; Italian trans.: *L'Episcopato y la Chisea universale,* R, 1966; Spanish trans.: *Episcopado y la Iglesia universal,* Ba, 1967 (cf. n. 751).

711. *Quelques expressions traditionelles du service chrétien* in *L'épiscopat et l'Eglise universelle,* Ed. du Cerf, P, 1962, 101-132; German, Italian, Spanish translations (cf. n. 710).

712. *De la communion des Eglises à une ecclésiologie de l'Eglise universelle,* in *L'épiscopat et l'Eglise universelle,* Ed. du Cerf, P, 1962, 227-260; German, Italian, Spanish trans. (cf. n. 710).

713. *Kirche,* in *Handbuch theologischer Grundbegriffe,* I, 801-812, Munich, 1962 (cf. n. 874).

714. *Die Achtung der Priester und Ordensleute vor dem Laien-apostolat,* in *Sorge um alle,* H. Borgmann, Dortmund, 1962, 154-174; French text in Recherches et Débats, March, 1963, 117-142; reprinted in SL, 267-294.

715. *Essai de clarification de la notion de Tradition.* Verbum Caro, 64 (1962), 284-294.

716. *Les saints Pères, organes privilégiés de la Tradition.* Ir, 35 (1962), 479-498.

717. *L'Evangile source de la Tradition apostolique.* Proche-Orient chrétien, 1962, 305-318.

718. LA FOI ET LA THEOLOGIE. Ed. Desclée, Tou, 1962, XVI + 281 pp., "Le Mystère Chrétien," 1; Italian, Polish, American, Spanish trans.

719. LES VOIES DU DIEU VIVANT. THEOLOGIE ET VIE SPIRITUELLE. Ed. du Cerf, P, 1962, 447 pp. German trans.: *Wege des lebendigen Gottes,* Fr, 1964; Italian trans.: *Le Vie del Dio vivo,* Brescia, 1965; Spanish trans.: *Los caminos del Dios vivo,* Ed. Estela, Ba, 1965.

720. SACERDOCE ET LAICAT DEVANT LEURS TACHES D'EVANGELISATION ET DE CIVILISATION. Ed. du Cerf, P, 1962, 499 pp.; German trans.: *Priester und Laien,* Fr, 1965, Dutch trans.: *Evangelie en Beschaving,* I, Anvers, 1963; *Naar een dynamisch Laicat,* II, Anvers, 1965; English trans.: *Priest and Layman,* London, 1966; Italian trans.: *Sacerdozio e Laicato,* Brescia, 1966; Castilian trans., Ba, 1964.

721. *Les laïcs et le Concile.* TC, December 22, 1962; reprinted in *Vatican II. Le Concile au jour le jour,* Ed. du Cerf, P, 1963, 89-96.

722. *Quelques aspects de l'Eglise remis en lumière par le Concile.* Fiches Vérité et Vie, series 57, Str, 1962-1963, 4-11.

723. *Interview.* Il Mattino, Firenze.

1963

724. VATICAN II. LE CONCILE AU JOUR LE JOUR. Ed. du Cerf, P, 1963, 144 pp.: recueil des articles parus in ICI, translated in Dutch in De Bazuin (n. cf. 708); English trans.: *Report from Rome,* London, 1963; Castilian trans.: *El Concilio dia tras dia,* Ba, 1963; Catalan trans.: *El Concili al dia,* Ba, 1963.

725. *Pour une apologétique.* Revue Montalembert, n. spécial 4-5, February, 1963 : *Jean Guitton vu par . . .,* 264-274.

726. *La déclaration de paix de Jean XXIII.* TC, March 18, 1963.

727. *Pour un sens vrai de l'Eglise.* Christus, April, 1963, 207-220; English trans.: *Seeing the Church,* in Doctrine and Life, October, 1963, 507-518; German trans. in *Der grosse Entschluss,* May, 1964, 347-351.

728. *De Vatican I à Vatican II. Infallibilité de l'Eglise.* La Croix, April 30, 1963.

729. *"La pincée d'épices."* Réforme, n. 946, May 4, 1963; numéro spécial consacré à Kierkegarad.

730. *Du bon usage de Denzinger.* L'Ami du Clergé, May 23, 1963, 321-329.

731. *Réflexions.* ICI, June 15, 1963.

732. *Lendemain d'élections.* Le Monde, June 22-23, 1963; reprinted in *Vatican II. Le Concile au jour le jour, 2ᵉ session,* 51-56.

733. *L'unité chrétienne et le nouveau pape.* Les Dernières Nouvelles d'Alsace, June 25, 1963, 1, et 6.

734. *27 théologiens présentent aux hommes d'aujourd'hui le mystère chrétien.* La Croix, June 28, 1963.

735. *Qu'est-ce qu'un évêque?* Le Nouvel Alascien, June 30, 1963.

736. *Préface à: Frank B. Norris: God's own People,* Helicon Press, Baltimore, 1963, II-V.

737. *Secouer la poussière impériale.* ICI, July 15, 1963.

738. *Langage des spirituels et langage des théologiens,* in *La Mystique rhénane,* P.U.F., P, 1963, 15-34; Swedish trans.: *Mystikernas sprack och teologernas sprack. Föredrag vid Tauler-kongressen,* Str, 1960, Lumen, January, 1966, 1-22.

228 YVES CONGAR

739. *Ecumenical experience and conversion: a personal testimony*, in
*The Sufficiency of God. Essays in honour of W. A. Visser't
Hooft*, London, 1963, 71-87; German trans.: *Oekumenische
Erfahrung und Bekehrung:ein Bekenntnis*, in *Gelebte Einheit
(Festschrift für W. A. Visser't Hooft)*, Evang. Missions Verlag,
G.M.B.H., St, 1963, 67-81; French text in CED, 123-139.

740. *Préface à: J. Colson: L'épiscopat catholique*, P, 1963, 7-13,
"Unam Sanctam," 43; reprinted in TC, October 10, 1963.

741. *La predicazione sociale nelle prospettive del messaggio della
salvezza.* Temi di predicazione (Napoli), n. 36 (1963), 11-34.

742. *Saint Paul et l'autorité de l'Eglise romaine d'après la Tradition.*
Acta Studiorum Paulinorum. Congressus internationalis catholicus, Rome, 1961, published in 1963, 491-516.

743. *Ce que Jésus a appris.* VS, 109 (1963) 694-706, reproduced in
Jésus-Christ (cf. n. 877), 50-67.

744. *Priesterum (allgemeines).* LTK, 8 (1963), 753-756.

745. *Un moyen privilégié d'échange entre chrétiens et incroyants.*
TC, September 5, 1963.

746. *Le dialogue, loi du travail œcuménique.* Choisir, September,
1963, 15-20; reprinted in CED, 1-17.

747. *Le bloc-notes du Père Congar.* ICI, nn. 201-206, October 1-
December 15, 1963; Dutch trans. in De Bazuin, October-December, 1963 (cf. n. 826).

748. LA TRADITION ET LA VIE DE L'EGLISE. Ed. Fayard, P, 1963, 136
pp.; English translation: *Tradition and the Life of the Church*,
London, 1964; Italian trans.: *La Tradizione e la vita della Chiesa*, Catania, 1964; Castilian trans.: *Tradicion y vida de la
Iglesia*, Andorre, 1964; Catalan trans.: *La Tradicio i la vida de
l'esglesia*, Ba, 1965; German trans.: *Tradition und Kirche*,
Aschaffenburg, 1964.

749. LA TRADITION ET LES TRADITIONS. ESSAI THEOLOGIQUE. Ed. Fayard, P, 1963, 367 pp.; Italian trans.: *La Tradizione e le tradizioni*, Ed. Paoline, R, 1965; German trans.: *Die Tradition und
die Traditionen*, Mainz, 1965; English trans.: *Tradition and
Traditions*, London, 1966.

750. SAINTE EGLISE. ETUDES ET APPROCHES ECCLESIOLOGIQUES. Ed.
du Cerf, P, 1963, 719 pp. "Unam Sanctam," 41; 2nd ed.,
June, 1964; Spanish trans.: *Santa Iglesia*, Ba, 1965; Italian
trans.: *Santa Chisea*, Brescia, 1966; German trans.: *Heilige
Kirche*, St, 1966.

751. POUR UNE EGLISE SERVANTE ET PAUVRE. Ed. du Cerf, P, 1963,
152 pp.; English trans.: *Power and Poverty in the Church*,
London, Baltimore, 1964; Castilian trans.: *El servicio y la
pobreza en la Iglesia*, Ba, 1964; Catalan trans.: *Vers una*

Església de server i de pobresa, Ba, 1964; Italian trans.: *Servizio e povertà della Chiesa,* T, 1964; Dutch trans., *Voor een arme en dienende Kerk,* Anvers, 1964; Portuguese trans.: *Igreja serva e pobre,* Lisbon, 1964; German trans.: *Für eine dienende und arme Kirche,* Mainz, 1965.

752. *Pour une Eglise servante et pauvre.* TC, September 26, 1963.

753. *Réponse à une enquête.* L'Arche, P, 1963, November.

754. *Introduction et notes pour les Traités antidonatistes de saint Augustin,* vol. I, Ed. Desclée de Brouwer, P, 1963, 9-124.

755. *Le P. Sertillanges.* Le Monde, December 10, 1963.

756. *Interview.* Les Dernières Nouvelles d'Alsace, December 10, 1963.

757. *Eglise et Monde.* Testimonianze, Firenze, 1963.

Contributions à : *CATHOLICISME, HIER, AUJOURD'HUI, DEMAIN,* encyclopédia directed by G. Jacquemet, Letouzey et Ané P, V, 1963:

758. *Gillet (Martin-Stanislas),* cols. 24-25.

759. *Glaives (Théorie des deux),* cols. 39-42.

760. *Gnésioluthérien,* col. 69.

761. *Gogarten (Friedrich),* col. 90.

762. *Goguel (Maurice),* cols. 90-91.

763. *Gomar (François),* cols. 92-93.

764. *Gore (Charles),* cols. 105-106.

765. *Gratieux (Albert),* cols. 206-207.

766. *Grundtvig (Nicolas-Frédéric-Séverin),* col. 319.

767. *Guettée (Vladimir),* col. 365.

768. *Gugler (Joseph-Henri-Alois),* col. 365.

769. *Günther (Anton),* cols. 430-431.

770. *Gustav-Adolf-Verein,* col. 433.

771. *Gustave-Adolphe de Suède,* cols. 433-434.

772. *Halifax (Lord)* cols. 496-497.

773. *Haller (Karl Ludwig von),* col. 499.

774. *Harnack (Adolf von),* cols. 516-519.

775. *Hase (Karl August von),* cols. 524-525.

776. *Hatch (Edwin),* col. 528.

777. *Hauck (Albert),* col. 528.

778. *HauteEglise,* cols. 533-534.

779. *Hébert (Marcel),* col. 545.
780. *Hefele (Karl-Joseph),* cols. 560-561.
781. *Heiler (Friedrich),* col. 570.
782. *Heinrich (Jean-Baptiste),* col. 572.
783. *Hemmer (Marie-Hippolyte),* col. 596.
784. *Henri VI, d'Angleterre,* col. 606.
785. *Henri VIII, d'Angleterre,* cols. 606-607.
786. *Herbigny (Michel d'),* col. 633.
787. *Hérésie,* cols. 640-642.
788. *Hergenröther (Joseph),* cols. 648-649.
789. *Hermann, de Metz,* cols. 658-659.
790. *Herrmann (Wilhelm),* col. 687.
791. *Herzog (Edouard),* col. 697.
792. *Herzog (Johann Jakob),* cols. 697-698.
793. *Hettinger (Franz),* cols. 708-709.
794. *Hilgenfeld (Adolphe),* cols. 745-746.
795. *Hilversum (Convent ou Groupe d'),* col. 747.
796. *Hinschiste (Eglise évangélique),* col. 753.
797. *Hirscher (Jean-Baptiste),* cols. 765-766.
798. *Histoire,* cols. 767-783.
799. *Holl (Karl),* col. 822.
800. *Hontheim (Jean-Nicolas von),* col. 933.
801. *Hooker (Richard),* cols. 935-937.
802. *"Hors de l'Eglise pas de salut,"* cols. 948-956.
803. *Hubmaier (Balthasar),* cols. 999-1000.
804. *Hughes (Mgr Philip),* cols. 1006-1007.
805. *Huguenot,* cols. 1016-1017.
806. *Hugueny (François-Henri),* cols. 1017-1018.
807. *Hugues, de Fleury,* col. 1033.
808. *Huizinga (Johan),* cols. 1063-1064.
809. *Humbert, de Moyenmoutier (ou de Silva Candida),* cols. 1090-1093.
810. *Hurter (Friedrich von),* col. 1106.
811. *Hutten (Ulrich de),* col. 1113.
812. *Hutter (Léonard),* col. 1114.

813. *Infralapsaire*, col. 1621.

814. *Innocent III*, cols. 1650-1658.

815. *Innocent IV*, cols. 1658-1661.

1964

816. *Hochachtung vor dem Laienapostolat*. Theologie der Genewart in Auswahl, 7, July, 1964, n. 1.

817. *Interview*. Les Dernières Nouvelles d'Alsace, January 10, 1964.

818. *Le pèlerinage de Paul VI. Une nouvelle époque commence.* TC, January 16, 1964; reprinted in *Le Concile au jour le jour, 2e session*, 161-165.

819. *Tradition, épiscopat, laïcat dans l'Eglise du Concile.* Cahiers Lacordaire, n. 20, Dijon (ronéotypé).

820. *Le dialogue, loi du travail, œcuménique, structure de l'intelligence humaine*, in *Dialogue ou violence?* Rencontres internationales de Genève, Neuchâtel 1964, 37-54; reprinted in CED, 1-17.

821. *Osnavne ideje teoloske antropolojia*. Bogoslovska Smotra, 34/1, Zagreb 1964, 23-39.

822. *Les paraboles révélatrices du Dieu qui vient*. PM (1964), 24, 19-38.

823. *Interview*. La Rocca, Assise, February 15, 1964, 22-28.

824. *La prière de Jésus*. VS, 110 (1964), 157-174; American trans. in Review for Religious, March, 1965, 221-238, and in Cross and Crown, March, 1966, 49-67.

825. *Konzil als Versammlung und grundsätzliche Konzilizrität der Kirche*, in *Gott in Welt, Festgabe für Karl Rahner*, II, 135-165; reprinted in *Le Concile au jour le jour*, 2nd session, 9-39.

826. LE CONCILE AU JOUR, 2nd session. Ed. du Cerf, P, 1964, 221 pp.: recueil des articles parus in ICI et in De Bazuin (cf. n. 747); English trans.: *Report from Rome*, London, 1964; Castilian trans.: *Diario del Concilio*, Ba, 1964; Catalan trans.: *Diari del Concili*, Ba, 1964; Portuguese trans. in *Vaticano II, Ingreja em dialogo, Igreja e Missâo*, 13-14, 1964, 95-144.

827. *Le débat sur la question du rapport entre Ecriture et Tradition, au point de vue de leur contenu matériel*. RSPT, 48 (1964), 645-657; English trans. in *A Theology Reader*, ed. R. W. Gleason, NY et Londres, 1966, 115-129; Dutch trans. in DoC, Schrift en Traditie, Hilversum, 1965, 90-105.

828. *Le P. Clérissac 1864-1914 et le mypstère de l'Eglise*. VS, 111 (1964), 513-516. Preface for the Brazilian edition of: *Le mystère de l'Eglise du P. Clérissac*, Sâo Paulo, 1960.

829. *L'avenir de l'Eglise*, in *L'Avenir*, actes de la Semaine des Intellectuels catholiques 1963, P, 1964, 207-221; American trans. in *Ecumenism and the Future of the Church*, The Priory Press, Chicago, 1967, 154-181 (cf. n. 706).

830. *Chrétiens en dialogue*. La Croix, May 20, 1964.

831. *A l'heure du Concile: Perspectives catholiques*. Réforme, May 23, 1964, n. 1001.

832. CHRETIENS EN DIALOGUE. CONTRIBUTIONS CATHOLIQUES A L'OECU-MENISME. Ed. du Cerf, P, 1964, LXIV + 577 pp., "Unam Sanctam," 50; The Preface of this volume: *Appels et acheminements* has been reproduced in ICI, May 15, 1964, in Ecclesia (extracts): *Comment je vins à l'oecuménisme*, n. 185, August, 1964, 37-46; reprinted in Cahiers saint Dominique, April, 1965, 321-329 (cf. n. 858); Dutch trans. in DeBazuin, July 18, 1964; English trans. in Continuum, 2 (1965), n. 4, 184-193; complete translation: *Dialogue between Christians*, London, 1966.

833. *Le schéma sur l'Eglise. Le chapitre sur le peuple de Dieu va définir la relation entre laïcat et hiérarchie*. TC, June 11, 1964; reprinted in *Le Concile au jour le jour* (cf. n. 826), and in Cahiers bibliques de Foi et Vie, 2 (1964) 410-419.

834. *Dialog-prawo ekumenizmu*. Tagodnik Powszechna, Kraków, July, 1964.

835. *Jalons d'une reflexion sur le mystère des pauvres*. PM, 26, July 15, 1964, 470-487; reprinted in *Consolez mon peuple*, P. Gauthier, Ed. du Cerf, P, 1965, 307-327; German trans. in *Theologische Brennpunkte. II, Kirche Heute*, Frankfort, 1965, 44-53; partial trans. in *Theologie der Gegenwart*, 1965/8, 81-87.

836. *Il problema ecumenica e il Concilio Vaticano II*, in *L'unità dei cristiani*, Napoli, 1964, 31-53.

837. *Les ruptures de l'unité*. Istina, 1964, 133-178.

838. *Na czym Powinna Polegac Reforma i odnowa Kosciola katoliekiego?* Zo i Przeciw, 13 (366). Easter, 1964.

839. JALONS POUR UNE THEOLOGIE DU LAICAT. 3rd edition revised: addenda et corrigenda. Ed. du Cerf, P, (cf. n. 462).

840. *Preface à K. Delahaye: Ecclesia Mater chez les Pères des trois premiers siècles*. Ed du Cerf, P, 1964, "Unam Sanctam," 46, 7-32; reprinted in VS, 110 (1964), 315-342; Italian trans.: *Un nuovo volto della Chiesa*, Mi, 1964; German trans.: *Mutter Kirche*, in Theologie der Gegenwart, 3 (1963), 148-151; in Tübinger theologische Quartalschrift, 145 (1965), 68-100, and in *Theologische Brennpunkte. II. Kirche heute*, Frankfort, 1965, 30-38.

841. *Le thème du Dieu créateur et les explications de l'Hexameron dans la tradition chrétienne*, in *L'homme devant Dieu. Mélanges offerts au P. Henri de Lubac (I)*. Ed. Aubier, P, 1964, 189-222.

842. *Avant la 3ᵉ session du Concile*. Les Dernières Nouvelles d'Alsace, Str, September 1, 1964.

843. *Ministères et laïcat dans les recherches actuelles de la théologie catholique romaine*. Verbum Caro, 71-72 (1964), 127-148; reprinted in *Ministères et laïcat*, Taizé, 1964, 127-148.

844. *Le Bloc-notes du Père Congar*, ICI, nn. 224-229, September 15-December 1, 1964; Dutch trans. in De Bazuin, September-December, 1964 (cf. n. 878).

845. *Conquering our enmities*. Steps to Christian Unity, ed. by J. O'Brien, NY, 1964, 100-109.

846. *Le Christ, chef invisible de l'Eglise visible d'après saint Paul. Problèmes actuels de christologie*. Synposium de l'Arbresle held in 1961, Ed. Desclée de Brouwer, P, 1964, 367-395; reprinted in *Jésus Christ, notre Médiateur et notre Seigneur*, Ed. du Cerf, P, 1965, 147-179.

847. *La conscience des laïcs a progressé*. TC, December 17, 1964.

848. *Discours au Concile Vatican II*. Edited by Y. Congar, H. Küng, and D. O'Hanlon. Ed. du Cerf, P, 1964, 320 pp.; German trans.: *Konzilsreden*, Einsiedeln, 1964; English trans.: *Council Speeches of Vatican II*, London, 1964; American trans.: *Council Speeches of Vatican II*, Glen Rock, N.J., 1964; Spanish trans.: *Discursos conciliares*, Ma, 1964; Dutch trans.: *Concilie-toespraken*, Anvers, 1964.

1965

849. *L'Eglise comme peuple de Dieu*. Concilium 1 (1965), 15-32; German, English, Spanish, Dutch, Portuguese, Italian versions.

850. *Un initiateur: le P. M.-D. Chenu*. Le Monde, January 31-February 1, 1965, 11.

851. *Tradition and Scripture*. The Jews and Ourselves, 3 (1965), n. 1, 5-10; n. 2, 46-51.

852. *Eglise et monde*. Esprit, February, 1965, 337-359; Italian trans.: *Chiesa e mondo*, in Aggiornamenti Sociali, February, 1965, 81-102, and in pamphlet form, Mi, 1965; German trans.: *Kirche und Welt*, in *Weltverständnis im Glauben*, 1965, 102-126; reprinted in *Le Concile au jour le jour*, 3rd session, 143-176; reprinted in *Prêtres d'aujourd'hui*, October, 1965, 453-468; and November, 1965, 515-525.

853. *Concilium. Une nouvelle revue de théologie sous le signe du Concile*. La Croix, February 14-15, 1965.

854. *La théorie de la paix de Pie XII*. Le Monde, March 3, 1965.

855. *Sur le journal catholique.* La Croix, March 11, 1965.

856. *Die "letzen Dinge" und die Geschichte. Ein Kommentar zum 7. Kapitel der Konst. über die Kirche.* Der christliche Sonntag, March 14, 1965, 85-86; December 26, 1965, 413-414.

857. *Zum Dekret über den Oekumenismus.* Quatember, Easter, 1965, 82-85.

858. *Un homme se penche sur son passé,* in Semences d'unité. Ed. Casterman, P, 1965, 59-82; Spanish trans.: *Mis primeros pasos por el camino del Ecumenismo,* in Dialogos de la Cristiandad, Salamanca, 1964, 52-62 (cf. n. 832).

859. *"Strzasnac ten cesarski kurz."* Tagodnik Powszechna, Kraków, May 16, 1965, 1-2.

860. *L'exposition missionnaire de Strasbourg.* Les Dernières Nouvelles d'Alsace, May 23, 1965.

861. *Interview sur le schéma des Missions.* La Croix, June 17, 1965.

862. *L'Eglise est sainte.* Angelicum, XLII, fasc. 3, July-September, 1965, 273-298.

863. *La religion de Péguy (Un livre de P. Duployé).* Le Monde, August 17, 1965.

864. *Théologie et sciences humaines.* Esprit, August, 1965, 121-137.

865. *Zum Mysterium der Armen. Seine Begründung im Heilsgeheimnis Gottes und Christi.* Theologie der Gegenwart in Auswahl, 8 (1965), 81-87 (cf. n. 835).

866. *L'Eglise, sacrement universel du salut.* Eglise Vivante, 17, September-October, 1965, 339-355; reprinted in Evangelisation et Paroisse, September, 1966, 4-16; Spanish trans.: *La Iglesia, sacramento universal de salvacion,* Misiones extranjeras, 48, December, 1965, 508-520.

867. *Le bloc-notes du Père Congar.* ICI, nn. 248-255, September 15, 1965-January 1, 1966; Dutch trans. in De Bazuin, September 4, 11, October 2, 16, 30, November 13, 20, December 4, 18, 1965, and January 9, 1966; reprinted in *Le Concile au jour le jour,* 4th session (cf. n. 898).

868. *Note sur la conjoncture de la Déclaration de Vatican II sur les religions non chrétiennes.* L'Ami du clergé, October 14, 1965, 593-596; reprinted in *Le Concile au jour le jour,* 4th session (cf. n. 898), 155-167.

869. *Enfrances ardennaises.* La Grive, n. 128, October-December, 1965, 14-16.

870. *A mes frères prêtres.* VS, 113 (1965), 501-520; German trans.: *An meine Brüder im Priestertum, Zeugen des Evangeliums in der Einsamkeit,* in Lebendiges Zeugnis, nn. 2/3/4/1966, 52-66.

871. *Anthénagoras I. Der Patriarch spricht.* Einleitung, Vienna, 1965, 9-13.

872. *Un témoignage désaccord entre canonistes et théologiens,* in *Etudes d'histoire du Droit canonique dédiées à G. Le Bras,* II, 1965, 861-884.

873. *Préface à: Encyclopédie de la Foi.* Ed. du Cerf, P, 1965, I, 7-9.

874. *Eglise. II. Histoire dogmatique,* in *Encyclopédie de la Foi.* Ed. du Cerf, P, 1965, I, 421-432.

875. *Laïc,* in *Encyclopédie de la Foi.* Ed. du Cerf, P, 1965, II, 436-456.

876. *Introduction au décret sur l'œcuménisme,* in *Concile Vatican II: L'Eglise, l'OEcuménisme, Les Eglises orientales.* Ed. du Centurion, P, 1965, 165-192.

877. JESUS-CHRIST, NOTRE MEDIATEUR ET NOTRE SEIGNEUR. Ed. du Cerf, P, 1965, 255 pp., coll. "Foi Vivante," 1, 2nd ed., 1966; English trans.: *Jesus Christ,* London, 1966; American trans., NY, 1966; Catalan trans.: *Jesucrist,* Ba, 1966; Italian trans., Marietta, T, 1966; Castilian trans.: *Jesucristo,* Ed. Estela, Ba, 1966; Dutch trans.: *Jezus Christus; beeld van de onzichtbare God,* Hilversum, 1966.

878. LE CONCILE AU JOUR LE JOUR, 3RD SESSION. Ed. du Cerf, P, 1965, 181 pp., collection of articles that appeared in ICI, September 15-December 1, 1964, and trans. in Dutch in De Bazuin (cf. n. 844); Catalan trans.: *Diari del concili,* Ba, 1965; Portuguese trans. in Vaticano II: *Igreja em diálogo, Igreja e* Missâo, 17-18 (1965), 163-251.

879. ESQUISSES DU MYSTERE DE L'EGLISE. Ed. du Cerf, P, 1965; re-edited in the coll. "Foi Vivante," n. 18, of the 3rd edition, 1963 (cf. n. 148).

880. *La mission dans la théologie de l'Eglise,* in *Repenser la Mission,* 35ᵉ Semaine de Missiologie de Louvain; Louvain, 1965, 53-74; reprinted in *Missionnaires pour demain* (session de Lyon 1965), P, 1966, 11-40.

881. *Avant-Propos à: I. de la Potterie et S. Lyonnet: La vie selon l'Esprit, condition du chrétien.* Ed. du Cerf, P, 1965, "Unam Sanctam," 55, 7-11.

882. *Introduction à La Collégialité épiscopale. Histoire et théologie.* Ed. du Cerf, P, 1965, "Unam Sanctam," 52, 7-9.

883. *Notes sur le destin de l'idée de collégialité épiscopale en Occident au Moyen Age (VII-XVIᵉ siècles),* in *La Collégialité épiscopale.* Ed. du Cerf, P, 1965, "Unam Sanctam," 52, 99-129.

884. *Conclusion à A Igreja do Concilio Vaticano Segundo.* Rio de Janeiro, 1965; Italian trans.: *La Chiesa del Vaticano II,* Vallecchi, Florence, 1965; *In luogo di conclusione,* 1261-1268; French

text: *L'Eglise de Vatican II,* Ed. du Cerf, P, 1966, "Unam Sanctam," 51 c: *En guise de conclusion,* 1365-1373.

885. *L'application à l'Eglise comme telle des exigences évangéliques concernant la pauvreté. Les conditions et les motifs,* in Eglise et Pauvreté. Ed. du Cerf, P, 1965, "Unam Sanctam," 57, 135-155.

886. *Les biens temporels de l'Eglise d'après sa tradition théologique et canonique,* in Eglise et pauvreté. Ed. du Cerf, P, 1965, "Unam Sanctam," 57, 233-258.

887. *Une réalité traditionnelle: L'Eglise, recours des faibles et des pauvres,* in Eglise et Pauvreté. Ed. du Cerf, P, 1965, "Unam Sanctam," 57, 259-266.

888. *Interview: "La Iglesia tiene ahora necesidad de un momento de calma."* Palabra, December, 1965.

889. *Le Concile a atteint ses objectifs.* Les Dernières Nouvelles d'Alsace, December 23, 1965, 7.

890. *La théologie au Concile. Le "théologiser" du Concile.* Fiches Vérité et Vie, series 71, Str, 1965, 530 De; German trans.: *Theologie und Konzil,* in Der christliche Sonntag, 41, October, 1966, and 42, October, 1966, 333-334; Polish trans., in Znack, 1966; American trans.: *Theology in the Council,* in The American Ecclesiastical Review, October, 1966, 217-230.

1966

891. *Le Christ dans l'économie salutaire et dans nos traités dogmatiques.* Concilium,, 11 (1966), 11-26; German, English, Spanish, Dutch, Portuguese, Italian versions.

892. *Oecuménisme en 1966.* Le Rhin français, Str, January, 1966.

893. *Ein verjüngter und offener Katholizismus.* Der christliche Sonntag, 9 (1966), February.

894. *Ecriture et Tradition.* Ecclesia, February, 1966, 123-132.

895. *La missione e le missioni nelle prospettive del Concilio Vaticano II.* Sacra Doctrina, 41 (1966), 5-13.

896. *Ordinations invitus, coactus, de l'Eglise antique au canon 214.* RSPT, 50 (1966), 169-197.

897. *Vorschläge für den Dialog.* Kerygma und Dogma, 3 (1966), 181-187; French text: *Propos sur le dialogue* in Voix de Saint Paul, March, 1966, 6-7; Spanish trans.: *Proposiciones sobre el dialogo,* in Cuadernos para el dialogo, 28 (1966), 43-44.

898. LE CONCILE AU JOUR LE JOUR. 4TH SESSION. Ed. du Cerf, P, 1966, 272 pp.: collection of articles that appeared in ICI, September 15, 1965-January 1, 1966, and trans. in De Bazuin (cf. n. 867); German trans. of the last article: *Bilan du Concile,* in

Der christliche Sonntag, February 27, 1966, 69-70; March 6, 1966, 77-78; March 13, 1966, 85-86.

899. *Interview*. Panorama chrétien, March, 1966, 16-18.

900. *Sur le pluralisme culturel et théologique*. Sapienza, 3 (1966), 261-266.

901. *The Church, Seed of Unity and Hope for the Human Race*. Chicago Studies, 5 (1966), 25-40; Spanish trans.: *La Iglesia, germen de unidad y de esperanza para todo el genero humano*, in Misiones extranjeras, 49 (1966), 1-14.

902. *La recherche théologique*. Recherches et Débats, 54, April, 1966, 89-102.

903. PELLEGRINO DELL'ASSOLUTO. Mi, 1966 (cf. VDV, 247-264).

904. *La pauvreté dans la vie chrétienne au sein d'une civilisation du bien-être*. Concilium, 15 (1966), 45-62; German, English, Spanish, Dutch, Portuguese, Italian versions.

905. *Entretien avec le P.Y. Congar*. La Liberté, Fri, June 1, 1966; reprinted in part in DC, July 3, 1966, cols. 1248 ff.

906. *Prayer for Unity. A Meditation*. The Ecumenist, 4, May-June, 1966, 56-57; French trans.: *La prière pour l'Unité*, in L'Amitié, 4, October, 1966, 5-10.

907. *The Anatomy of Ecumenism*. Cross and Crown, 1966, 261-276.

908. *Mariages mixtes*. Signes du Temps, June 6, 1966, 10-12.

909. *Le Concile à votre portèe*. TC, June 30, 1966.

910. *Le ch. II du Décret sur l'Apostolat des laïcs: commentaire*, in *Laymen Vatican's Decree on the Apostolate of the Laity*. Chicago, 1966, 11 f.

911. *Kosciol i Swiat*. Tagodnik Powszechna, Kraków, June 5, 1966, 1-2.

912. *Interview: Les perspectives du renouveau dans l'Eglise*. Wiez, Varsovie, nn. 7/8, 1966, 105-106.

913. *Interview*. Les Dernières Nouvelles d'Alsace, Str, August 26, 1966.

914. *Protestants et catholiques s'interrogent. Réponse du P.Y. Congar au Pasteur J.L. Leuba*, in *Le courage des lendemains*. Ed. du Centurion, P, 1966, 98-113.

915. *Le diaconat dans la théologie des ministères*, in *Le diacre dans l'Eglise et la monde d'aujourd'hui*. Ed. du Cerf, P, 1966, "Unam Sanctam," 59, 121-141, and in Vocation, 234, April, 1966, 273-293 (DC, July 3, 1966, cols. 1247 ff.); German trans. in Catholica, 1966, and in *Die Autorität der Freiheit*, hrsg. J.C. Hampe, Munich, 1967.

916. *Une expérience à renouveler*. ICI, October 15, 1966.

917. *Le sacerdoce chrétien. Celui des laïcs et celui des prêtres.* Vocation, n. 236, October, 1966, 587-613.

918. *Points de vue actuels sur la vie monastique.* Montserrat, 1966, 67-69.

919. *Composantes et idée de la Succession apostolique,* in Oecumenica 1966, 61-80.

920. *Wer ist die Kirche?* Compte rendu de Hans Urs von Balthasar, in Der christliche Sonntag, August 21, 1966.

921. *L'Eglise catholique à Strasbourg,* in Présence de Strasbourg, n. 19, December, 1966, 34-35.

922. *Institutionalized Religion,* in *The Word in History.* The St. Xavier Symposium, NY, 1966, 133-153; French text: *Religion et Institution,* in *Théologie d'aujourd'hui et de demain,* Ed. du Cerf, P, 1967.

923. *Une nouvelle relation Eglise-Monde?* in Pax Romana Journal, n. 6, 1966, 3-5.

924. *Une certaine peine* (A propos de *Le Paysan de la Garonne* de J. Maritain), in Le Monde, December 28, 1966, 10.

925. *Avertissement,* in *La Liberté religieuse,* Unam Sanctam, 60, Ed. du Cerf, P, 1966, 11-14.

926. *Que faut-il entendre par "Déclaration"?* in *La Liberté religieuse,* Unam Sanctam, 60, Ed. du Cerf, P, 1966, 47-52.

927. *Préface à: A. Feuillet, Le Christ Sagesse de Dieu d'après les épîtres pauliniennes.* P. Gabalda, 1966, 7-15.

928. *Traditio thomistica in materia ecclesiologica,* in Angelicum, 43 (1966), fasc. 3-4, Roma, 405-428.

Contributions à *CATHOLICISME, HIER, AUJOURD'HUI, DEMAIN,* encyclopedia directed by G. Jacquemet, Letouzey et Ané, P, VI, 1963...

929. *Investitures,* cols. 41-46.

930. *Irvingiens,* cols. 113-114.

931. *Ivanios (Mar),* col. 228.

932. *Ivanov (Wenceslas),* col. 230.

933. *Jablonski (Daniel-Ernest),* col. 239.

934. *Jacobite (Eglise),* cols. 248-249.

935. *Jacobites,* col. 249.

936. *Jacques, de Viterbe,* cols. 266-267.

937. *Janséniste (Eglise),* dite *d'Utrecht,* cols. 331-332.

938. *Jean le Prêtre,* col. 617.

939. *Johnson (Humphrey)*, col. 922.
940. *Johnson (Vernon Cecil)*, col. 922.
941. *Jonas (Justus)*, col. 948.
942. *Journal of Theological Studies (The)*, col. 1088.
943. *Journet (Charles)*, cols. 1096-1097.
944. *Juridisme*, cols. 1273-1274.
945. *Jurieu (Pierre)*, cols. 1274-1276.
946. *Karrer (Otto)*, col. 1376.
947. *Kattenbusch (Ferdinand)*, cols. 1380-1381.
948. *Kénose*, cols. 1399-1403.
949. *Khomiakov (Alexis Stephanovitch)*, cols. 1427-1428.
950. *Kidd (B.-J.)*, col. 1428.
951. *Knox (Ronald Arbuthnot)*, cols. 1464-1465.

1967

952. *La prière pour l'unité.* VS, January, 1967, 9-22.
953. *La signification du salut et l'activité missionnaire.* PM, 36, January, 1967, 67-83.
954. *El apostolado de los laicos según el decreto del Concilio.* Sal Terrae, 55, January, 1967, 13-27.
955. *Lettre du Père Congar*, in Convergences (Bull. des étudiants de la Faculté de théologie), Str, January, 1967, 58-61.
956. *Conversion à l'homme?* in Civitas, 22 (1966/67), February, 355-359.
957. *Changements et continuité*, in L'Eglise en Alsace, February, 1967, 9-18; reprinted in *La France Catholique*, February 24 and March 3, 1967.
958. *L'Apostolat des laïcs.* VS, February, 1967, 129-160.

RECORDS

L'Eglise, une, sainte, catholique, apostolique, à l'heure du Concile. Conférence enregistrée au cours des Journées d'études 1961 des ICI (cf. n. 684). Jéricho JER 15, Paris, 1961.

L'avenir de l'Eglise. Conférence enregistrée à la Semaine des Intellectuels catholiques (CCIF), November, 1963 (cf. n. 829). Jéricho JER 20, Paris, 1964.

Situation de l'œcuménisme. Conférence-débat, avec le Pasteur H. Roux, enregistrée pendant la semaine de l'unité 1964 (CCIF). Jéricho JER 24, Paris, 1964.

Le Concile: esquisse d'un bilan. Conférence enregistrée à la Mutualité, December, 1964 (CCIF). Jéricho JER 33, Paris, 1965.

WORKS IN PREPARATION

In the volumes de commentaries on the texts de Vatican II, coll. "Unam Sanctam," Ed. du Cerf:
   Les Missions: Commentaire du ch. I: Principes doctrinaux.

   Gaudium et spes: L'Eglise et le Monde (commentaire du ch. IV, 1ʳᵉ partie).

   Les Prêtres: Le sacerdoce du N.T.: Mission et culte.

   L'Education chrétienne: Préface.

   La liturgie: Introduction; L' "ecclesia" ou communauté chrétienne, sujet intégral de l'action liturgique; Le sacré et le profane.

   La Vie religieuse: Avertissement.

In *Volk Gottes (Festgabe Höfer):*
   Apostolicité de ministère et apostolicité de doctrine. Réaction protestante et Tradition catholique, pp. 84-111.

In *Problèmes de l'autorité:*
   Le développement historique de l'autorité dans l'Eglise.

In *Theologie:*
   Préface.

In *La Foi et la Théologie:*
   Préface.

In *Euntes Docete: Mélanges en l'honneur de Mgr P. Parente:*
   La consécration épiscopale et la succession apostolique constituent-elles chef d'une Eglise locale ou membre du Collège?

In *Esprit:*
   Réponse à l'enquête sur "Nouveau monde et Parole de Dieu."

In *Rivista per la Storia della Chiesa in Italia:*
   Compte rendu de *Reformata reformanda (Festgabe H. Jedin).*

In *Actes du Congrès de Théologie de Rome 1966:*
   De fundamento dialogi in natura Catholicitatis ad effectum deducendae.

In *Actes de la Semaine théologique de Notre-Dame, U.S.A.:*
   Le Peuple de Dieu.
   Les laïcs.

In *Teachingall Nations* (Manila, Philippines).
   The Meaning of Salvation and the Missionary Apostolate.

In *La Théologie au XXᵉ siècle* (Tournai-Paris, Casterman et Freiburg, Herder):
   Le Père M.-D. Chenu.